Brevity 2

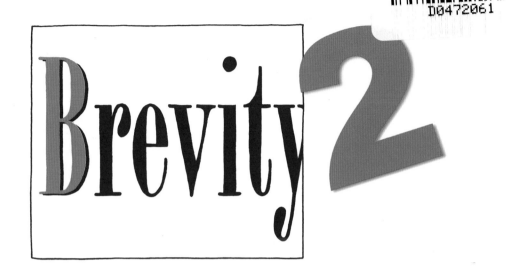

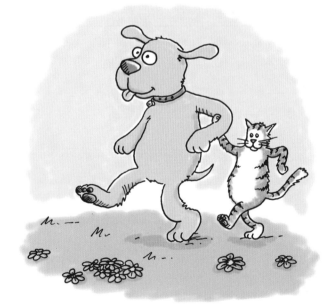

Other Books by

guy & rodd

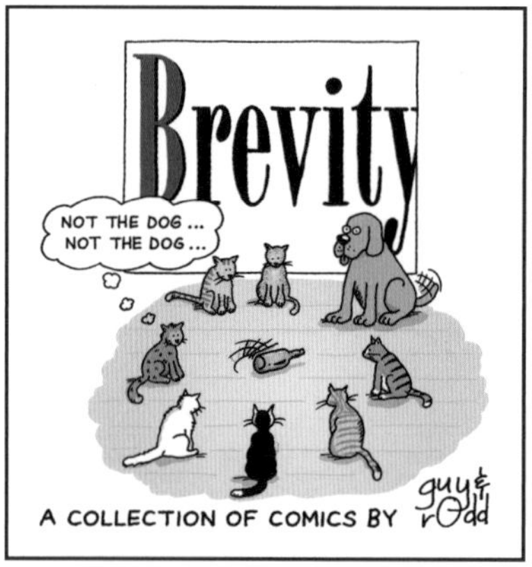
Brevity
NOT THE DOG ...
NOT THE DOG ...
A COLLECTION OF COMICS BY guy & rodd

Brevity 2

ANOTHER COLLECTION OF COMICS BY

guy & rOdd

Andrews McMeel
Publishing, LLC

Kansas City

Brevity is distributed by United Feature Syndicate, Inc.

Brevity 2 copyright © 2007 by Guy & Rodd. All rights reserved. Printed in China. No part of this book may be used or reproduced in any manner whatsoever without written permission except in the case of reprints in the context of reviews. For information, write Andrews McMeel Publishing, LLC, an Andrews McMeel Universal company, 4520 Main Street, Kansas City, Missouri 64111.

07 08 09 10 11 SDB 10 9 8 7 6 5 4 3 2 1

ISBN-13: 978-0-7407-6840-8
ISBN-10: 0-7407-6840-9

Library of Congress Control Number: 2007925460

www.andrewsmcmeel.com

────────── **ATTENTION: SCHOOLS AND BUSINESSES** ──────────

GUY DEDICATES THIS BOOK TO RENEE AND DEL.

RODD DEDICATES THIS BOOK TO MAURA, TOWNES, GUS, AND TED.
ALSO, HIS DAD FOR DRAWING WITH HIM ON SATURDAY
MORNINGS, AND HIS MUM, FOR POSING IN THE NUDE.

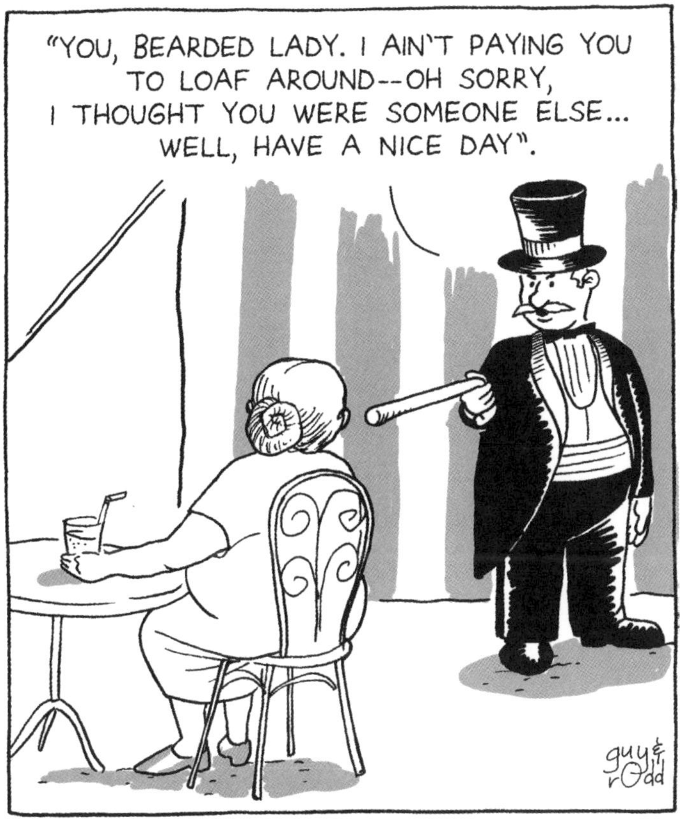
"YOU, BEARDED LADY. I AIN'T PAYING YOU TO LOAF AROUND--OH SORRY, I THOUGHT YOU WERE SOMEONE ELSE... WELL, HAVE A NICE DAY".
guy & rOdd

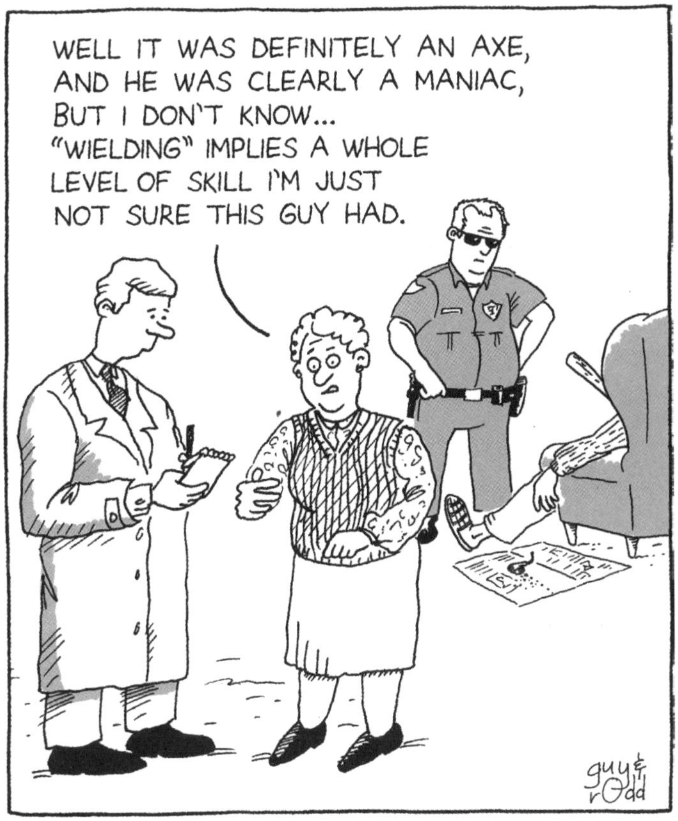
WELL IT WAS DEFINITELY AN AXE, AND HE WAS CLEARLY A MANIAC, BUT I DON'T KNOW... "WIELDING" IMPLIES A WHOLE LEVEL OF SKILL I'M JUST NOT SURE THIS GUY HAD.
guy & rOdd

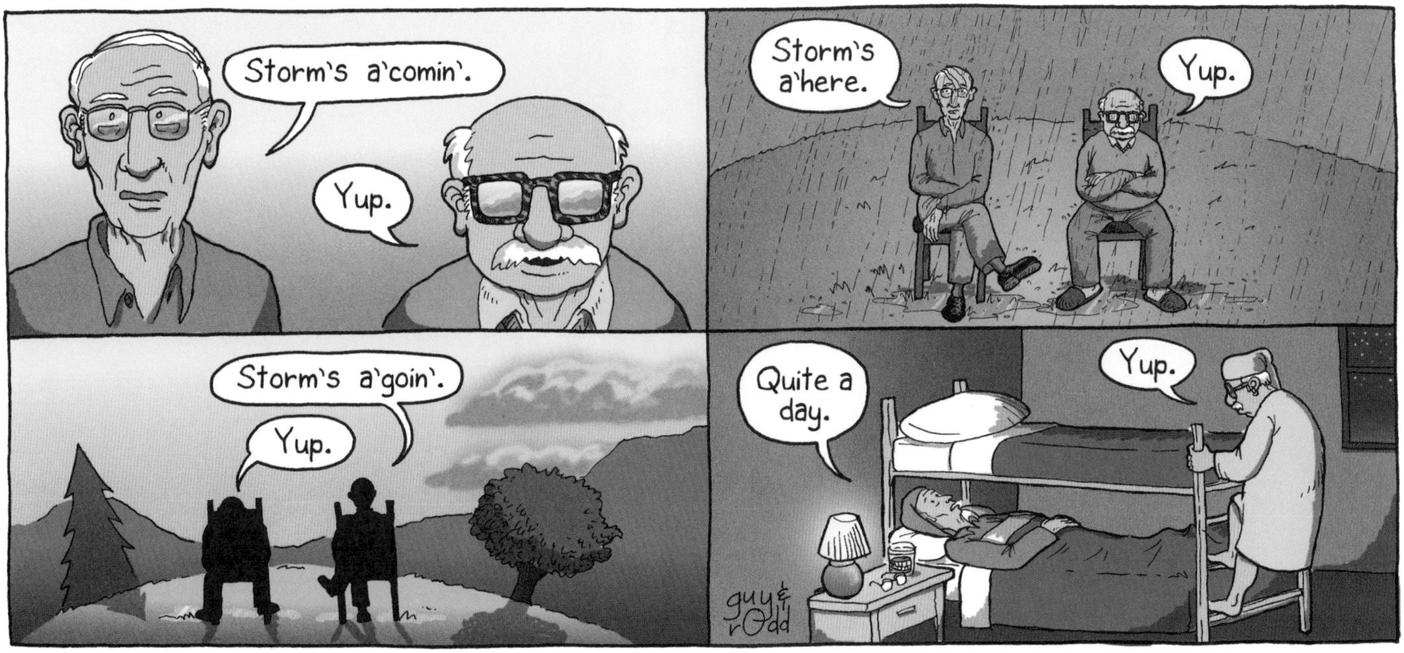
Storm's a'comin'.
Yup.
Storm's a'here.
Yup.
Storm's a'goin'.
Yup.
Quite a day.
Yup.
guy & rOdd

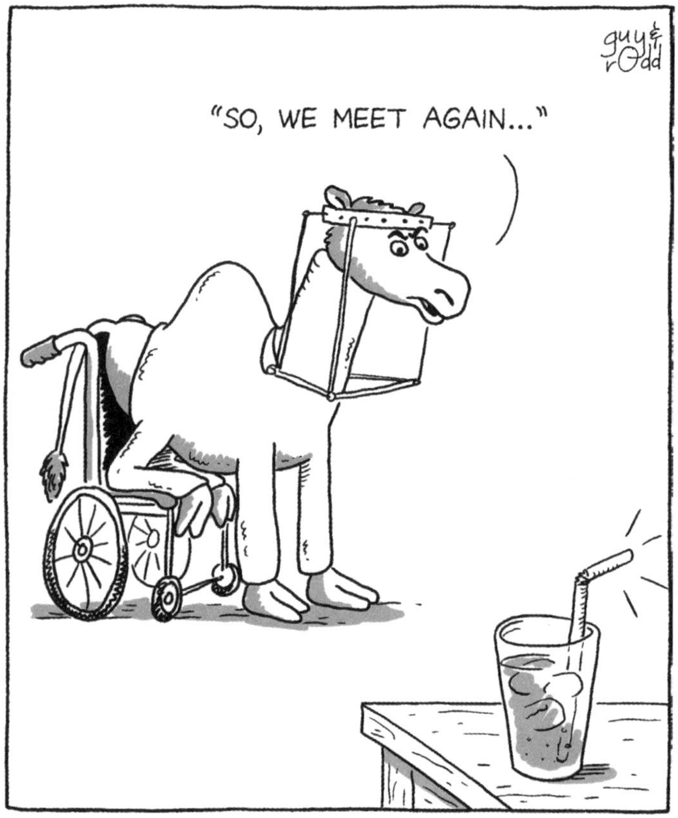
"SO, WE MEET AGAIN..."
guy & rodd

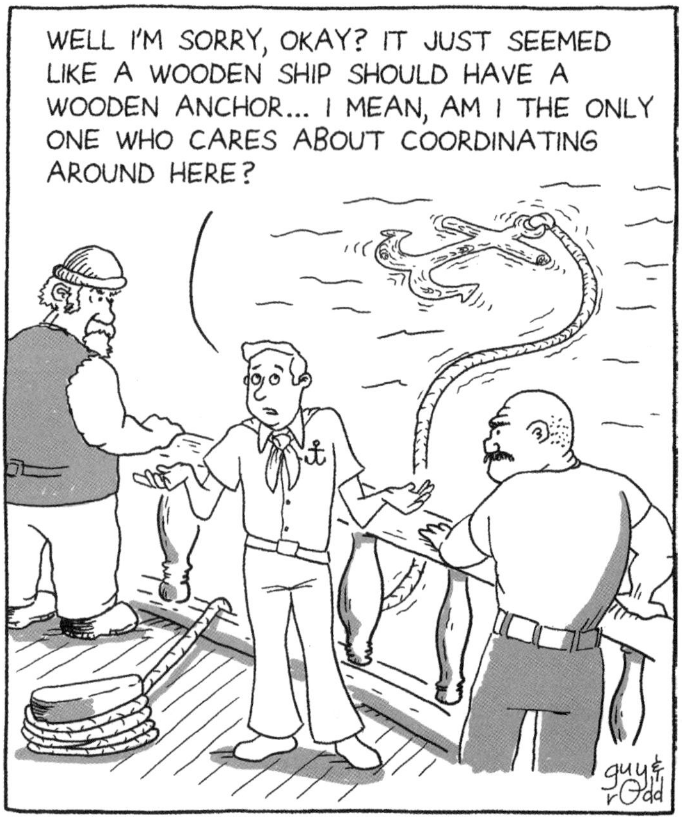
WELL I'M SORRY, OKAY? IT JUST SEEMED LIKE A WOODEN SHIP SHOULD HAVE A WOODEN ANCHOR... I MEAN, AM I THE ONLY ONE WHO CARES ABOUT COORDINATING AROUND HERE?
guy & rodd

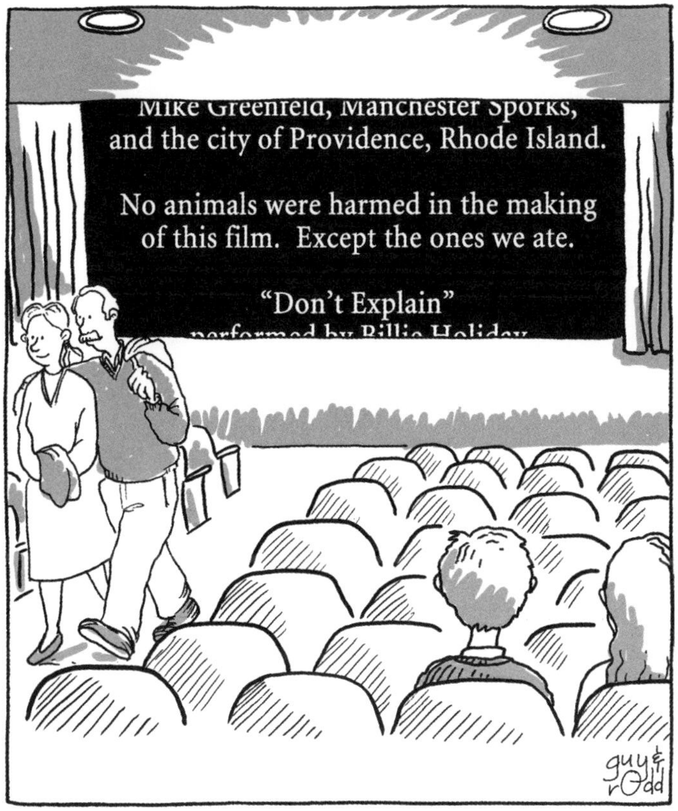
Mike Greenfeld, Manchester Sporks,
and the city of Providence, Rhode Island.
No animals were harmed in the making
of this film. Except the ones we ate.
“Don’t Explain”

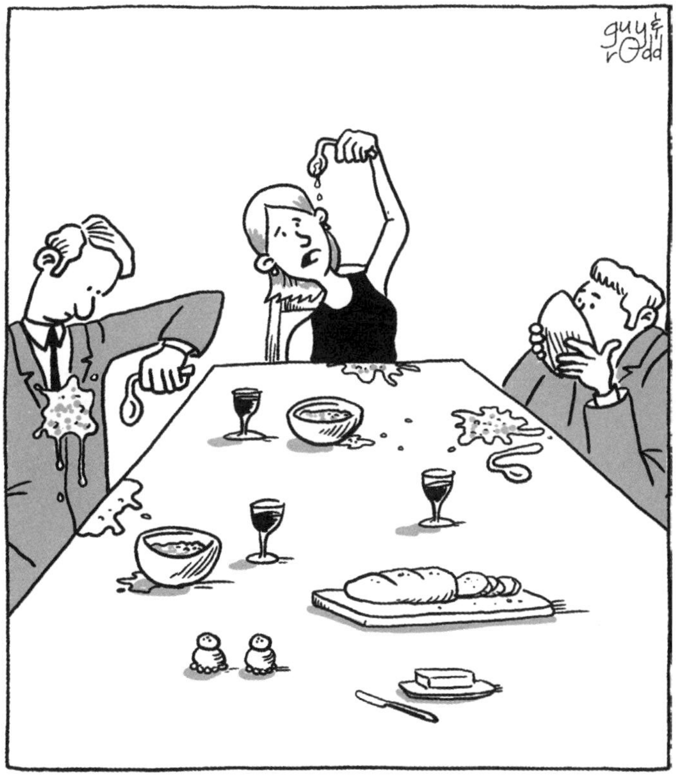

SOUP WAS ALWAYS DIFFICULT AT URI'S HOUSE.

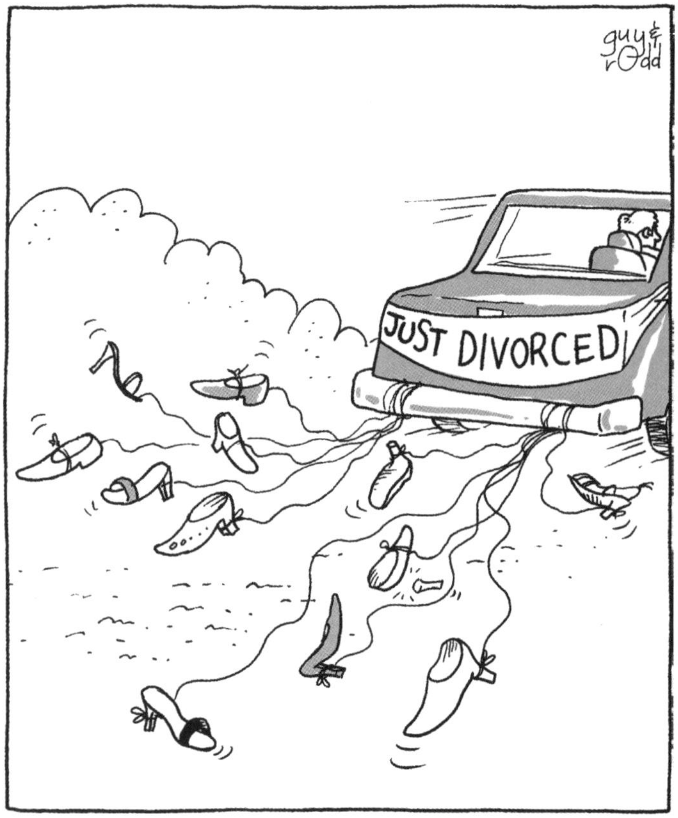
JUST DIVORCED

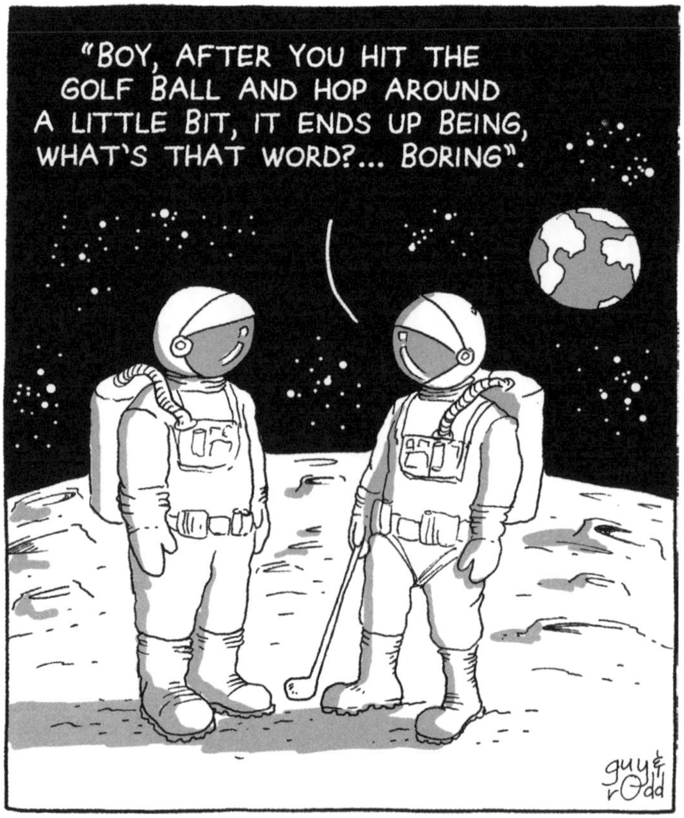
"BOY, AFTER YOU HIT THE GOLF BALL AND HOP AROUND A LITTLE BIT, IT ENDS UP BEING, WHAT'S THAT WORD?... BORING".

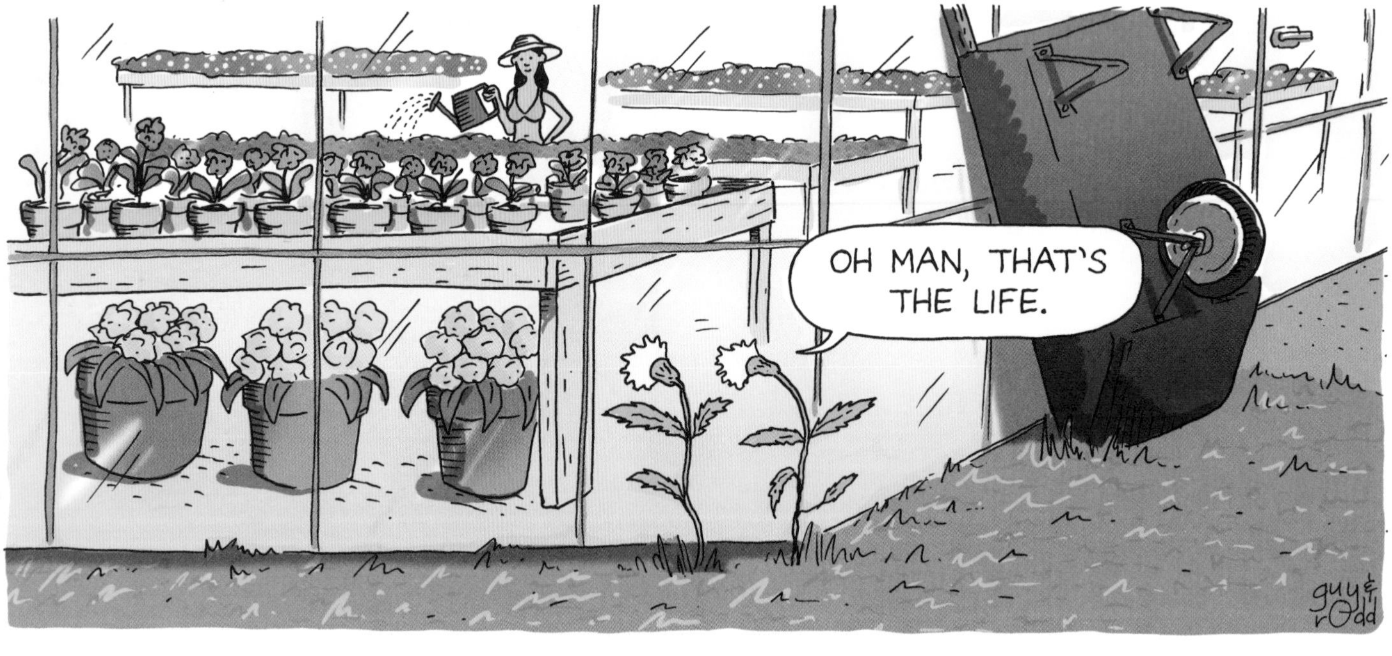
OH MAN, THAT'S THE LIFE.

ROBERTO PAUSED TO ADMIRE HIS WORK.
NEVER BEFORE HAD HE PLASTERED
A CEILING SO BEAUTIFULLY.
MINUTES LATER, A YOUNG PUNK NAMED
MICHELANGELO WOULD RUIN EVERYTHING.

"SOME OF THESE TREES HAVE BEEN HERE FOR
2000 YEARS... AND THEY STILL CAN'T TALK
...MAN, WE'RE AWESOME!"

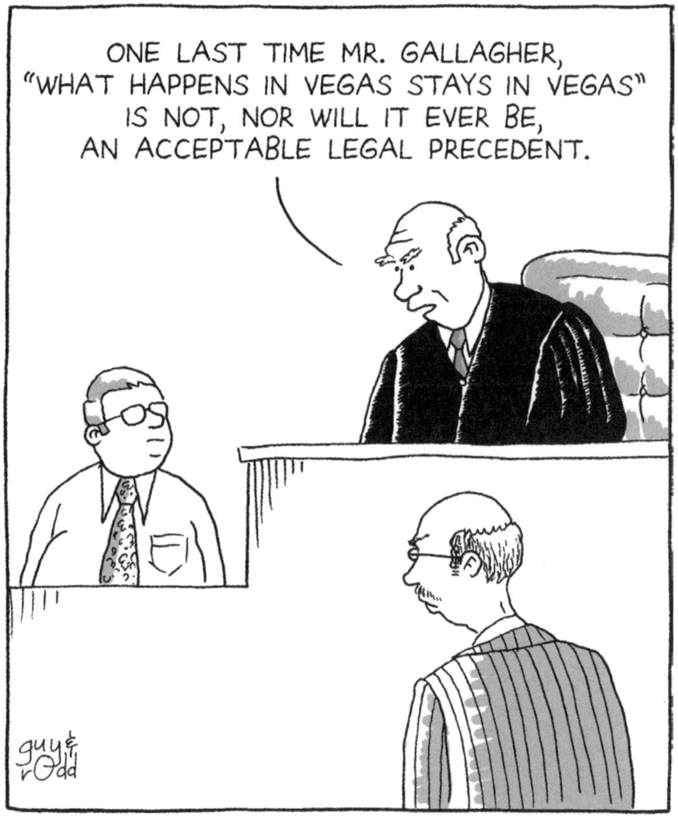
ONE LAST TIME MR. GALLAGHER, "WHAT HAPPENS IN VEGAS STAYS IN VEGAS" IS NOT, NOR WILL IT EVER BE, AN ACCEPTABLE LEGAL PRECEDENT.
guy & rodd

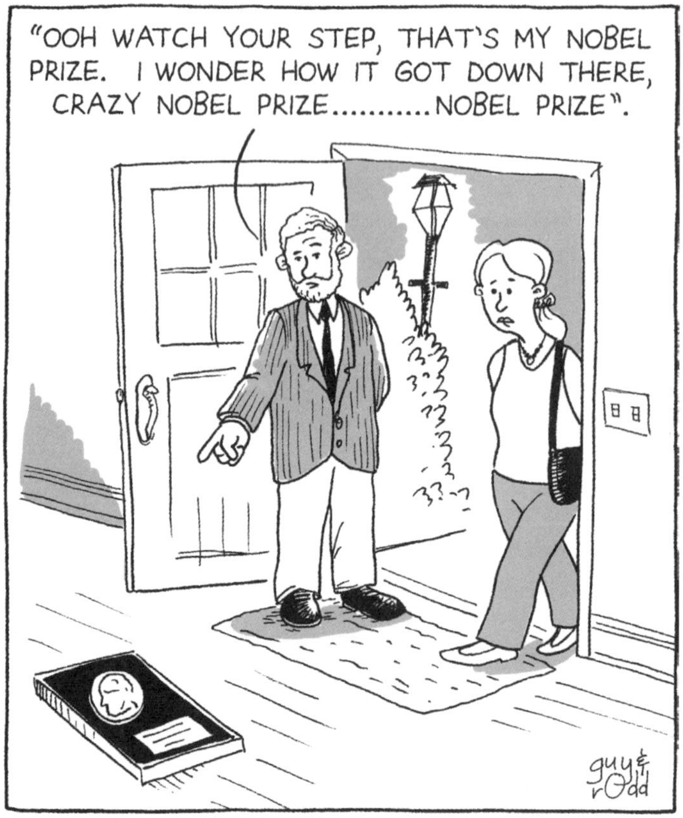
"OOH WATCH YOUR STEP, THAT'S MY NOBEL PRIZE. I WONDER HOW IT GOT DOWN THERE, CRAZY NOBEL PRIZE...........NOBEL PRIZE".
guy & rodd

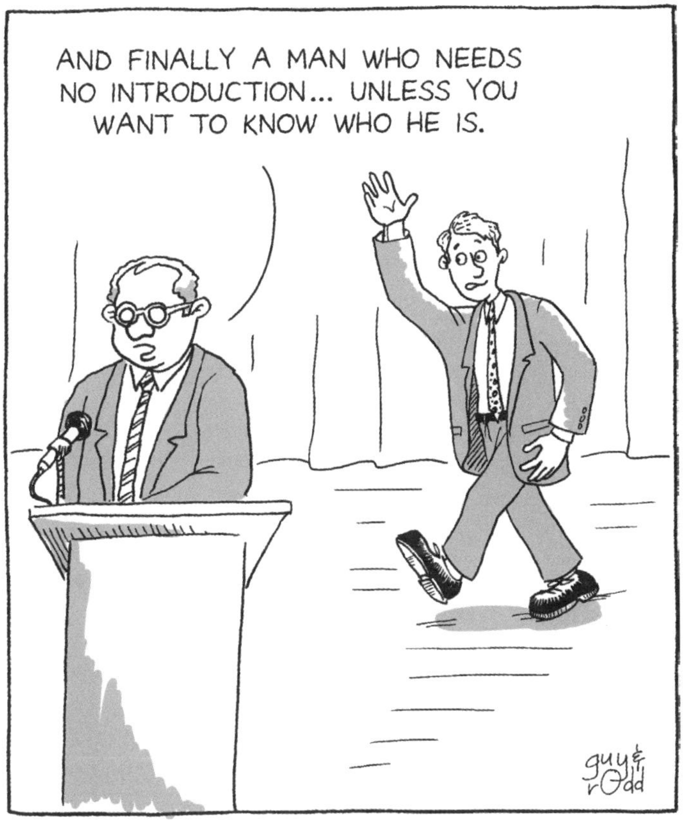
AND FINALLY A MAN WHO NEEDS NO INTRODUCTION... UNLESS YOU WANT TO KNOW WHO HE IS.
guy & rOdd

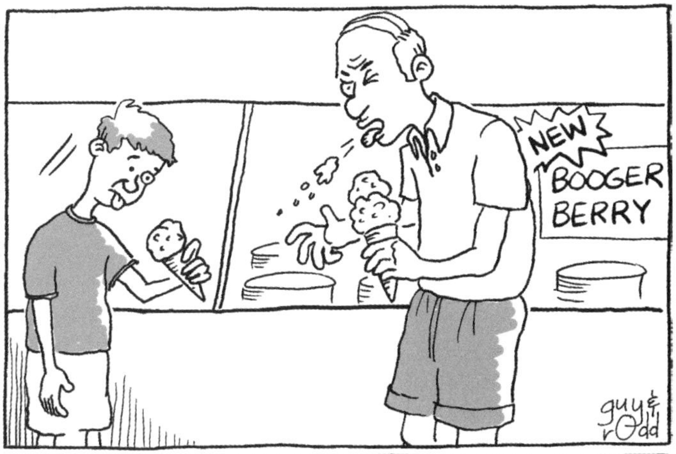
NEW
BOOGER BERRY
guy & rOdd

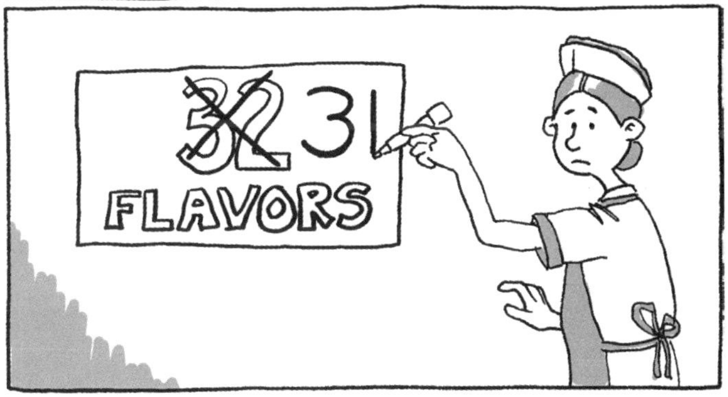
32 31
FLAVORS

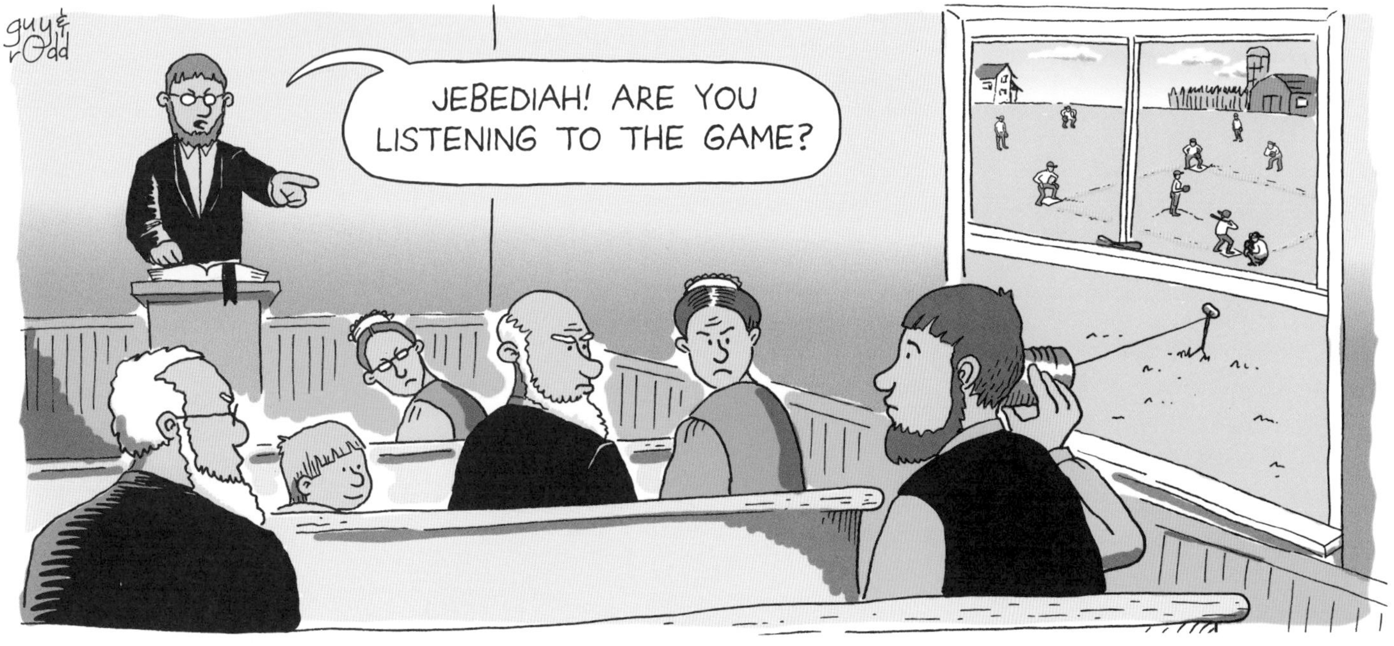
guy & rOdd
JEBEDIAH! ARE YOU LISTENING TO THE GAME?

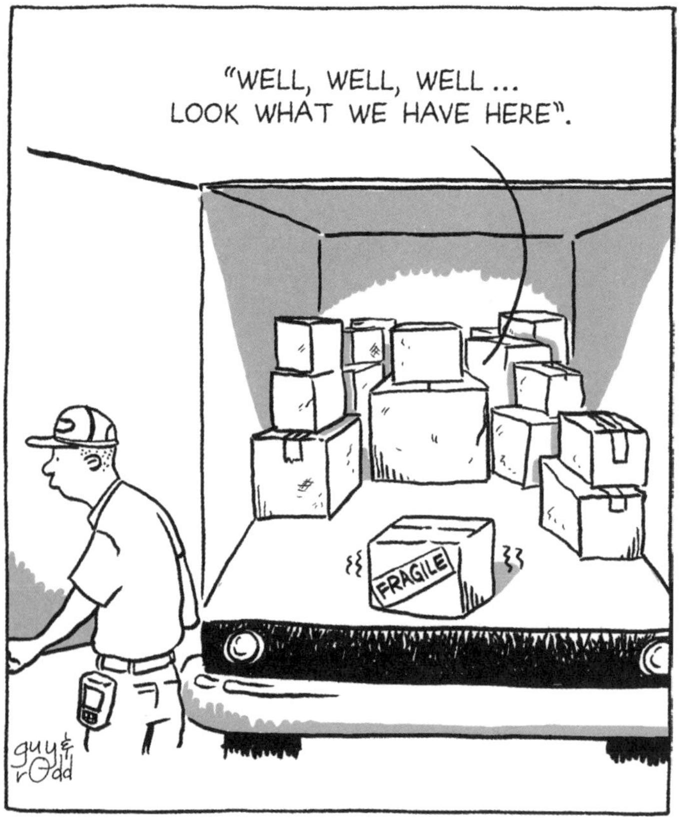
"WELL, WELL, WELL ...
LOOK WHAT WE HAVE HERE".
FRAGILE
guy & rOdd

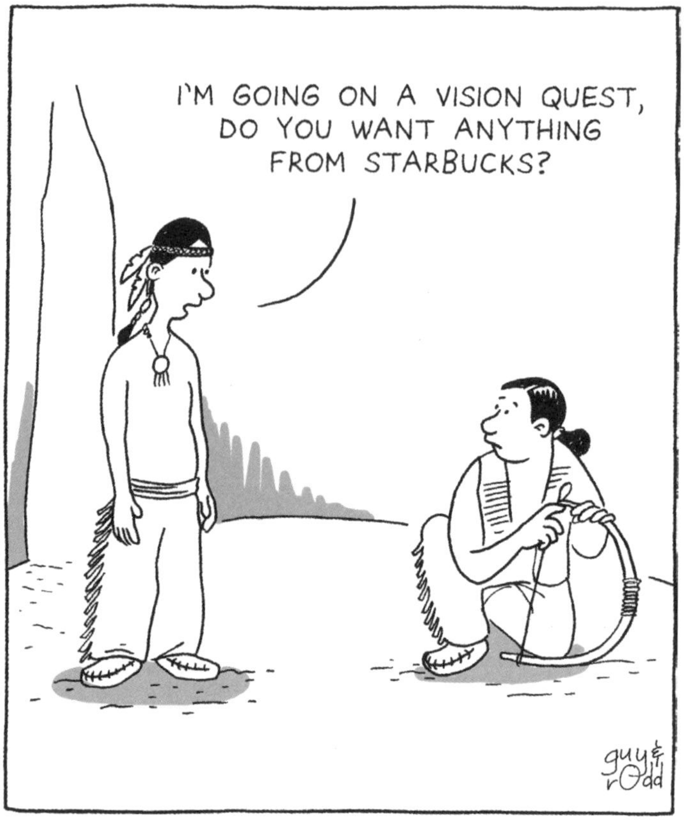
I'M GOING ON A VISION QUEST,
DO YOU WANT ANYTHING
FROM STARBUCKS?
guy & rOdd

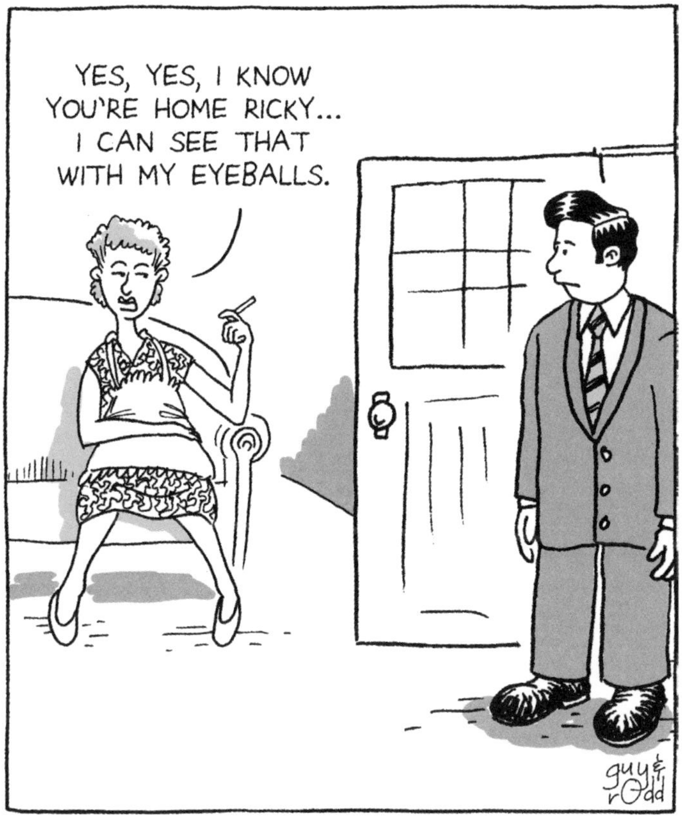
YES, YES, I KNOW YOU'RE HOME RICKY... I CAN SEE THAT WITH MY EYEBALLS.
guy & rOdd

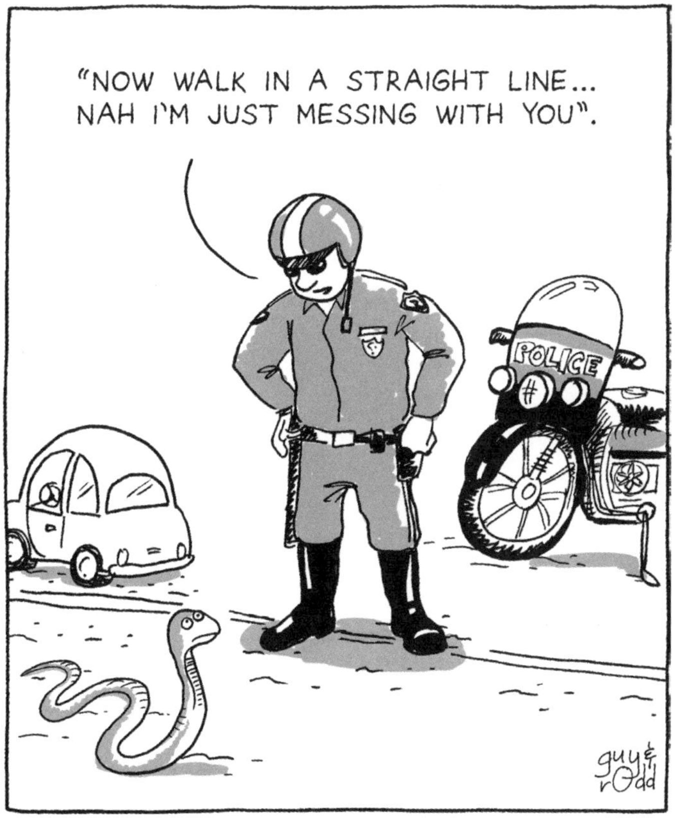
"NOW WALK IN A STRAIGHT LINE... NAH I'M JUST MESSING WITH YOU".
POLICE
guy & rOdd

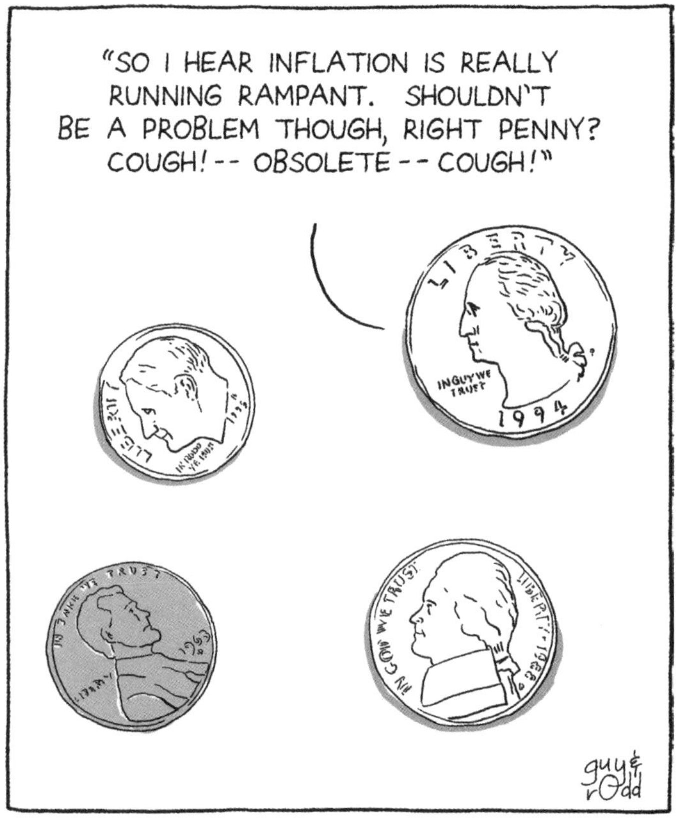
"SO I HEAR INFLATION IS REALLY RUNNING RAMPANT. SHOULDN'T BE A PROBLEM THOUGH, RIGHT PENNY? COUGH! -- OBSOLETE -- COUGH!"

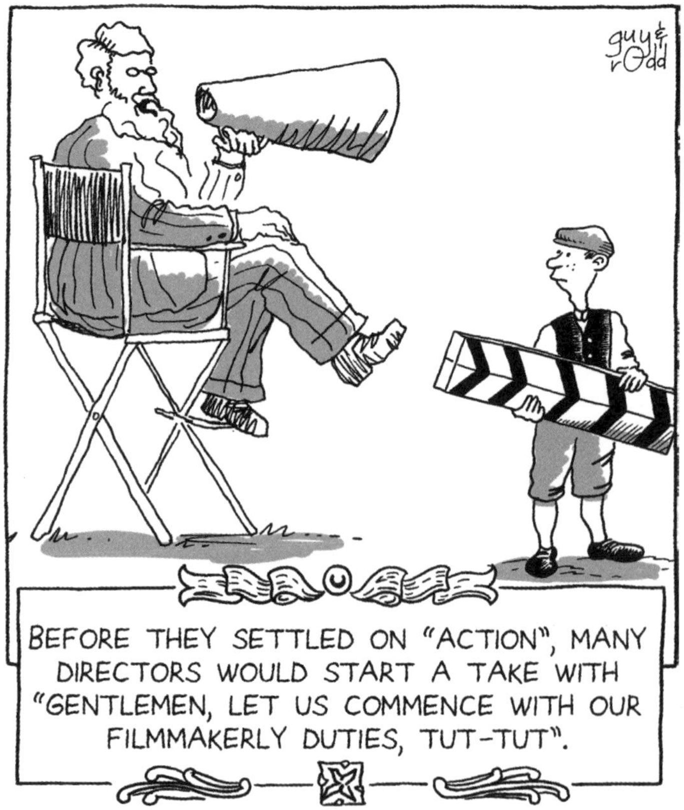
BEFORE THEY SETTLED ON "ACTION", MANY DIRECTORS WOULD START A TAKE WITH "GENTLEMEN, LET US COMMENCE WITH OUR FILMMAKERLY DUTIES, TUT-TUT".

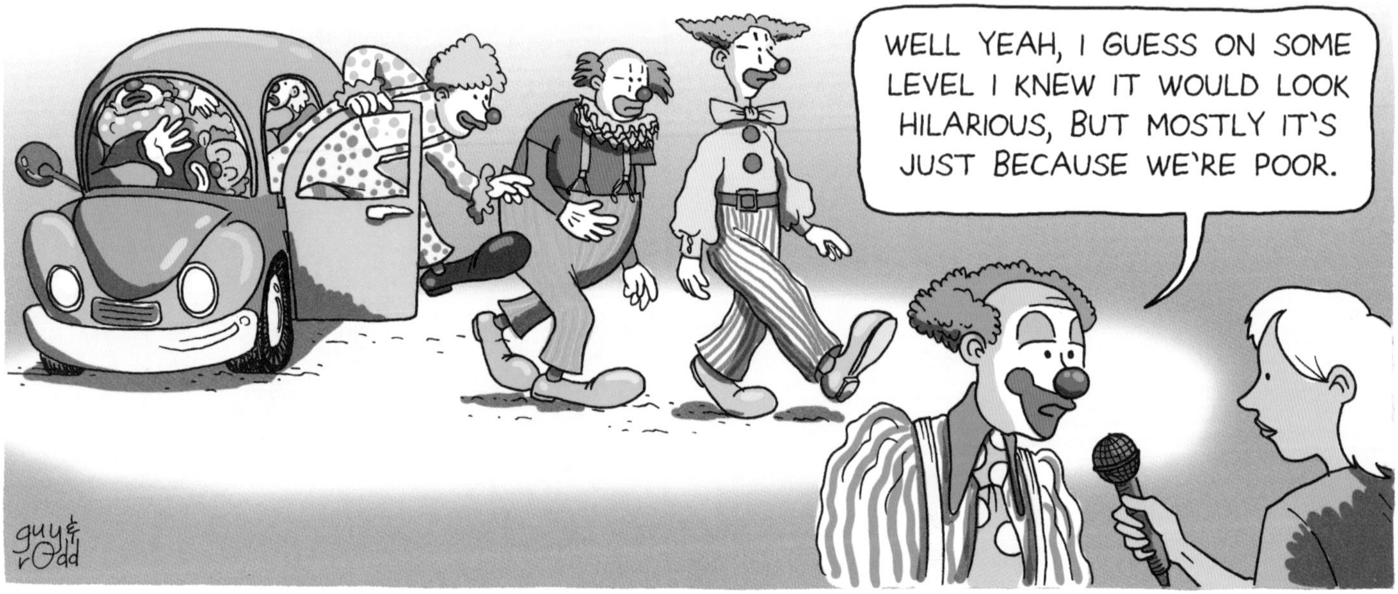
WELL YEAH, I GUESS ON SOME LEVEL I KNEW IT WOULD LOOK HILARIOUS, BUT MOSTLY IT'S JUST BECAUSE WE'RE POOR.

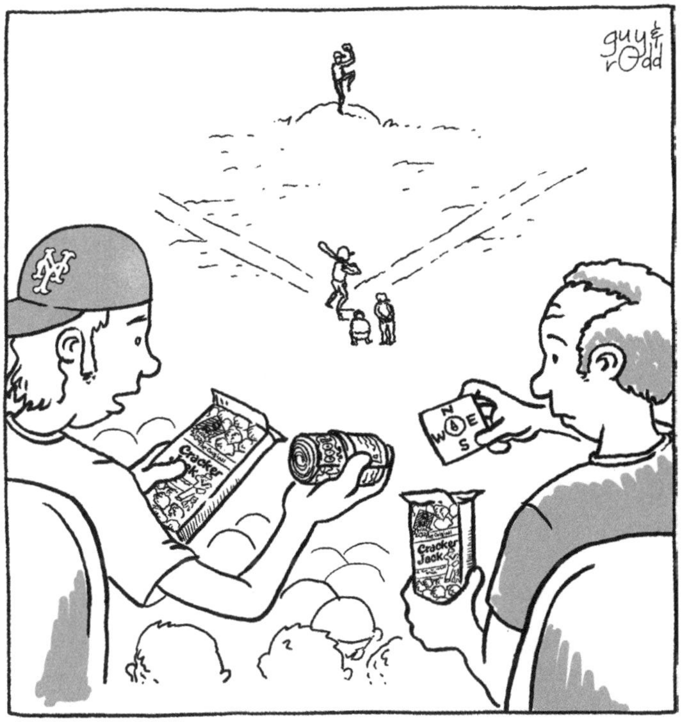
guy & rOdd
Cracker Jack
Cracker Jack
N
W
E
S
"HEY I GOT ANOTHER ROLL OF THOUSANDS,
THAT'S THE THIRD TIME THIS WEEK...
SO WHAT'D YOU GET?"

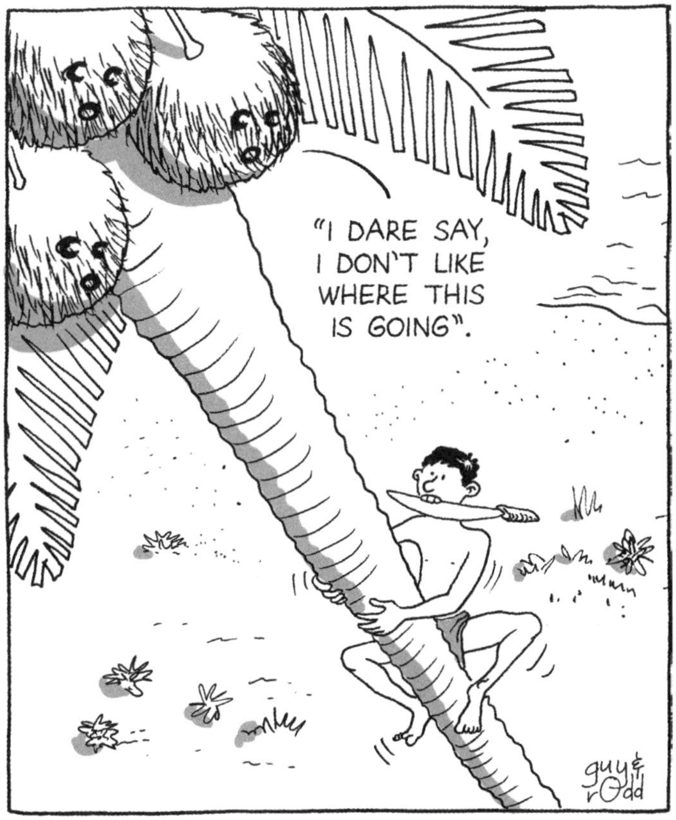
"I DARE SAY,
I DON'T LIKE
WHERE THIS
IS GOING".
guy & rOdd

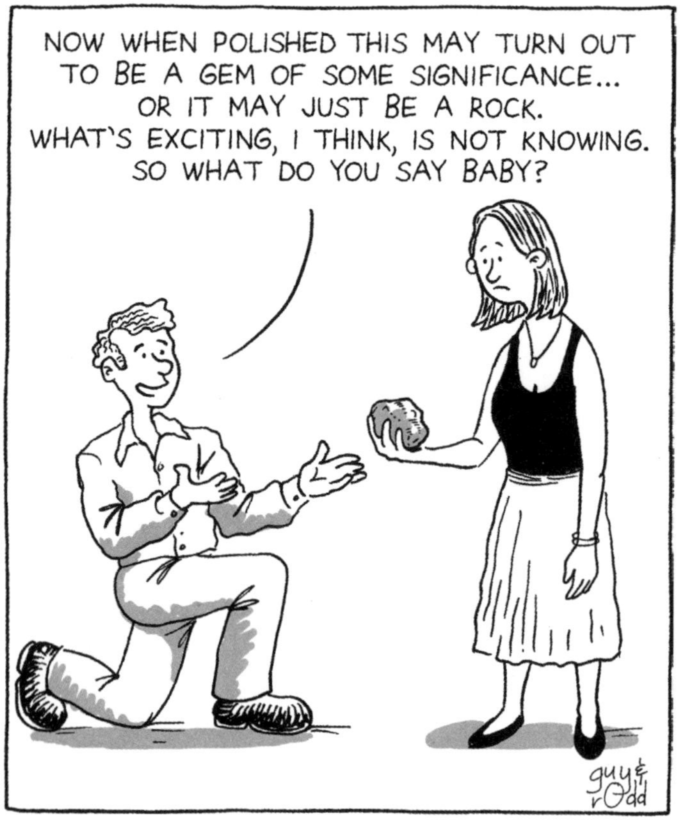
NOW WHEN POLISHED THIS MAY TURN OUT
TO BE A GEM OF SOME SIGNIFICANCE...
OR IT MAY JUST BE A ROCK.
WHAT'S EXCITING, I THINK, IS NOT KNOWING.
SO WHAT DO YOU SAY BABY?
guy & rodd

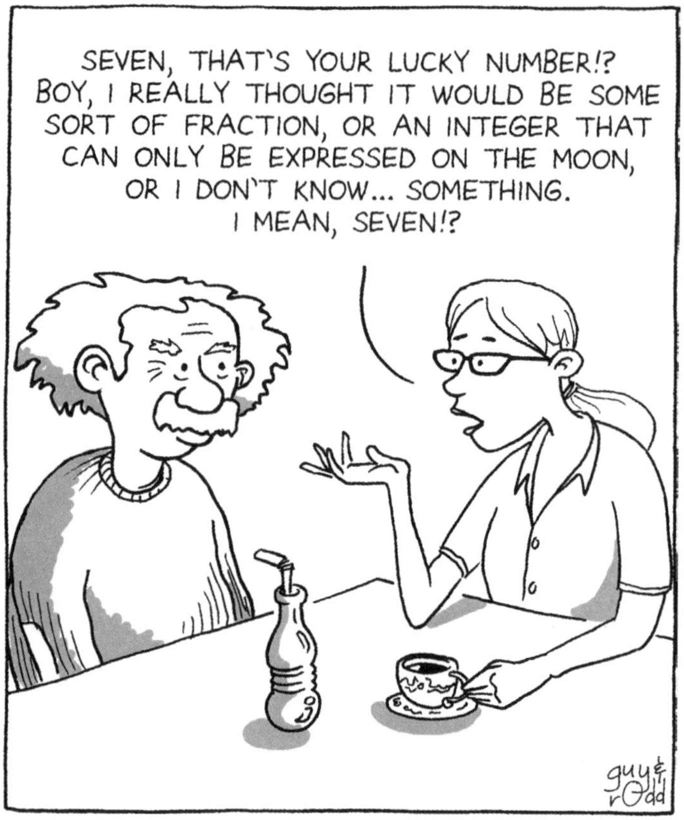
SEVEN, THAT'S YOUR LUCKY NUMBER!?
BOY, I REALLY THOUGHT IT WOULD BE SOME
SORT OF FRACTION, OR AN INTEGER THAT
CAN ONLY BE EXPRESSED ON THE MOON,
OR I DON'T KNOW... SOMETHING.
I MEAN, SEVEN!?
guy & rodd

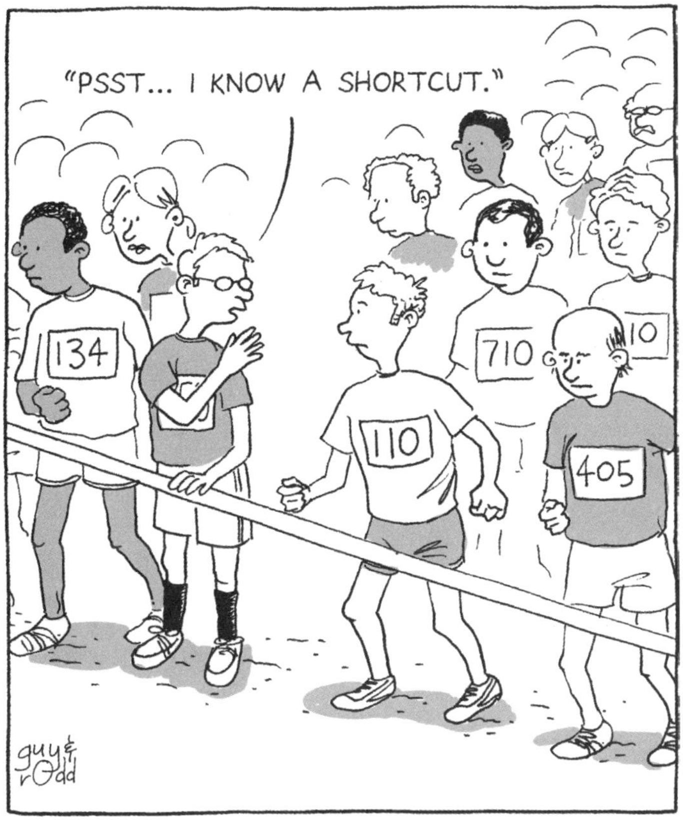
"PSST... I KNOW A SHORTCUT."
134
710
10
110
405
guy & rOdd

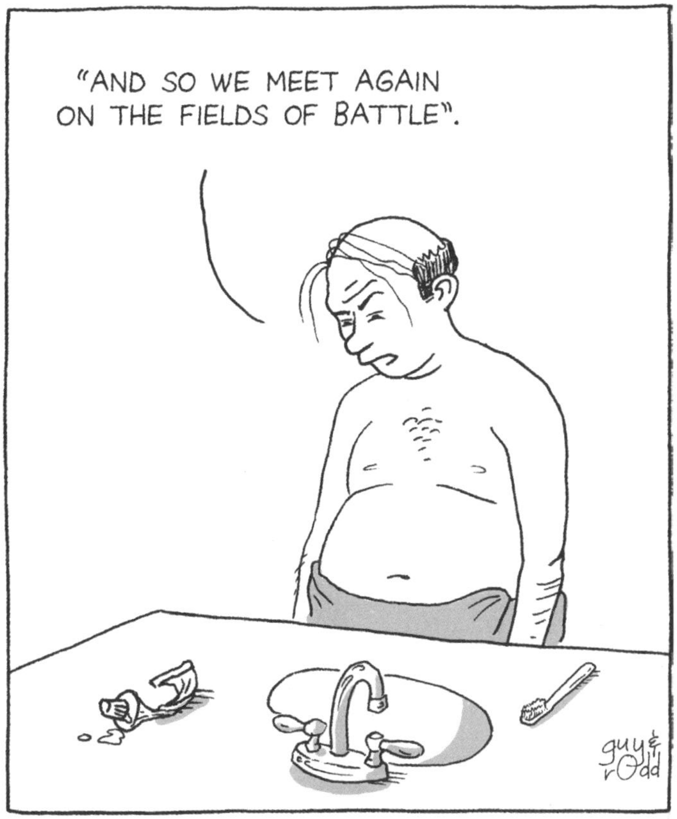
"AND SO WE MEET AGAIN ON THE FIELDS OF BATTLE".
guy & rOdd

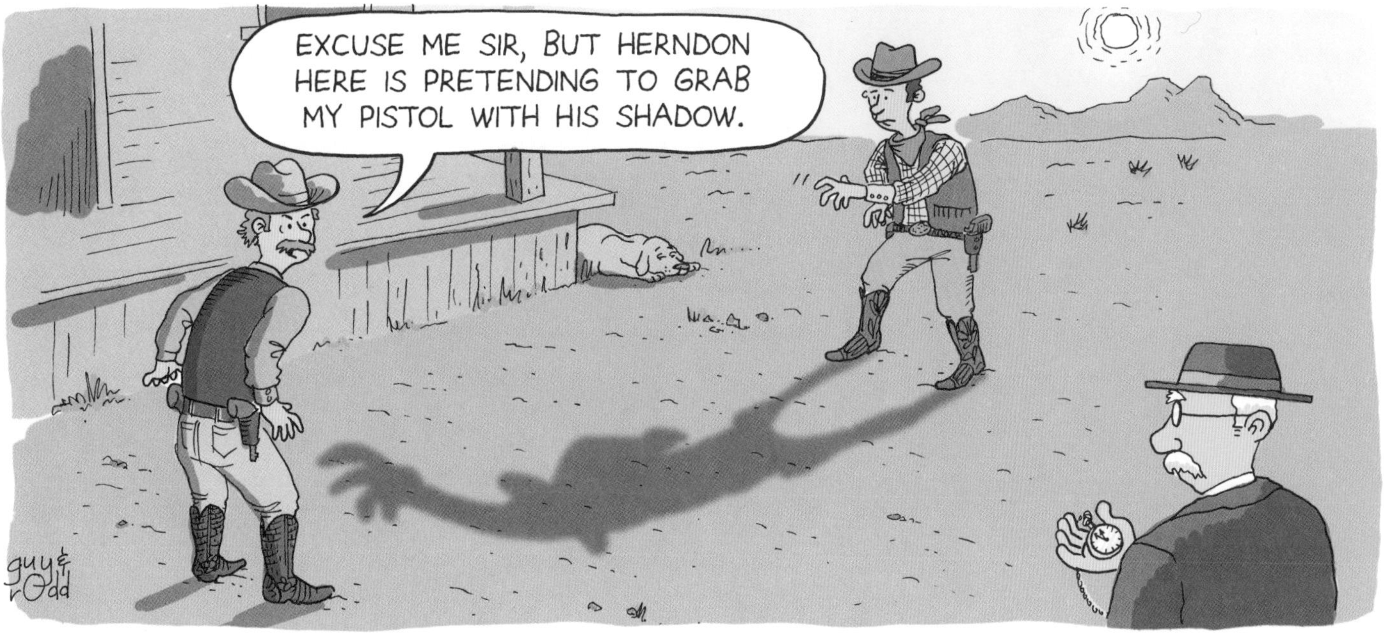
EXCUSE ME SIR, BUT HERNDON HERE IS PRETENDING TO GRAB MY PISTOL WITH HIS SHADOW.
guy & rOdd

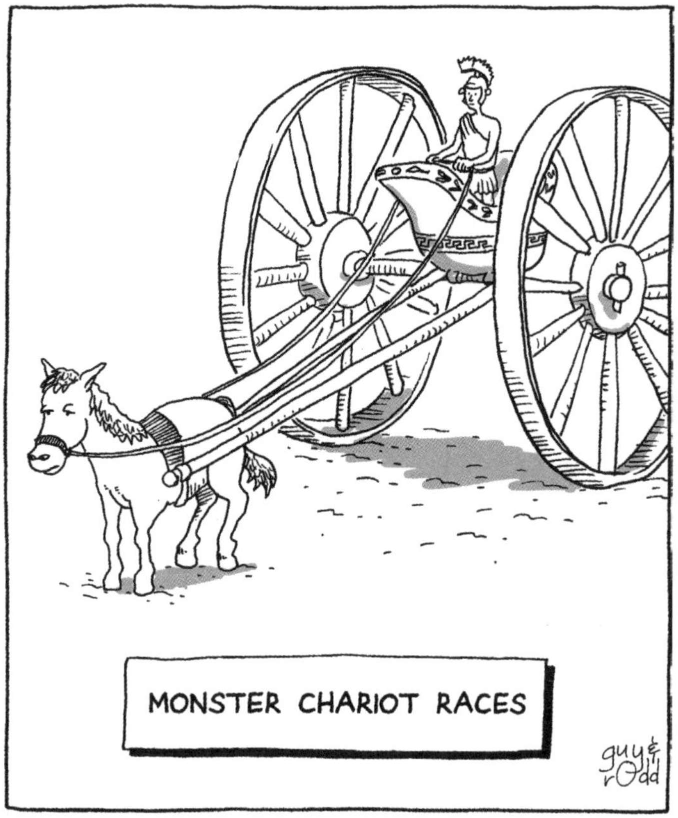
MONSTER CHARIOT RACES

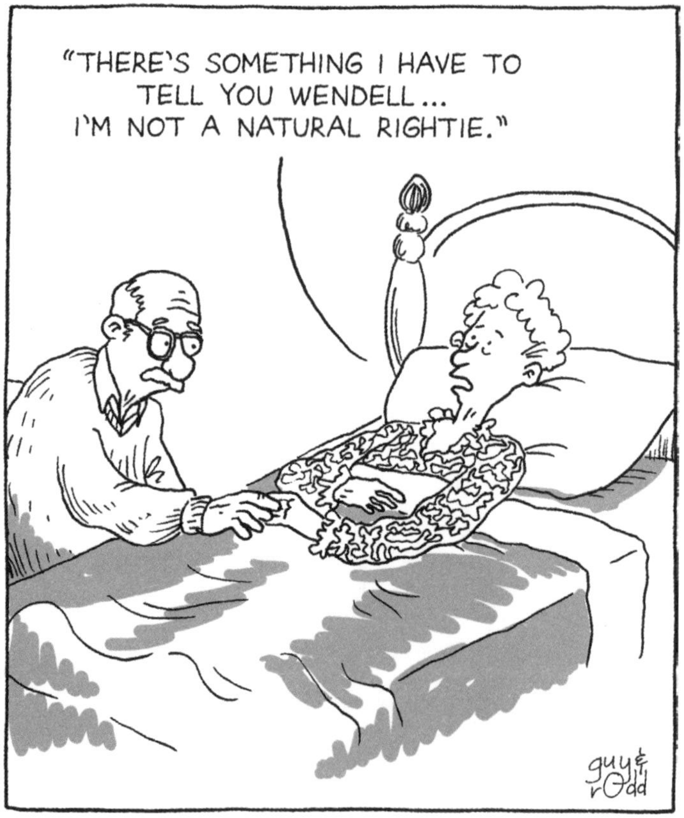
"THERE'S SOMETHING I HAVE TO TELL YOU WENDELL... I'M NOT A NATURAL RIGHTIE."

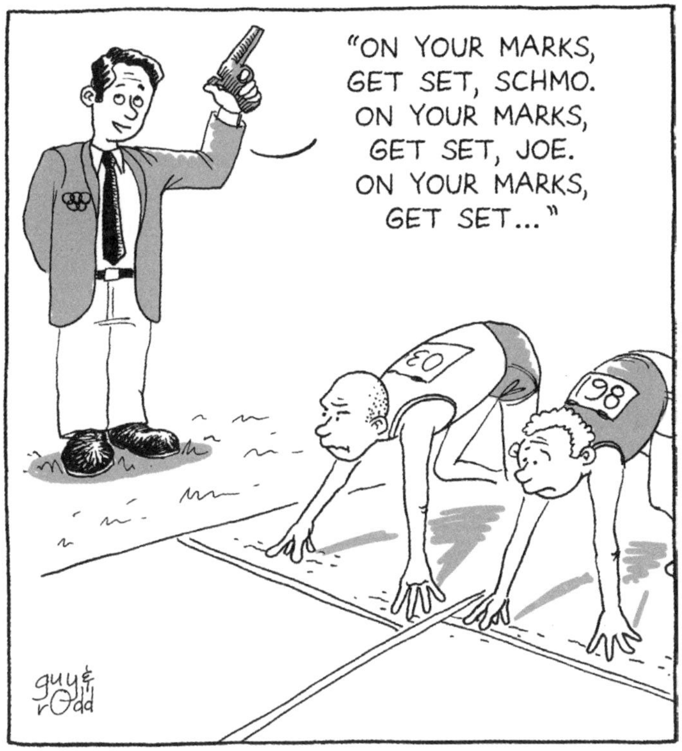
"ON YOUR MARKS, GET SET, SCHMO. ON YOUR MARKS, GET SET, JOE. ON YOUR MARKS, GET SET..."

SANDRO FAILED TO ANTICIPATE THE SERIOUSNESS OF THE OLYMPICS.

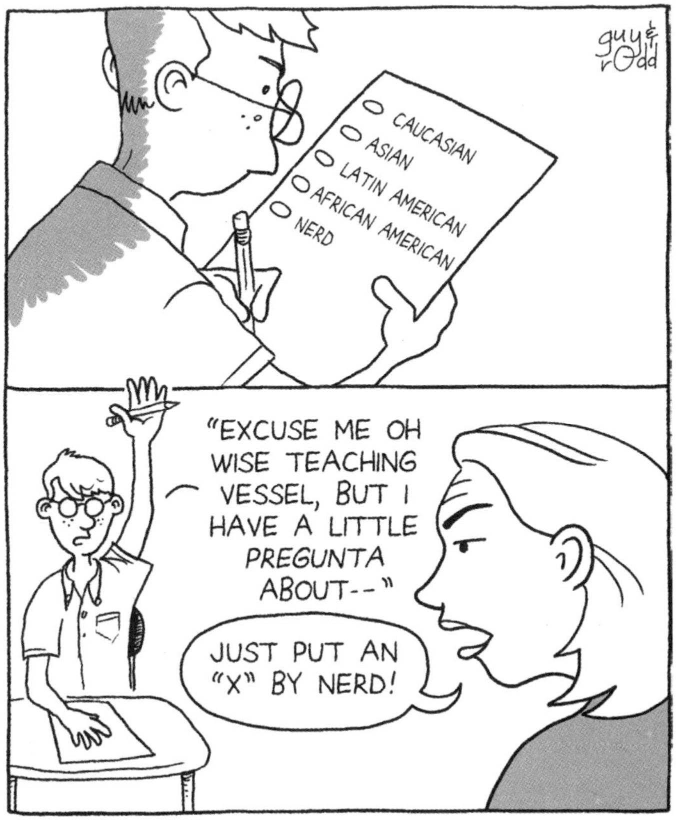
CAUCASIAN
ASIAN
LATIN AMERICAN
AFRICAN AMERICAN
NERD
"EXCUSE ME OH WISE TEACHING VESSEL, BUT I HAVE A LITTLE *PREGUNTA* ABOUT--"
JUST PUT AN "X" BY NERD!

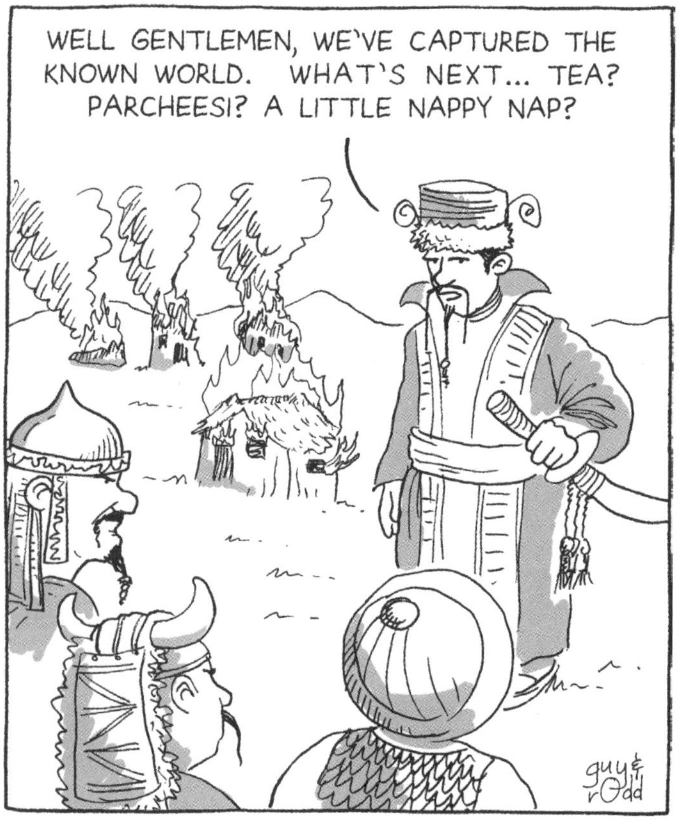
WELL GENTLEMEN, WE'VE CAPTURED THE KNOWN WORLD. WHAT'S NEXT... TEA? PARCHEESI? A LITTLE NAPPY NAP?
guy & rOdd

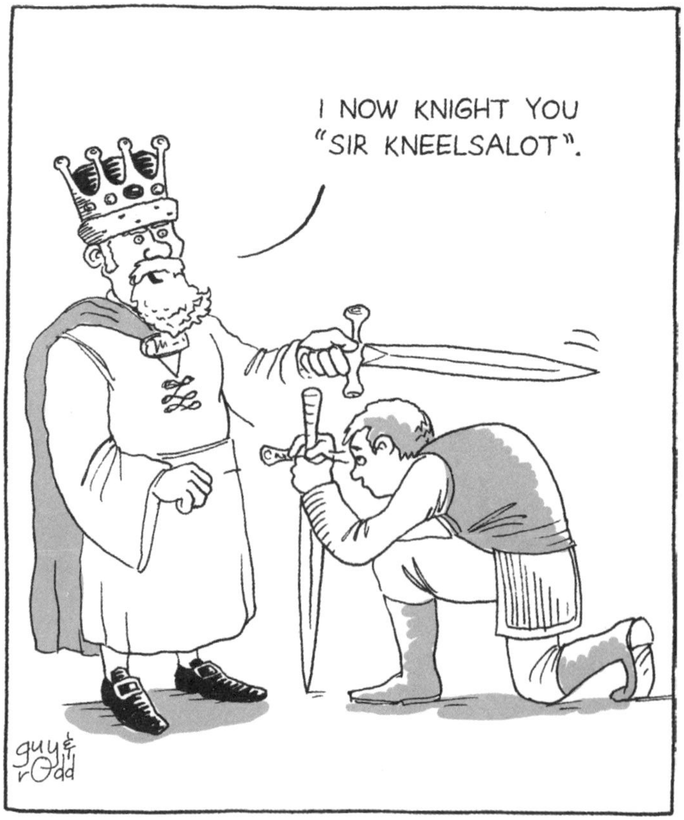
I NOW KNIGHT YOU "SIR KNEELSALOT".
guy & rOdd

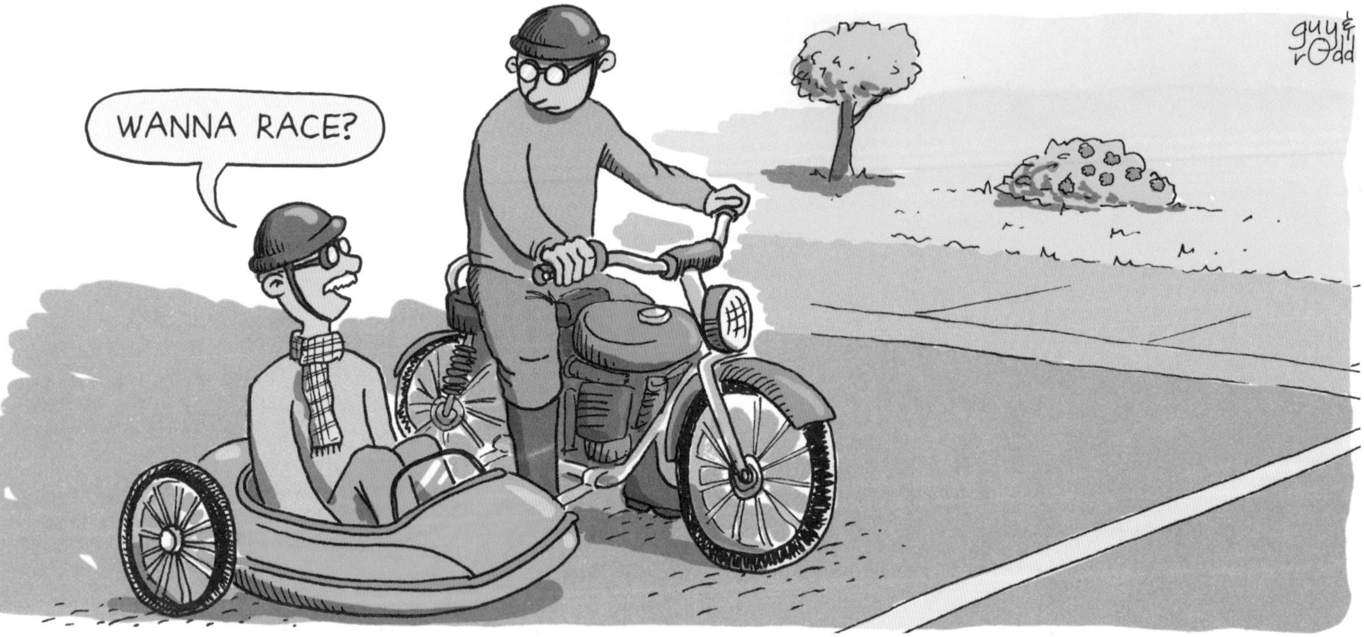
WANNA RACE?
guy & rOdd

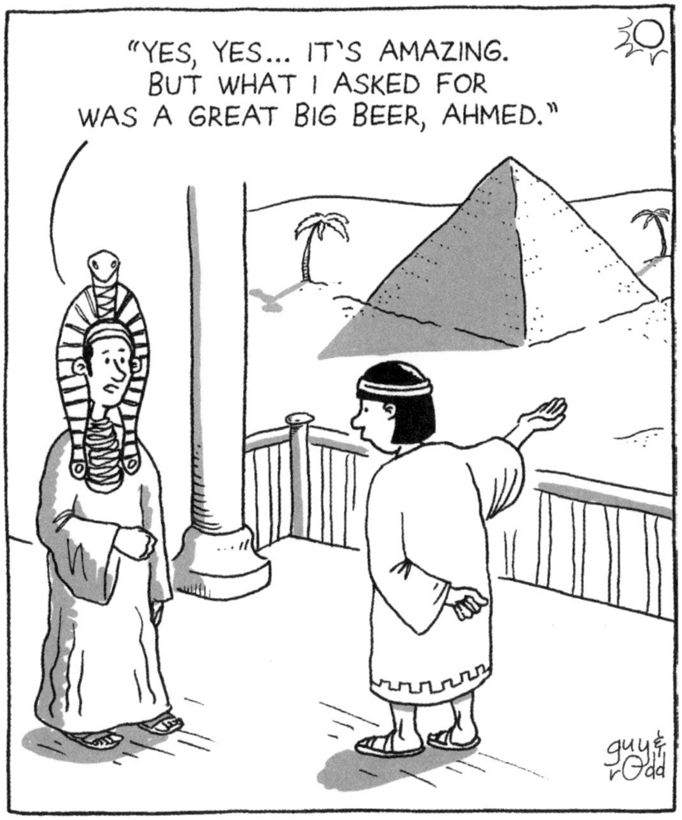
"YES, YES... IT'S AMAZING. BUT WHAT I ASKED FOR WAS A GREAT BIG BEER, AHMED."
guy & rOdd

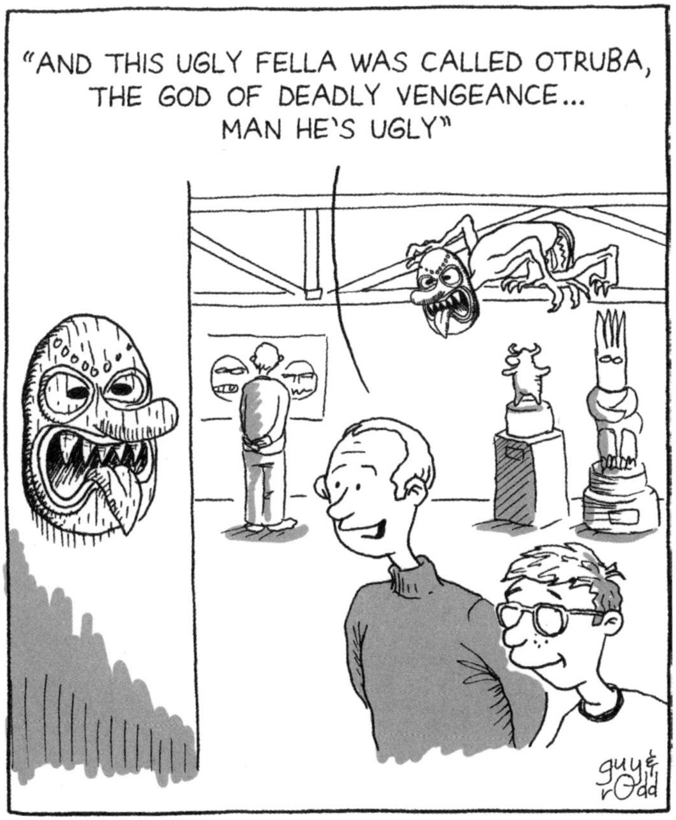
"AND THIS UGLY FELLA WAS CALLED OTRUBA, THE GOD OF DEADLY VENGEANCE... MAN HE'S UGLY"
guy & rOdd

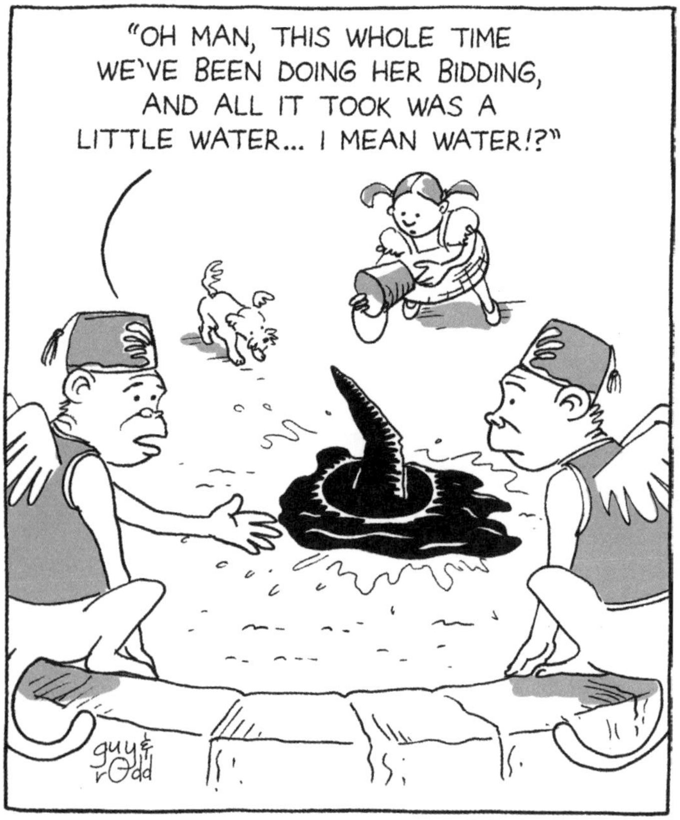
"OH MAN, THIS WHOLE TIME WE'VE BEEN DOING HER BIDDING, AND ALL IT TOOK WAS A LITTLE WATER... I MEAN WATER!?"
guy & rOdd

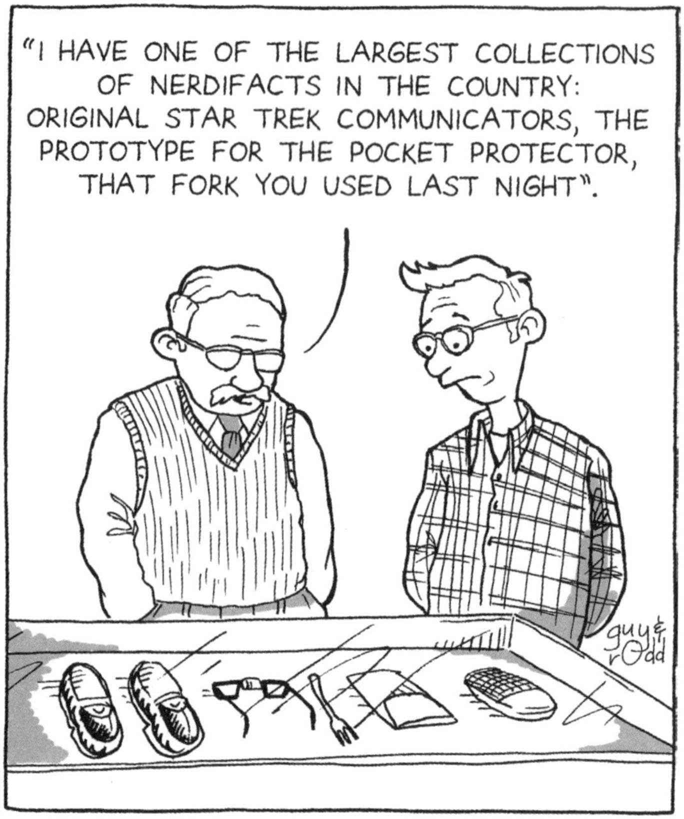
"I HAVE ONE OF THE LARGEST COLLECTIONS OF NERDIFACTS IN THE COUNTRY: ORIGINAL STAR TREK COMMUNICATORS, THE PROTOTYPE FOR THE POCKET PROTECTOR, THAT FORK YOU USED LAST NIGHT".
guy & rOdd

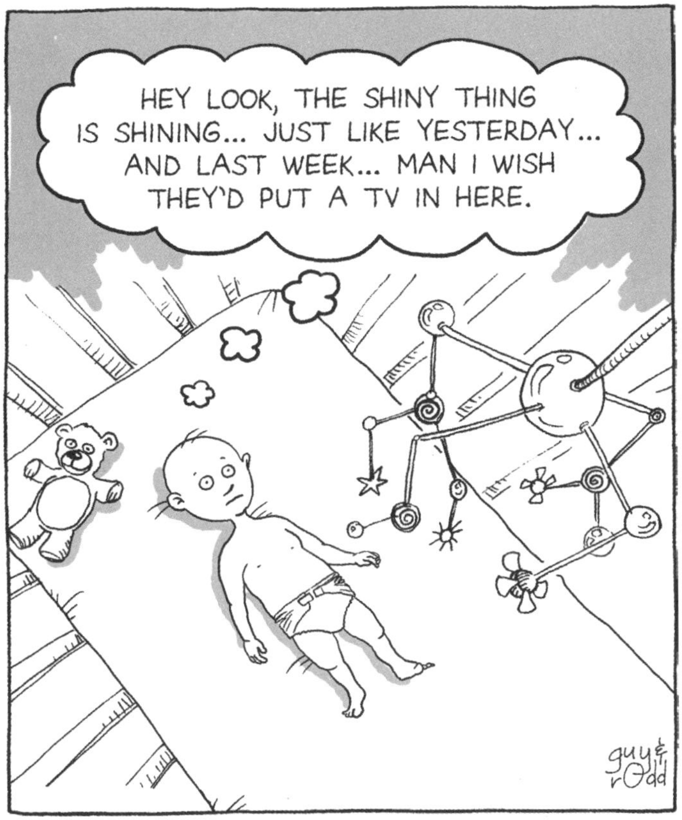
HEY LOOK, THE SHINY THING IS SHINING... JUST LIKE YESTERDAY... AND LAST WEEK... MAN I WISH THEY'D PUT A TV IN HERE.

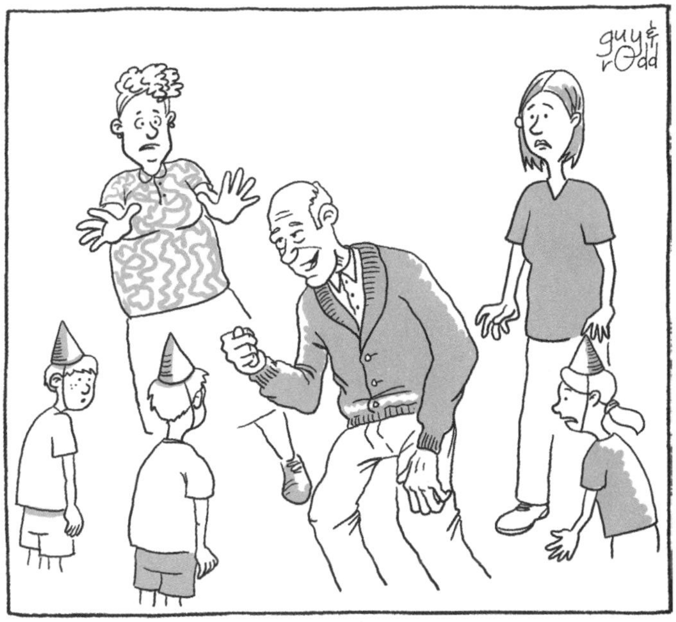

GRANDPA WAS PROUD OF THE EFFECT HIS SIGNATURE STOLEN NOSE TRICK WAS HAVING ON THE YOUNG CROWD. IT WASN'T UNTIL LATER THAT ANYONE EXPLAINED TO HIM HOW DYLAN HAD LOST HIS REAL NOSE IN A HORRIBLE SLEDDING ACCIDENT.

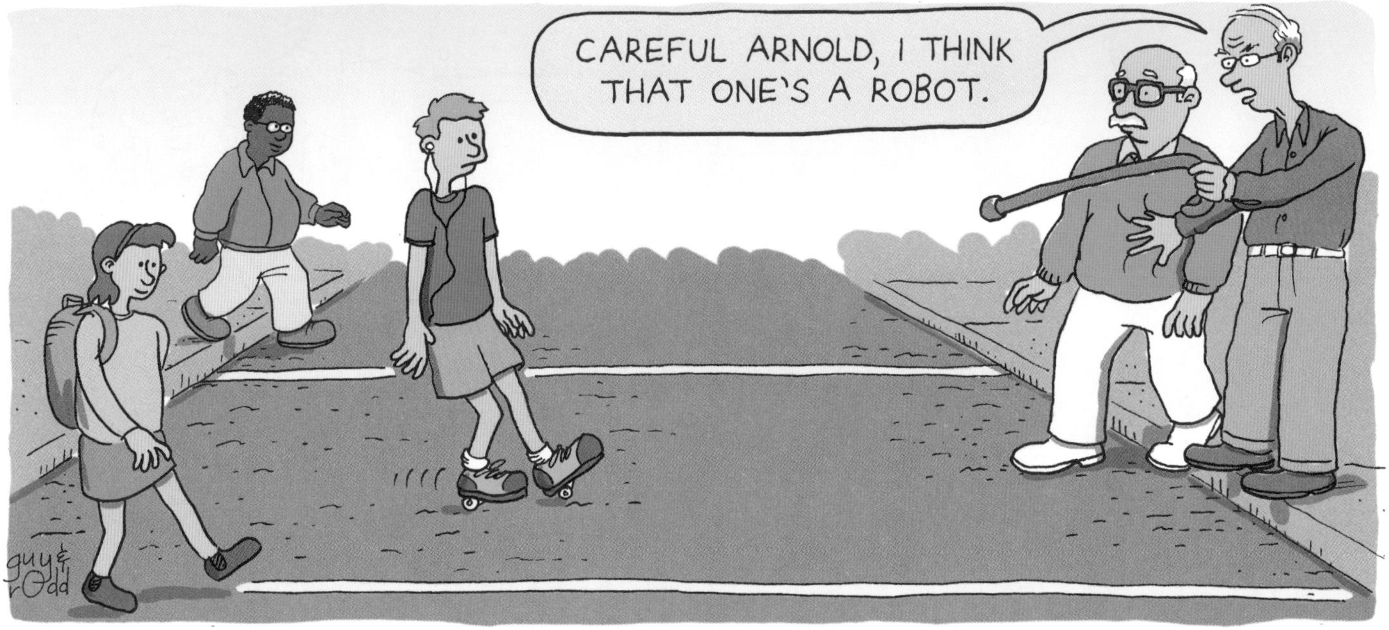
CAREFUL ARNOLD, I THINK THAT ONE'S A ROBOT.

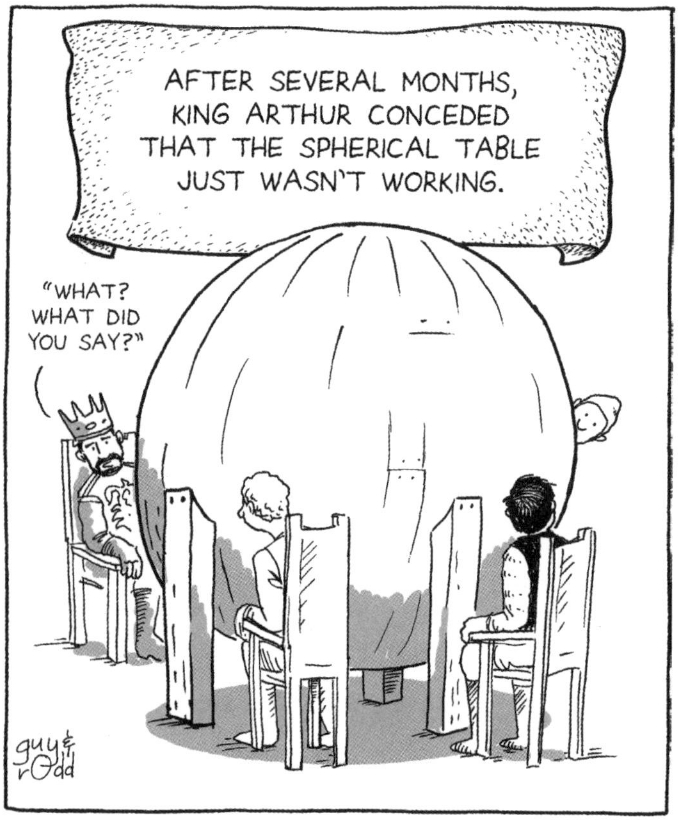
AFTER SEVERAL MONTHS, KING ARTHUR CONCEDED THAT THE SPHERICAL TABLE JUST WASN'T WORKING.
"WHAT? WHAT DID YOU SAY?"
guy & rOdd

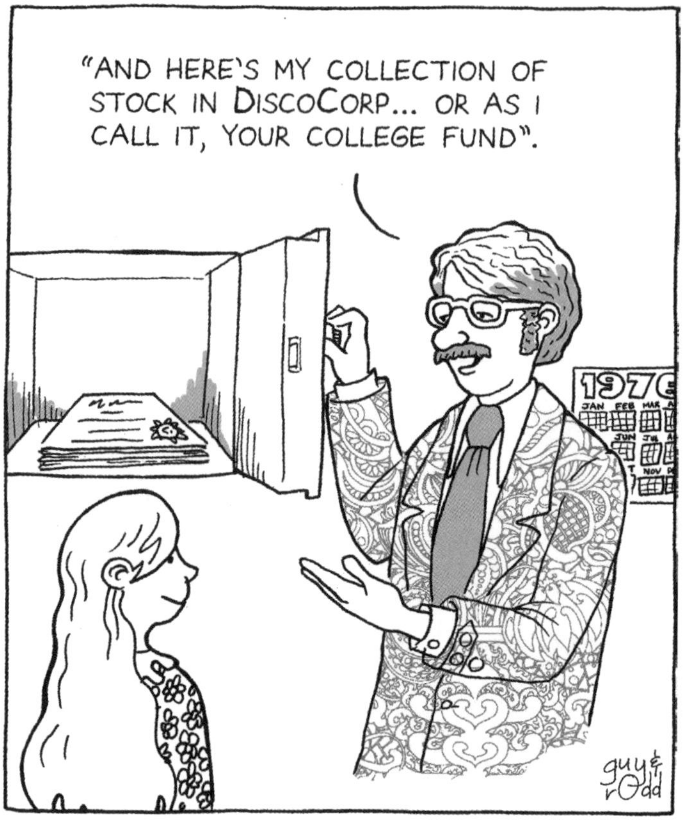
"AND HERE'S MY COLLECTION OF STOCK IN DISCOCORP... OR AS I CALL IT, YOUR COLLEGE FUND".
guy & rOdd

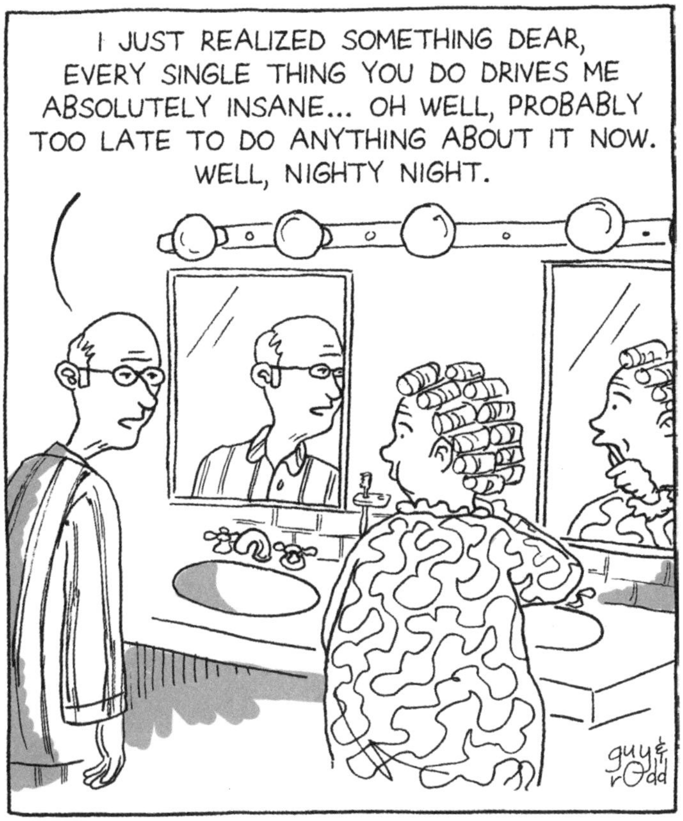
I JUST REALIZED SOMETHING DEAR, EVERY SINGLE THING YOU DO DRIVES ME ABSOLUTELY INSANE... OH WELL, PROBABLY TOO LATE TO DO ANYTHING ABOUT IT NOW. WELL, NIGHTY NIGHT.
guy & rOdd

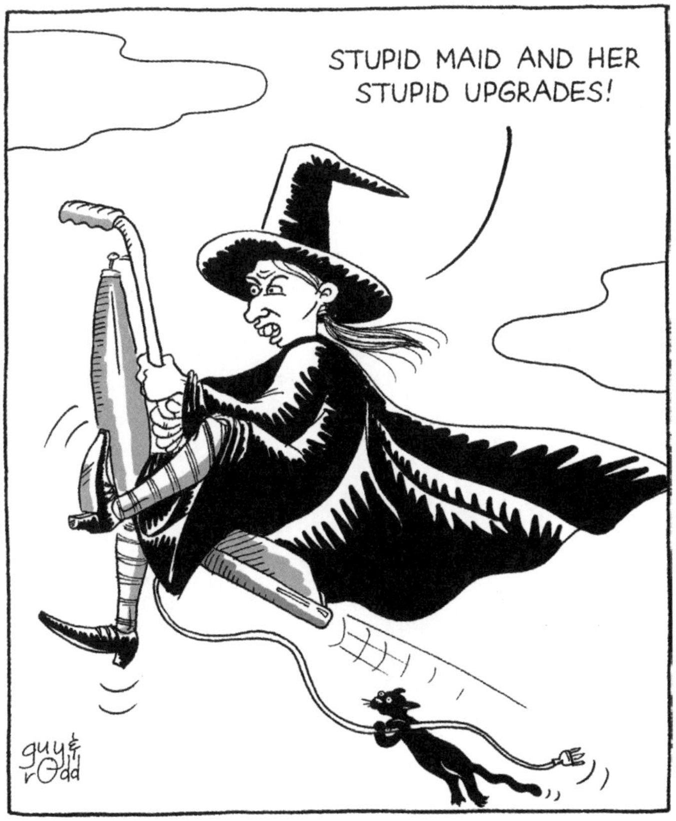
STUPID MAID AND HER STUPID UPGRADES!
guy & rOdd

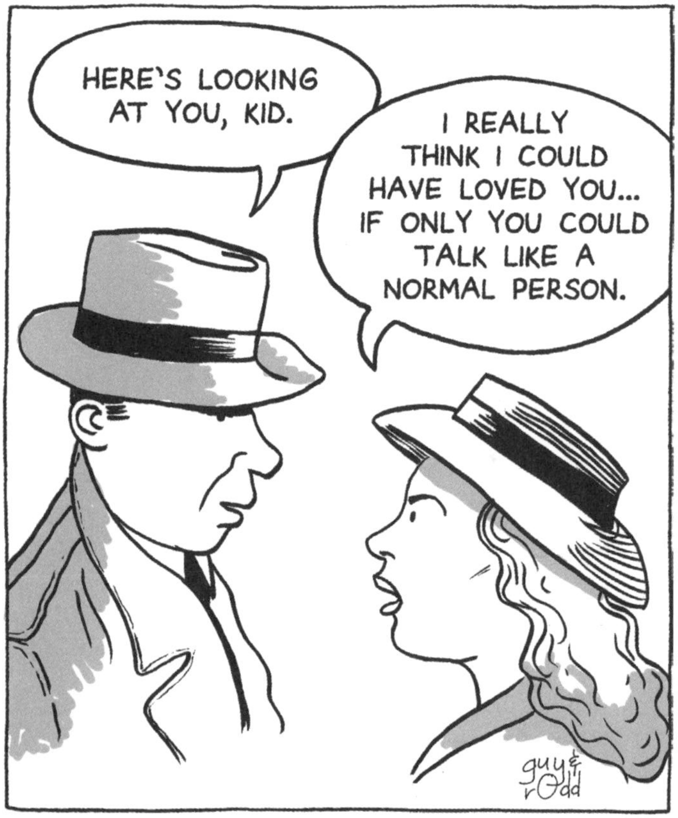
HERE'S LOOKING AT YOU, KID.
I REALLY THINK I COULD HAVE LOVED YOU... IF ONLY YOU COULD TALK LIKE A NORMAL PERSON.

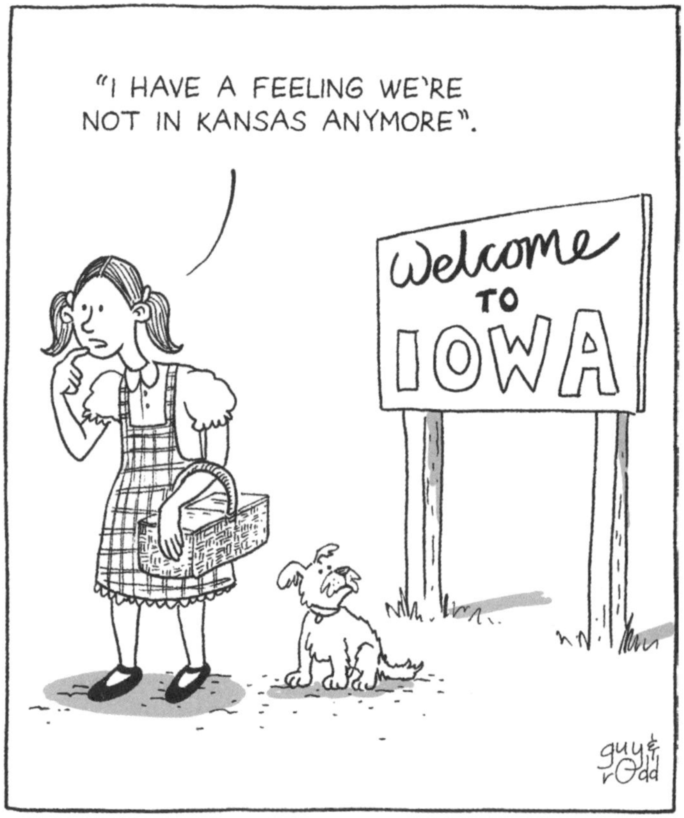
"I HAVE A FEELING WE'RE NOT IN KANSAS ANYMORE".
Welcome TO IOWA

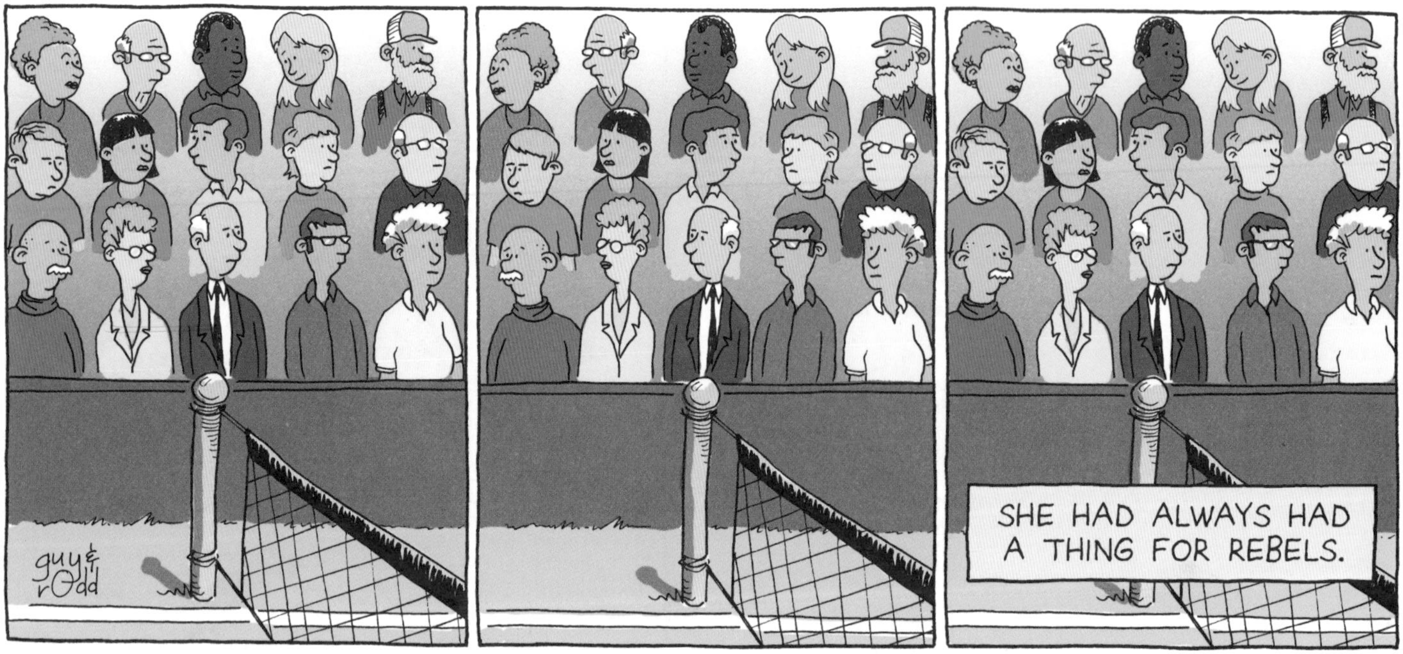
SHE HAD ALWAYS HAD A THING FOR REBELS.

SOON THE HUNTER-GATHERERS WOULD SPREAD FROM SEA TO SEA, WHILE THE SCROUNGER-BREAKDANCERS WOULD FADE INTO OBLIVION.

"NOW REMEMBER, HE SPENT $400 ON THAT, SO NO MATTER WHAT, WE CAN NEVER PLAY WITH IT".

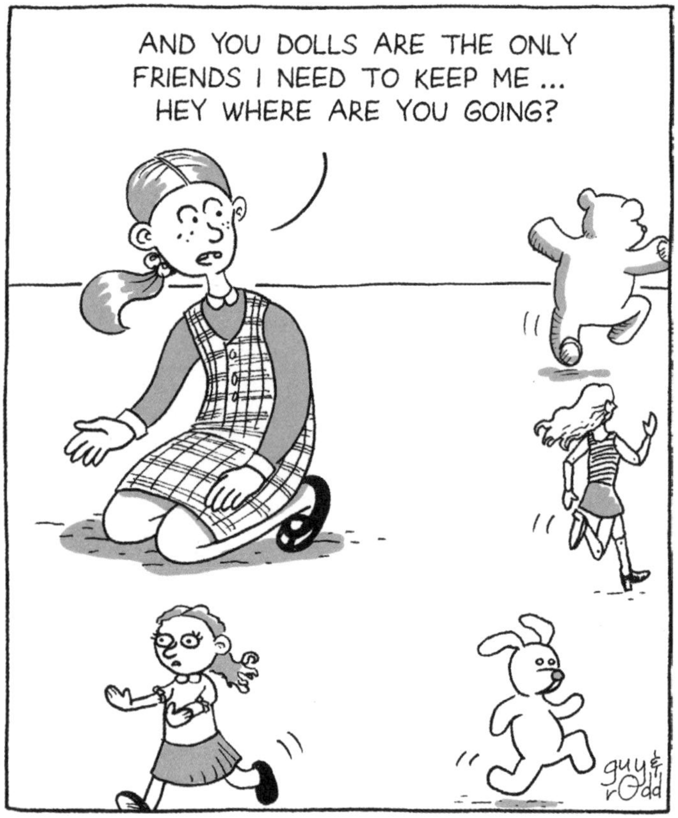
AND YOU DOLLS ARE THE ONLY FRIENDS I NEED TO KEEP ME ... HEY WHERE ARE YOU GOING?
guy & rodd

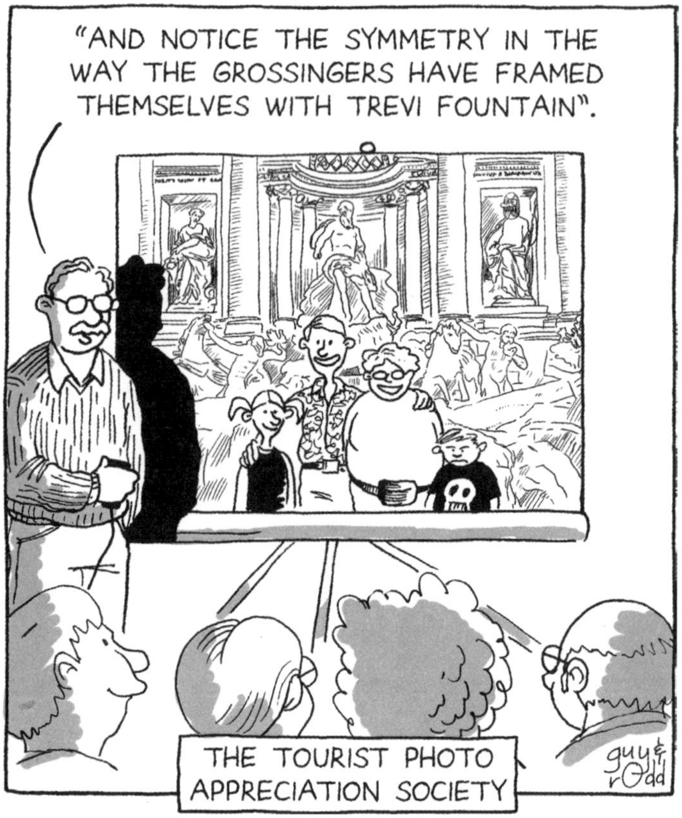
"AND NOTICE THE SYMMETRY IN THE WAY THE GROSSINGERS HAVE FRAMED THEMSELVES WITH TREVI FOUNTAIN".
THE TOURIST PHOTO APPRECIATION SOCIETY
guy & rodd

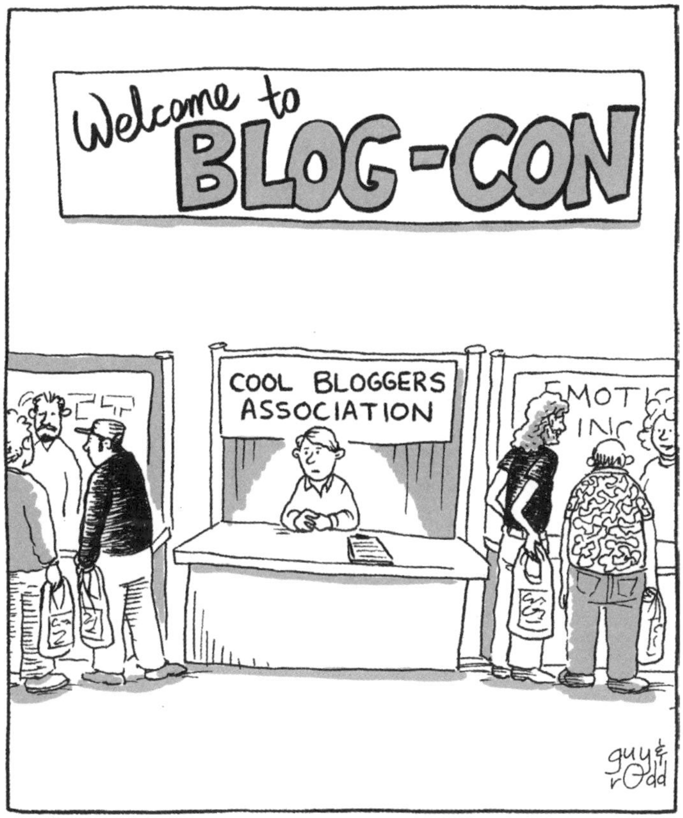
Welcome to
BLOG-CON
COOL BLOGGERS ASSOCIATION

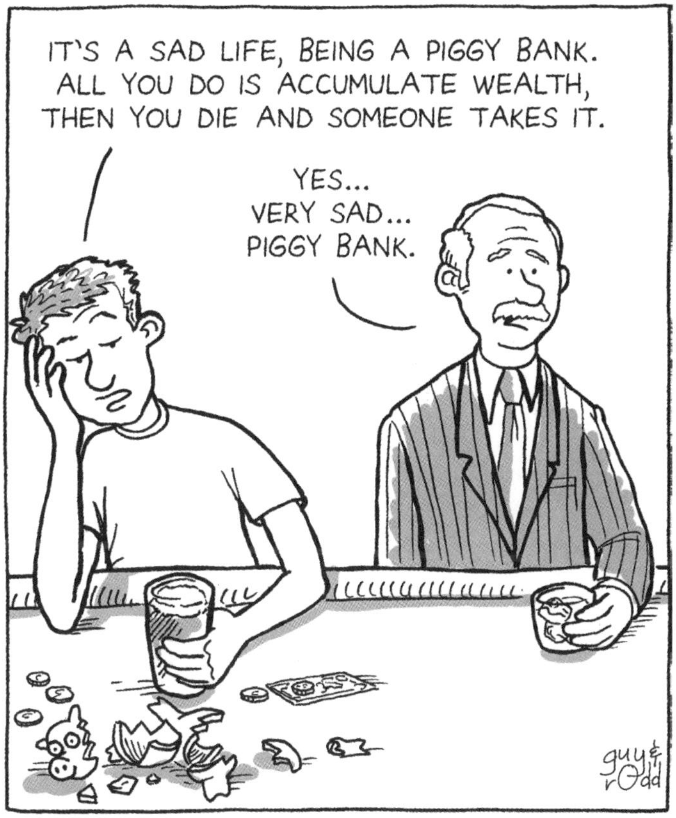
IT'S A SAD LIFE, BEING A PIGGY BANK. ALL YOU DO IS ACCUMULATE WEALTH, THEN YOU DIE AND SOMEONE TAKES IT.
YES... VERY SAD... PIGGY BANK.

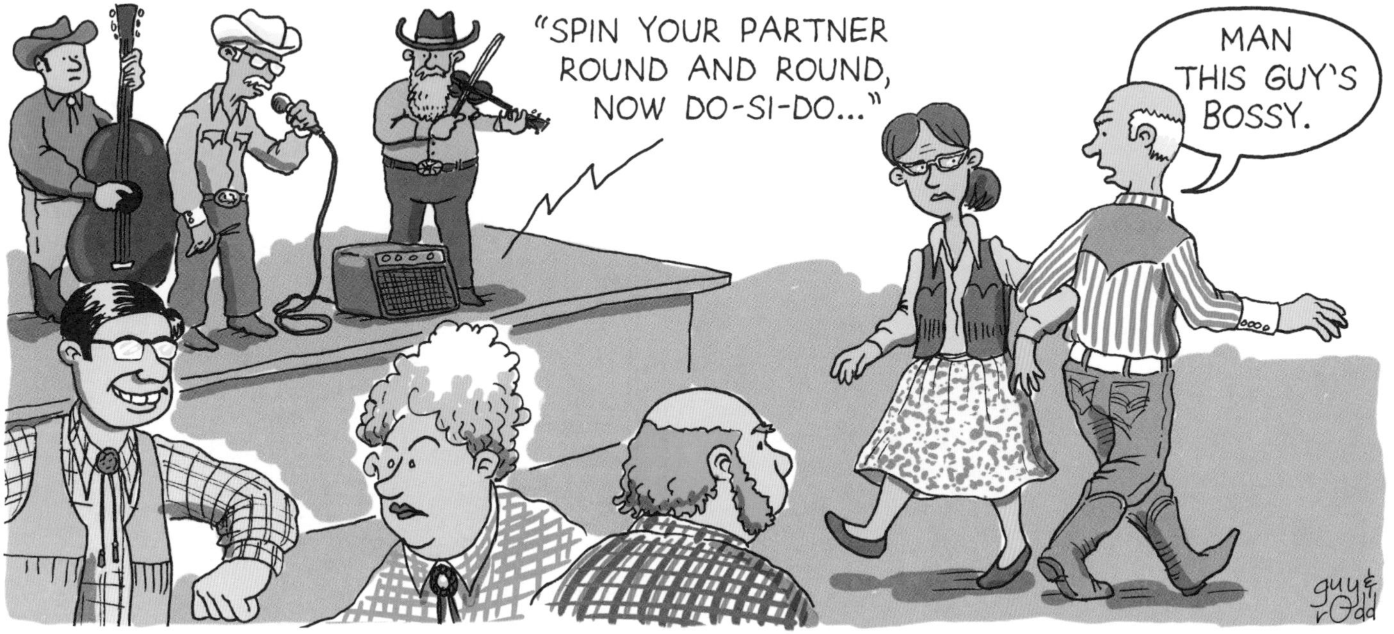
"SPIN YOUR PARTNER ROUND AND ROUND, NOW DO-SI-DO..."
MAN THIS GUY'S BOSSY.

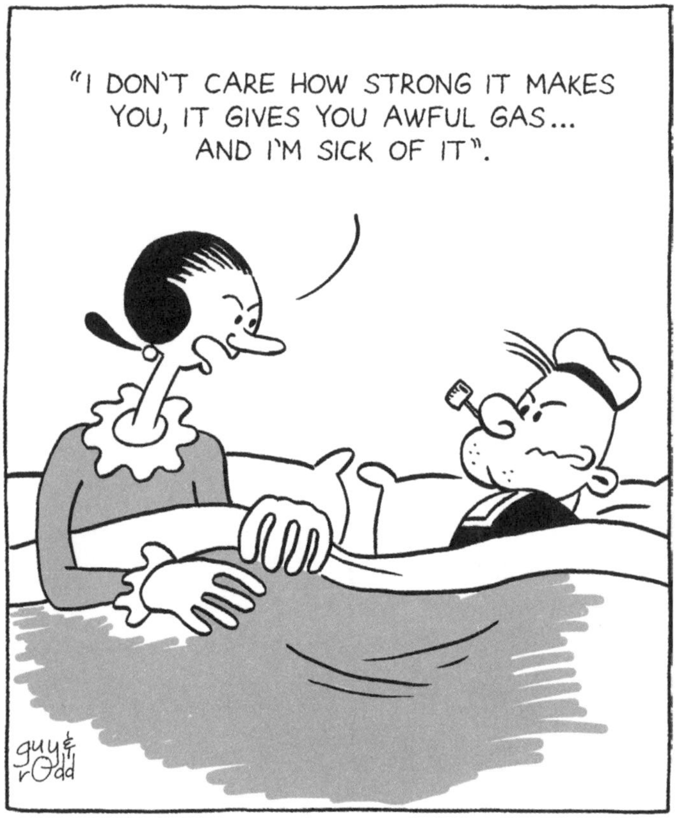
"I DON'T CARE HOW STRONG IT MAKES YOU, IT GIVES YOU AWFUL GAS... AND I'M SICK OF IT".
guy & rodd

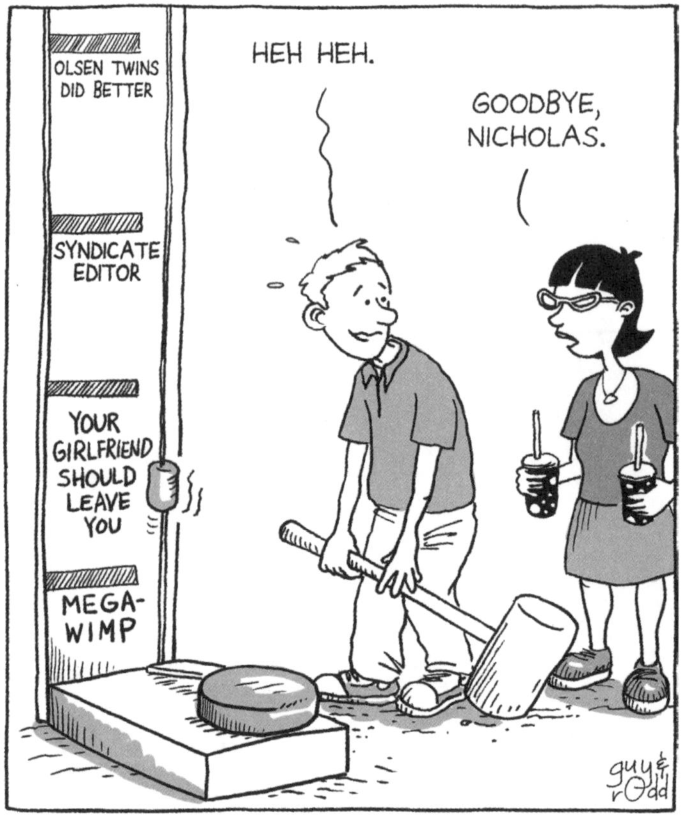
OLSEN TWINS DID BETTER
SYNDICATE EDITOR
YOUR GIRLFRIEND SHOULD LEAVE YOU
MEGA-WIMP
HEH HEH.
GOODBYE, NICHOLAS.
guy & rodd

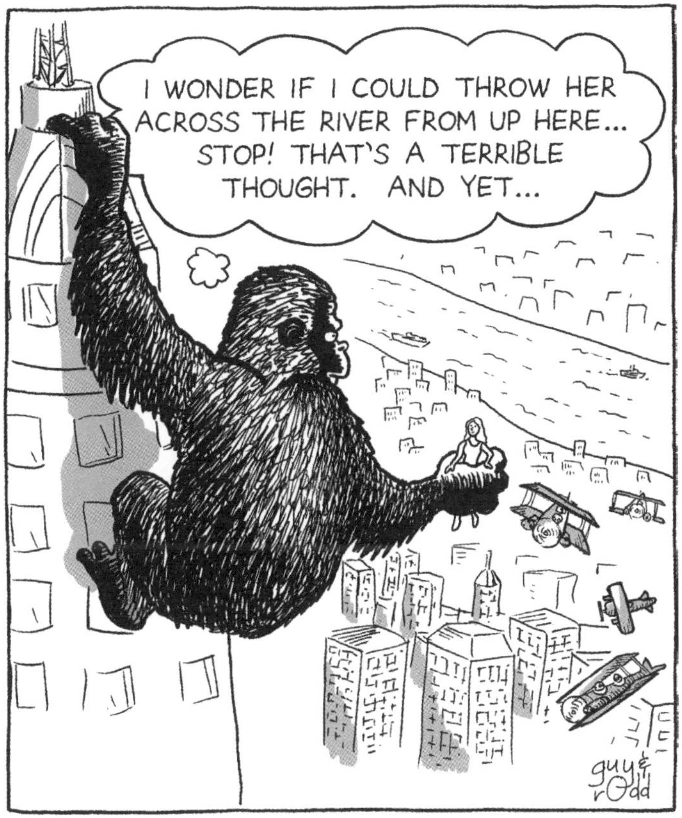
I WONDER IF I COULD THROW HER ACROSS THE RIVER FROM UP HERE... STOP! THAT'S A TERRIBLE THOUGHT. AND YET...
guy & rOdd

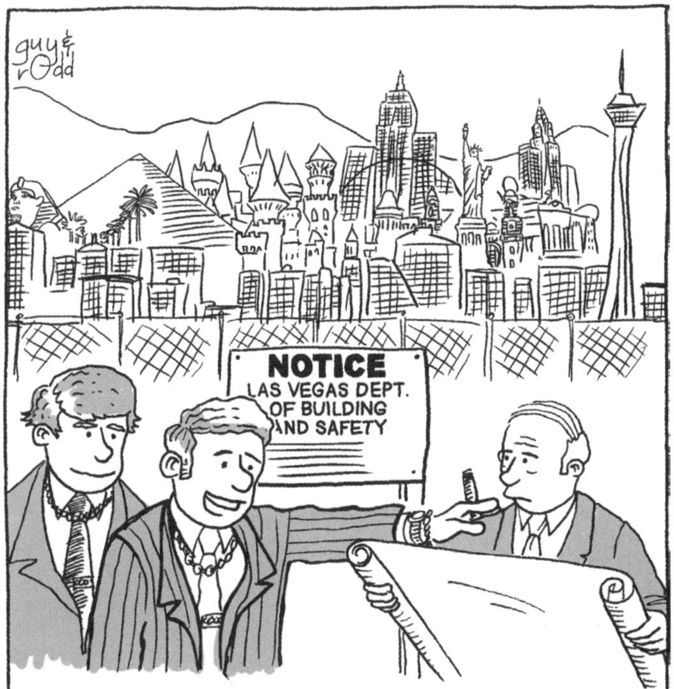
guy & rOdd
NOTICE
LAS VEGAS DEPT. OF BUILDING AND SAFETY

"WE WERE THINKING OF BUILDING SOMETHING A LITTLE SUBTLE THIS TIME... HA HA, JUST KIDDING, MAKE IT HORRIBLE".

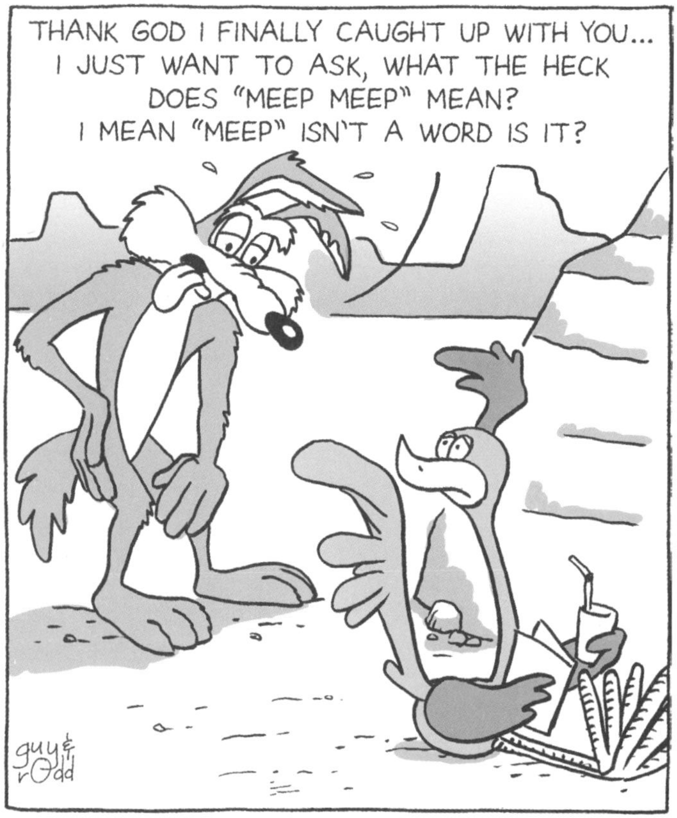
THANK GOD I FINALLY CAUGHT UP WITH YOU... I JUST WANT TO ASK, WHAT THE HECK DOES "MEEP MEEP" MEAN? I MEAN "MEEP" ISN'T A WORD IS IT?
guy & rOdd

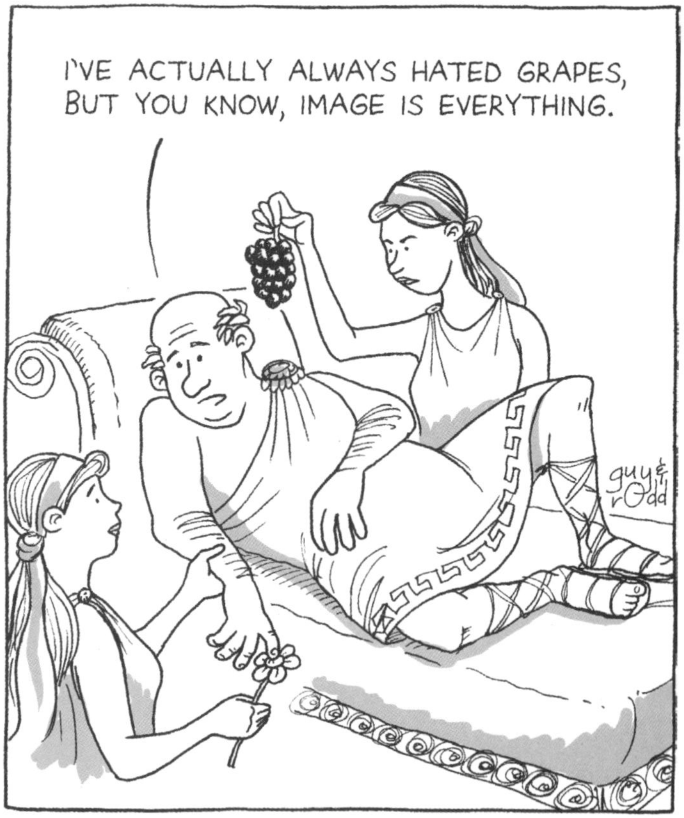
I'VE ACTUALLY ALWAYS HATED GRAPES, BUT YOU KNOW, IMAGE IS EVERYTHING.
guy & rOdd

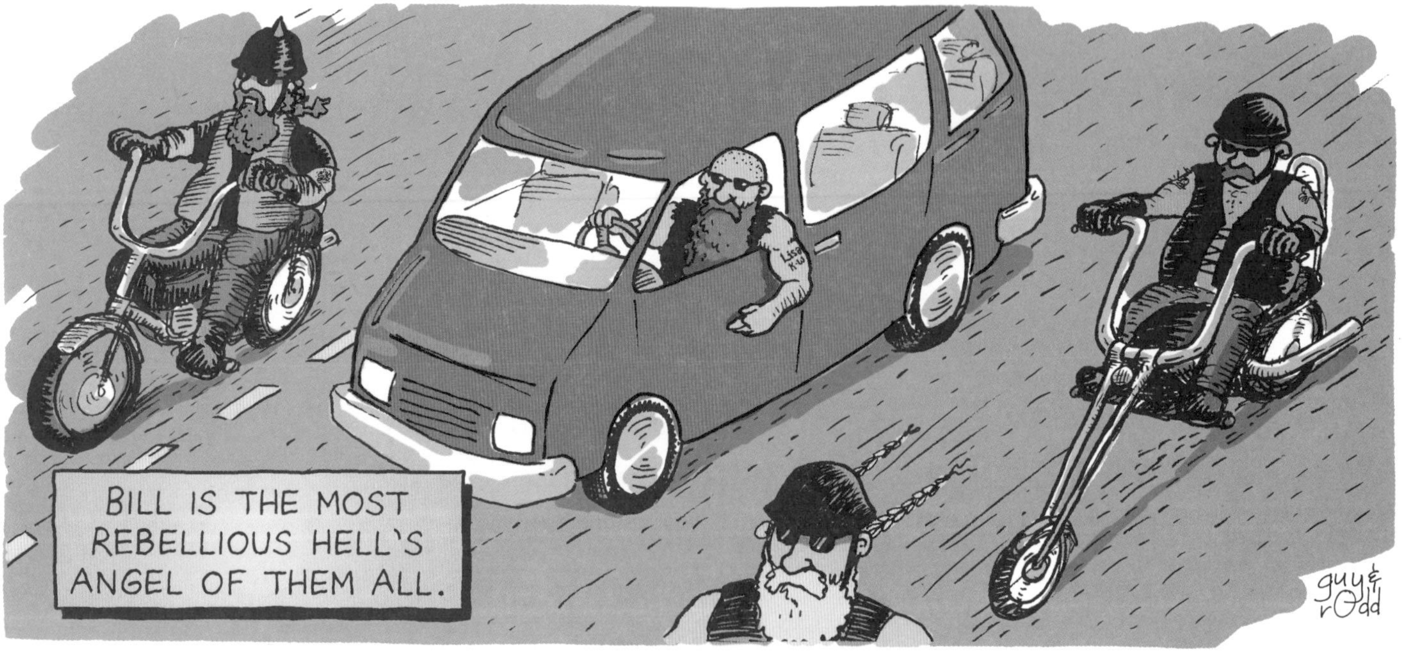
BILL IS THE MOST REBELLIOUS HELL'S ANGEL OF THEM ALL.
guy & rOdd

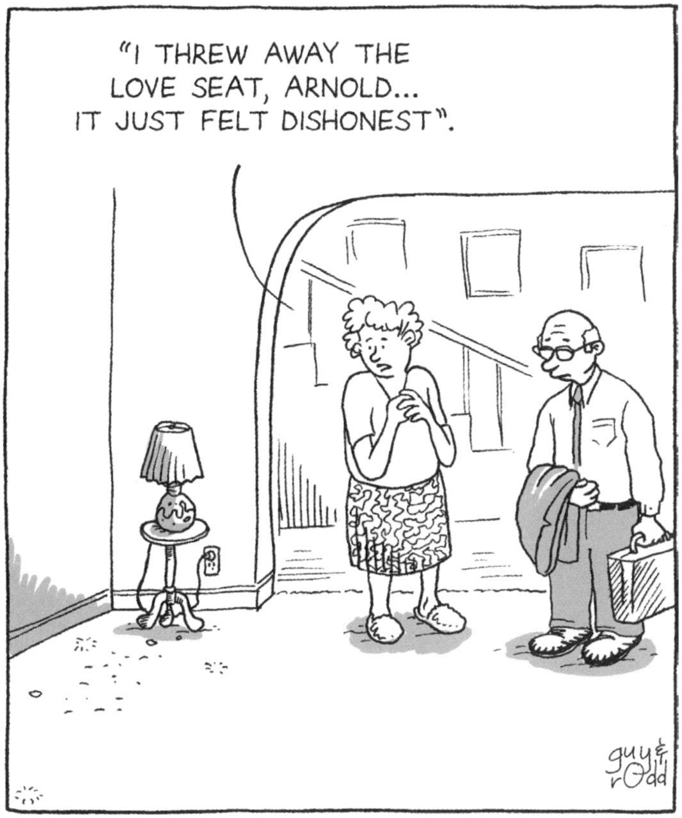
"I THREW AWAY THE
LOVE SEAT, ARNOLD...
IT JUST FELT DISHONEST".
guy & rOdd

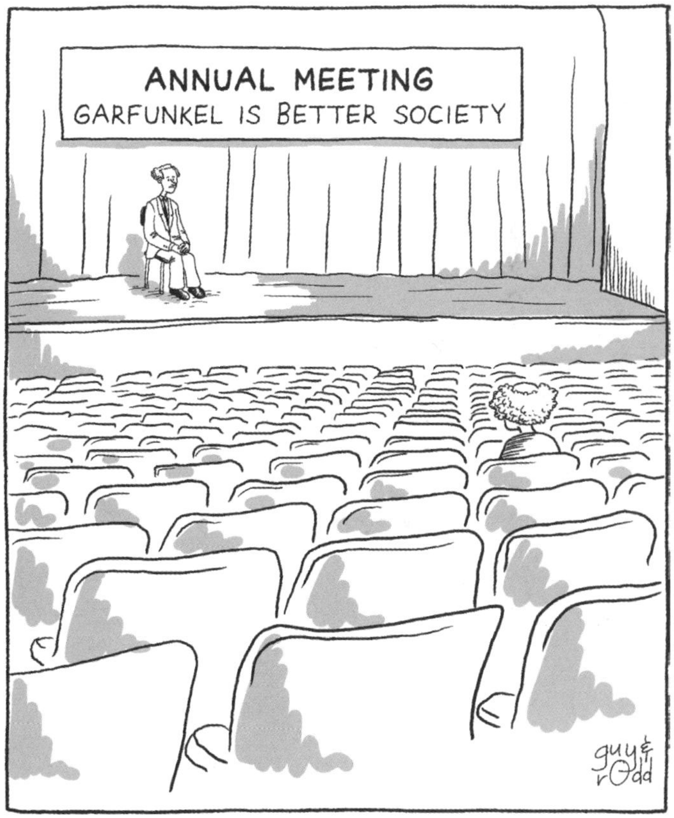
ANNUAL MEETING
GARFUNKEL IS BETTER SOCIETY
guy & rOdd

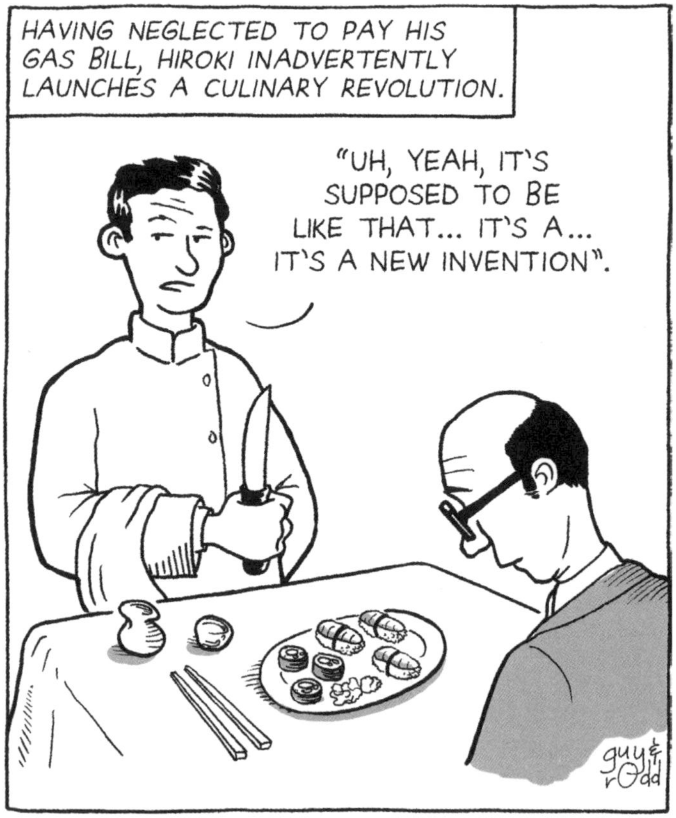
HAVING NEGLECTED TO PAY HIS GAS BILL, HIROKI INADVERTENTLY LAUNCHES A CULINARY REVOLUTION.
"UH, YEAH, IT'S SUPPOSED TO BE LIKE THAT... IT'S A... IT'S A NEW INVENTION".

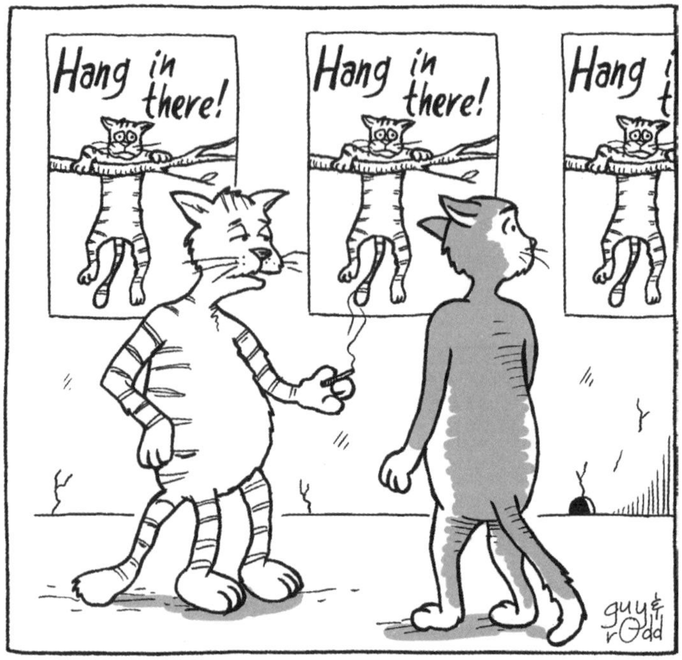
Hang in there!
Hang in there!
Hang

"IT'S ONE OF THE MOST SUCCESSFUL MOTIVATIONAL POSTERS OF ALL TIME, OR WHATEVER... I DON'T LIKE TO MAKE A BIG DEAL OUT OF IT... TOP FIVE IF YOU HAVE TO KNOW".

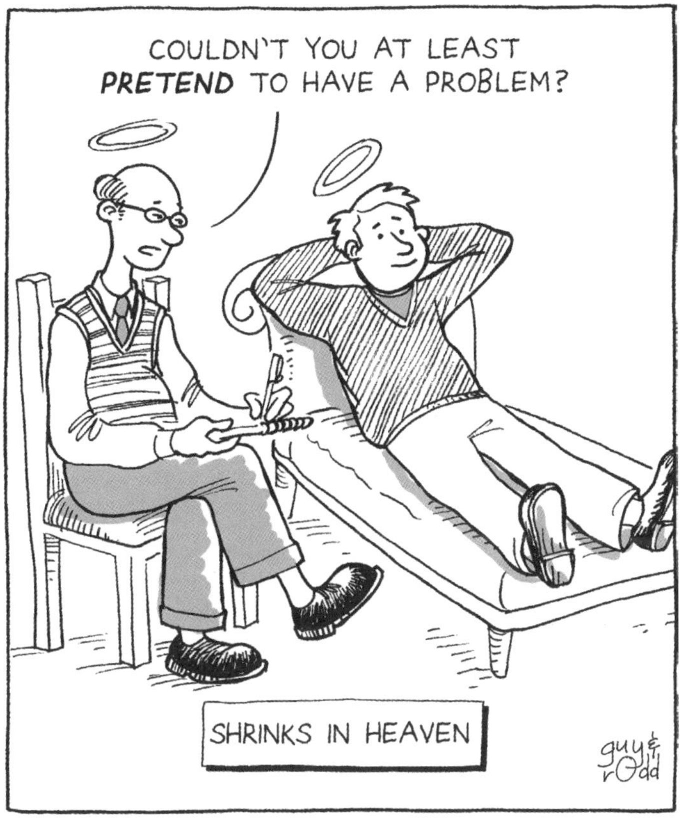
COULDN'T YOU AT LEAST **PRETEND** TO HAVE A PROBLEM?
SHRINKS IN HEAVEN
guy & rOdd

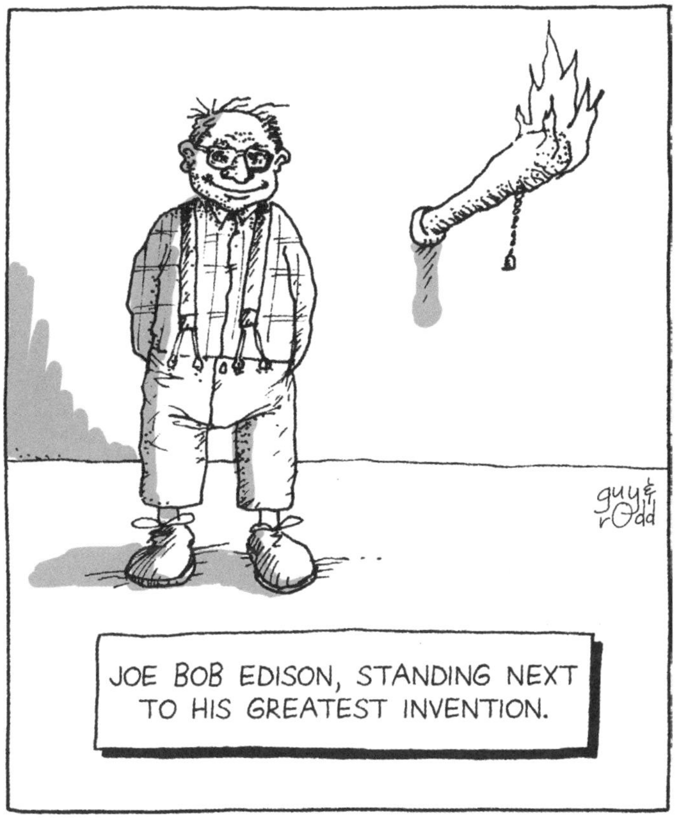
JOE BOB EDISON, STANDING NEXT TO HIS GREATEST INVENTION.
guy & rOdd

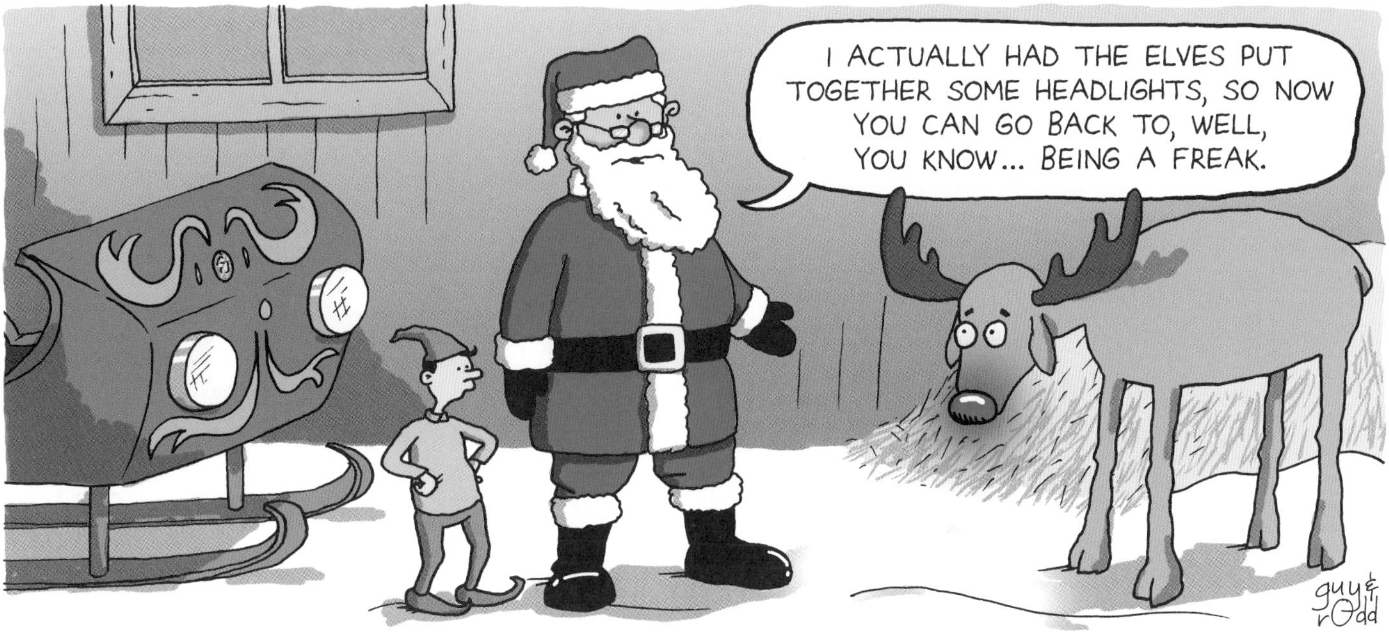
I ACTUALLY HAD THE ELVES PUT TOGETHER SOME HEADLIGHTS, SO NOW YOU CAN GO BACK TO, WELL, YOU KNOW... BEING A FREAK.
guy & rOdd

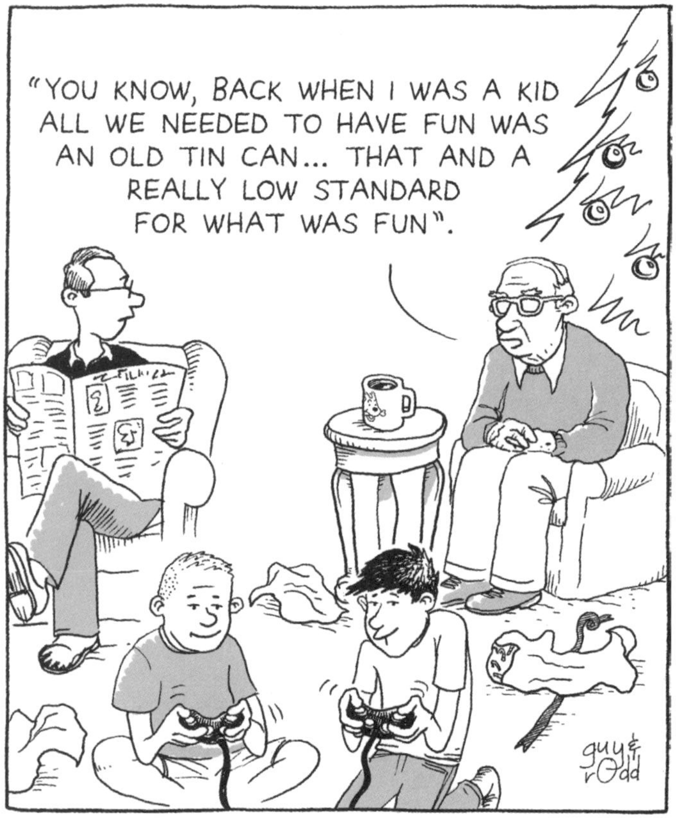
guy & rodd

"YOU KNOW, BACK WHEN I WAS A KID ALL WE NEEDED TO HAVE FUN WAS AN OLD TIN CAN... THAT AND A REALLY LOW STANDARD FOR WHAT WAS FUN".

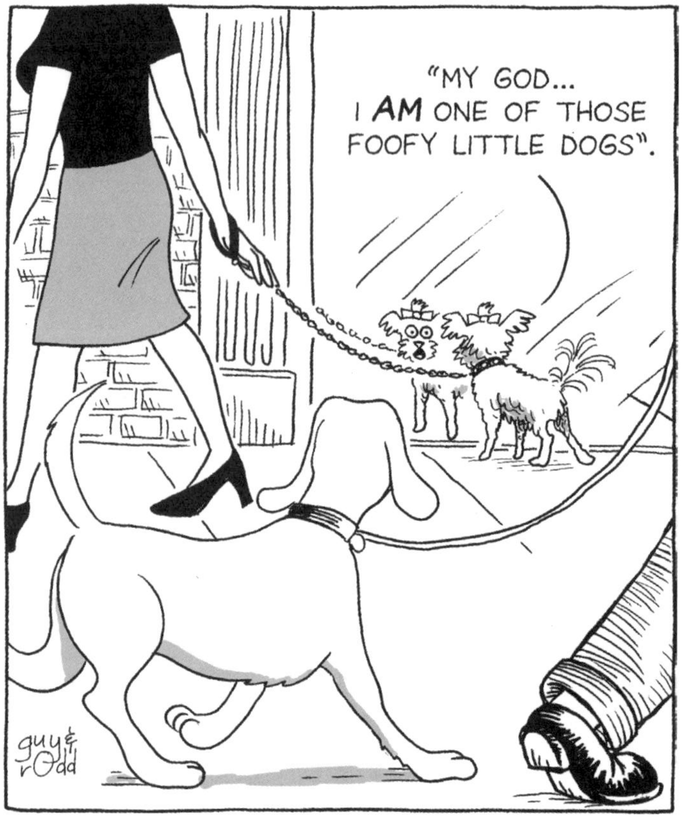
guy & rodd

"MY GOD... I **AM** ONE OF THOSE FOOFY LITTLE DOGS".

WOULD YOU CARE FOR SOME FRESH PEPPER?... WELL TOO BAD, BECAUSE ALL WE HAVE ARE THESE DRIED UP OLD PEPPERCORNS.

GROCERY BAGGERS HALL OF FAME

"THAT'S JEB LAMBERT. HE WAS ACTUALLY THE FIRST ONE TO SAY 'PAPER OR PLASTIC'. BEFORE THAT EVERYONE SAID 'PLASTIC OR PAPER'... I MEAN, CAN YOU IMAGINE?"

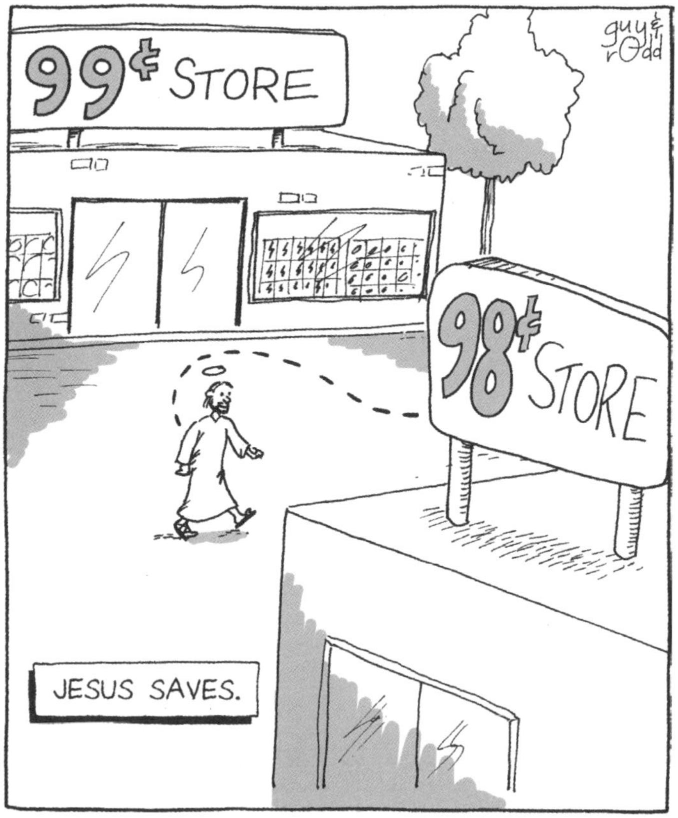

99¢ STORE
98¢ STORE
JESUS SAVES.

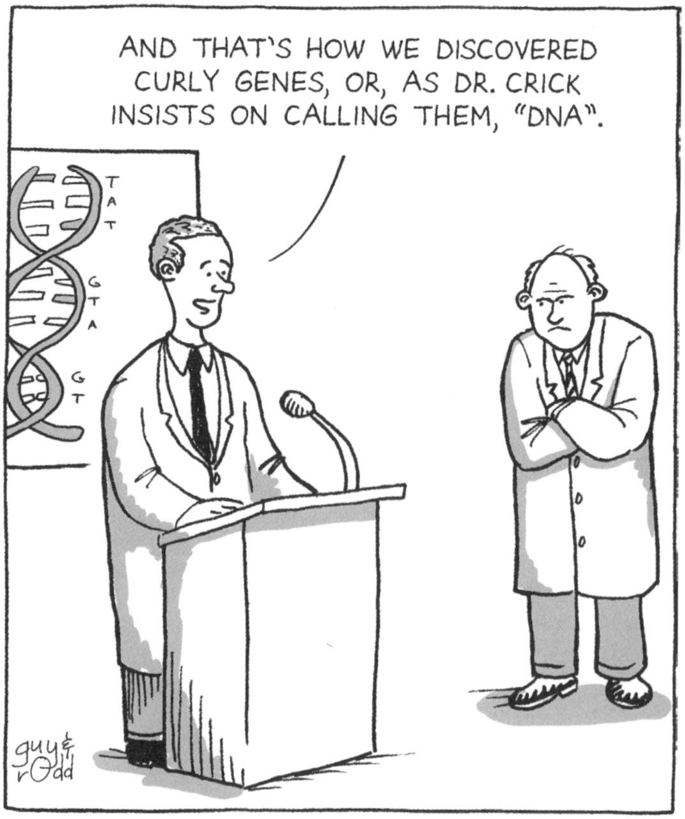

AND THAT'S HOW WE DISCOVERED CURLY GENES, OR, AS DR. CRICK INSISTS ON CALLING THEM, "DNA".

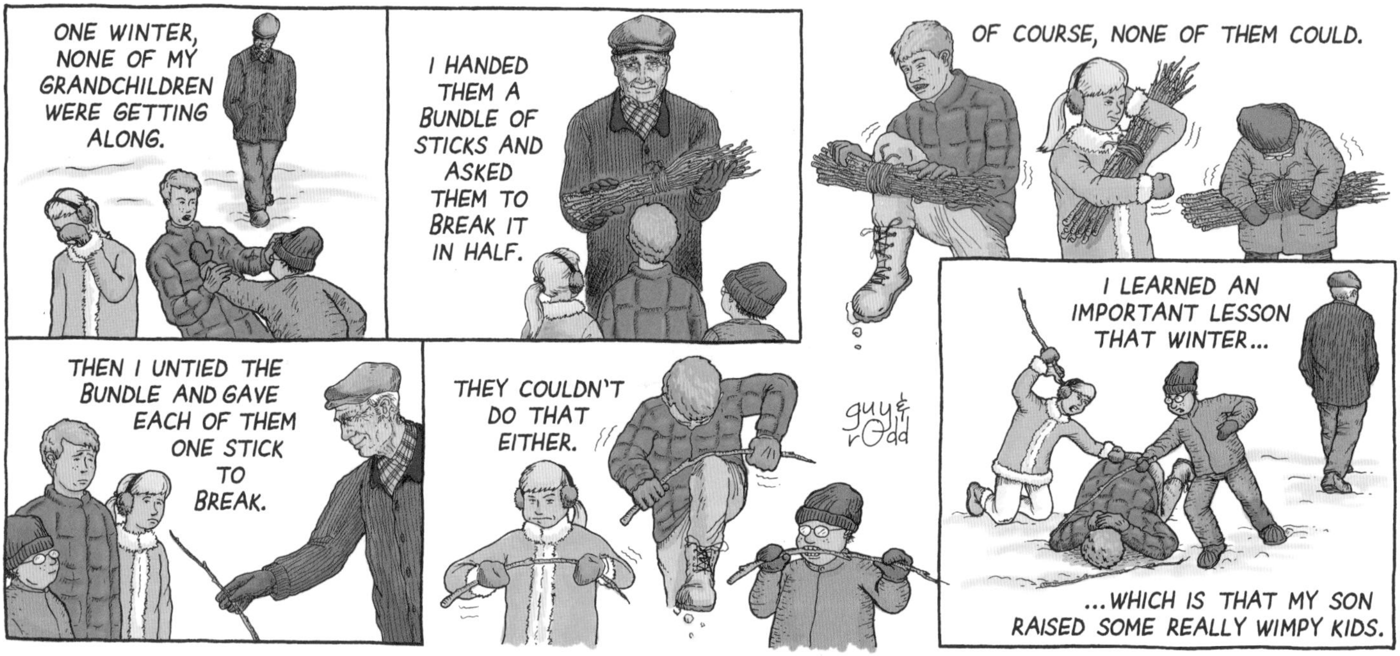

ONE WINTER, NONE OF MY GRANDCHILDREN WERE GETTING ALONG.
I HANDED THEM A BUNDLE OF STICKS AND ASKED THEM TO BREAK IT IN HALF.
OF COURSE, NONE OF THEM COULD.
THEN I UNTIED THE BUNDLE AND GAVE EACH OF THEM ONE STICK TO BREAK.
THEY COULDN'T DO THAT EITHER.
I LEARNED AN IMPORTANT LESSON THAT WINTER...
...WHICH IS THAT MY SON RAISED SOME REALLY WIMPY KIDS.

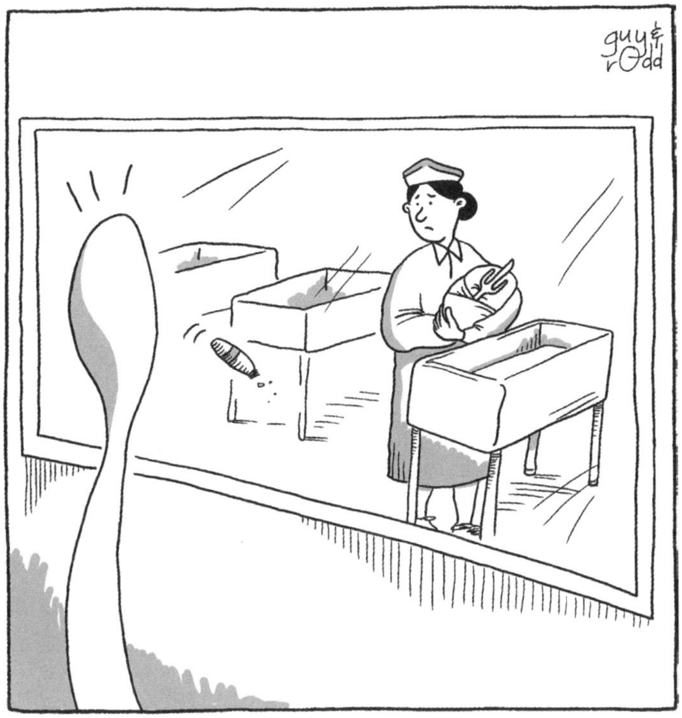
guy & rOdd

THE NURSE HELD UP A BEAUTIFUL BABY KNORK... NEEDLESS TO SAY, THE SPOON WAS DEVASTATED.

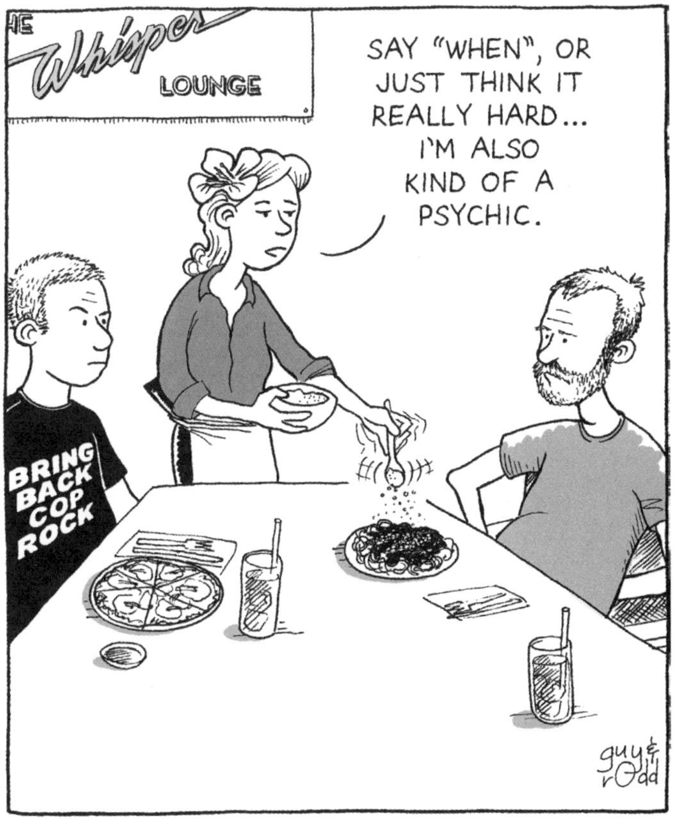
Whisper
LOUNGE
SAY "WHEN", OR JUST THINK IT REALLY HARD... I'M ALSO KIND OF A PSYCHIC.
BRING BACK COP ROCK
guy & rOdd

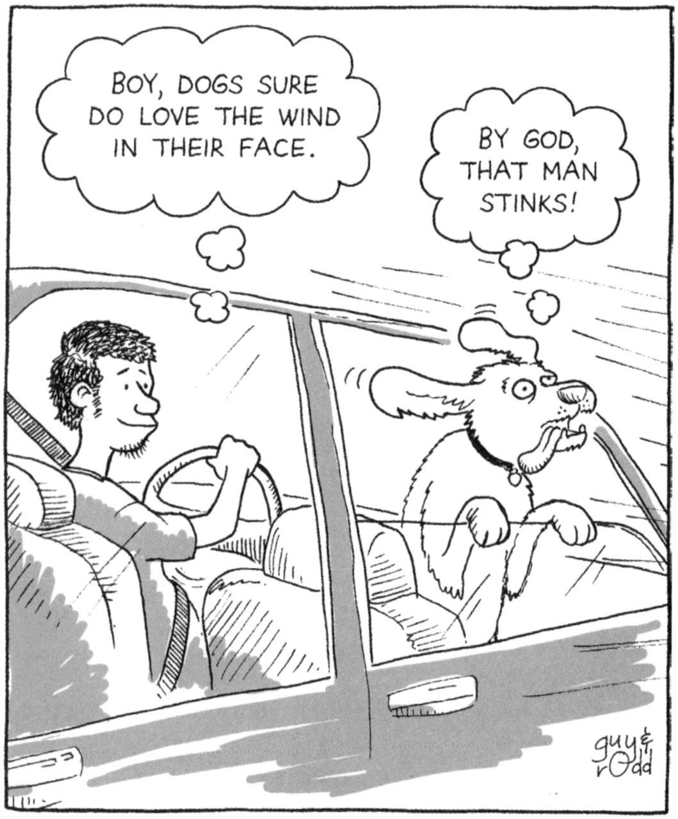
BOY, DOGS SURE DO LOVE THE WIND IN THEIR FACE.
BY GOD, THAT MAN STINKS!

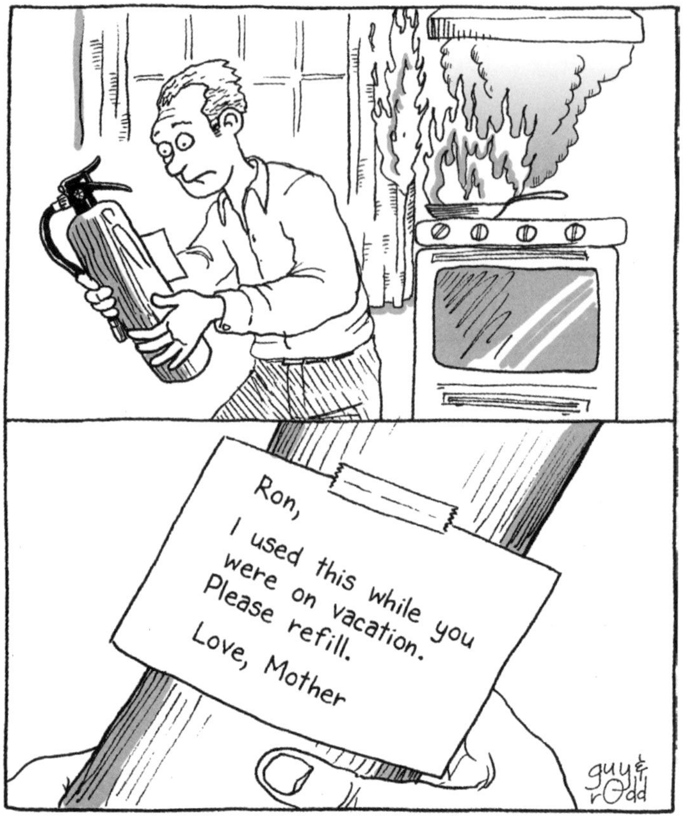
Ron,
I used this while you were on vacation. Please refill.
Love, Mother

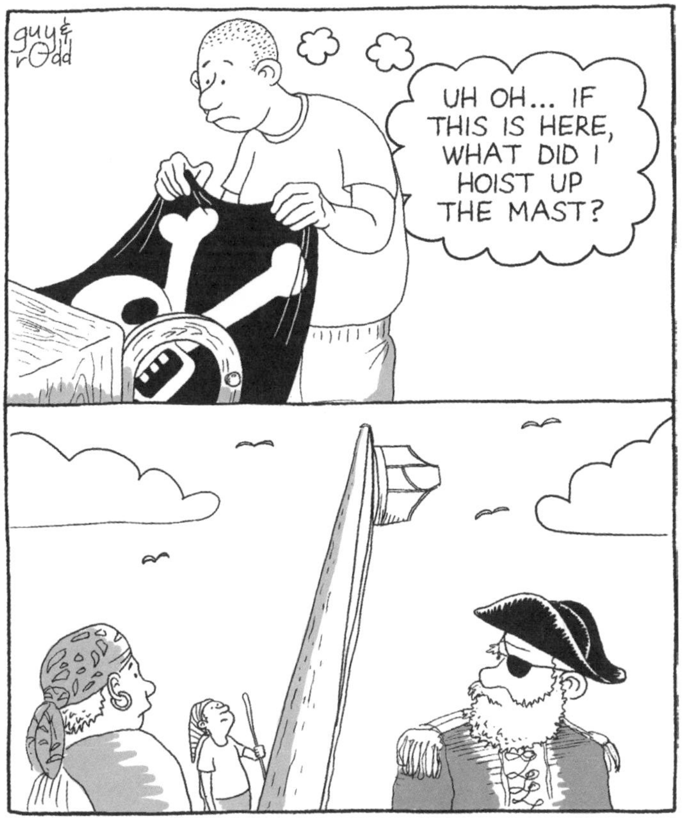
UH OH... IF THIS IS HERE, WHAT DID I HOIST UP THE MAST?

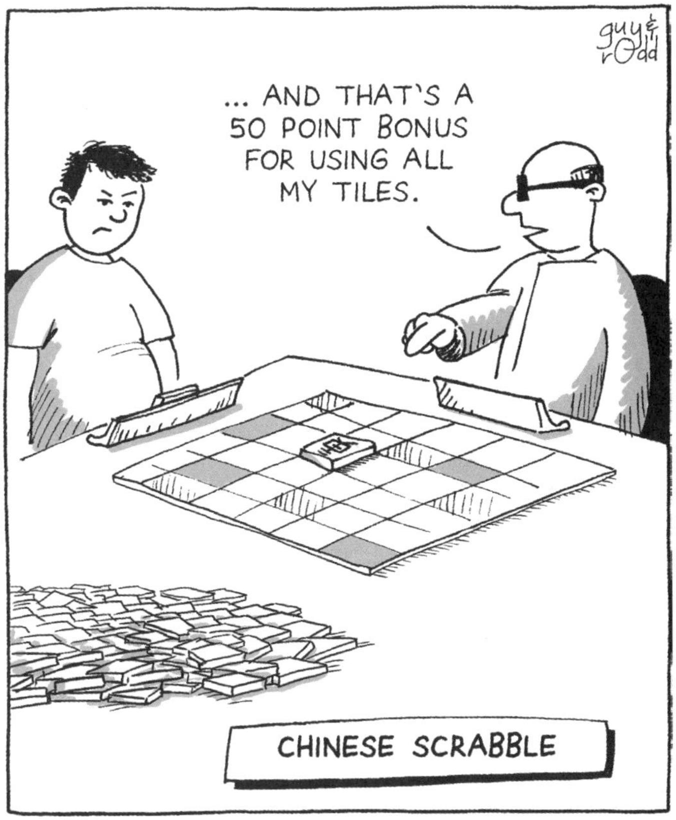
... AND THAT'S A 50 POINT BONUS FOR USING ALL MY TILES.
CHINESE SCRABBLE

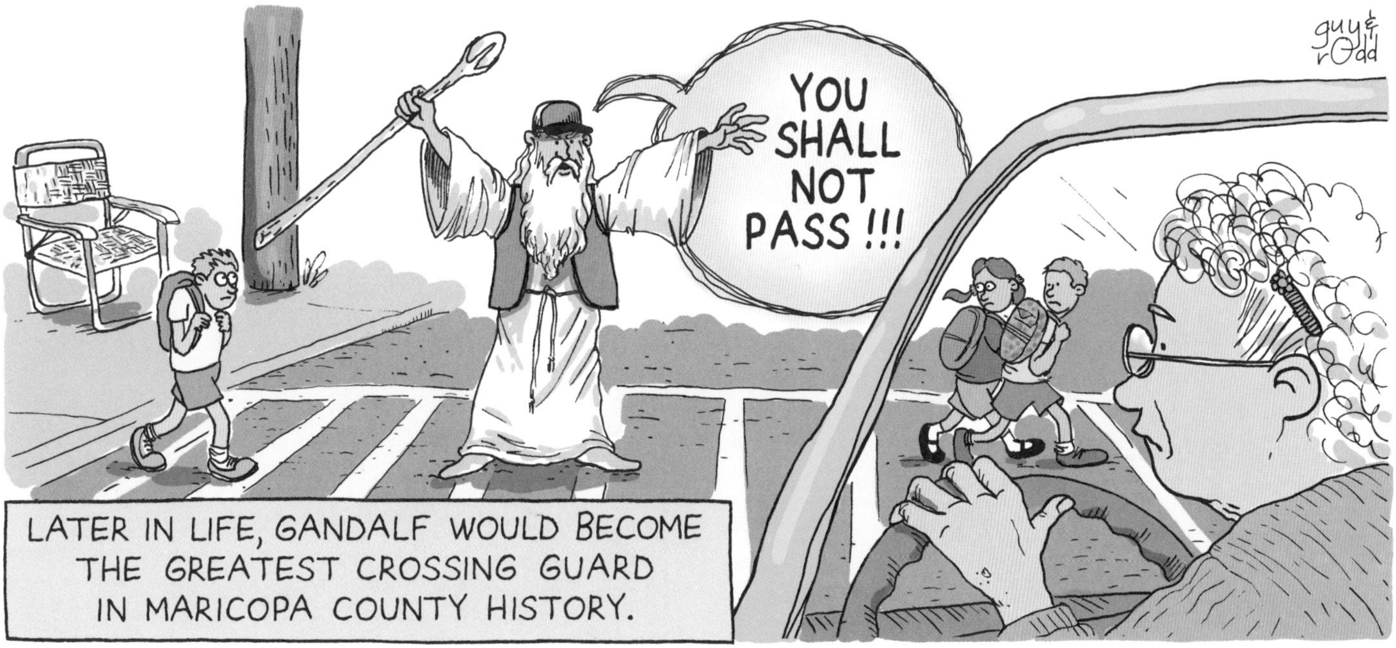
YOU SHALL NOT PASS !!!
LATER IN LIFE, GANDALF WOULD BECOME THE GREATEST CROSSING GUARD IN MARICOPA COUNTY HISTORY.

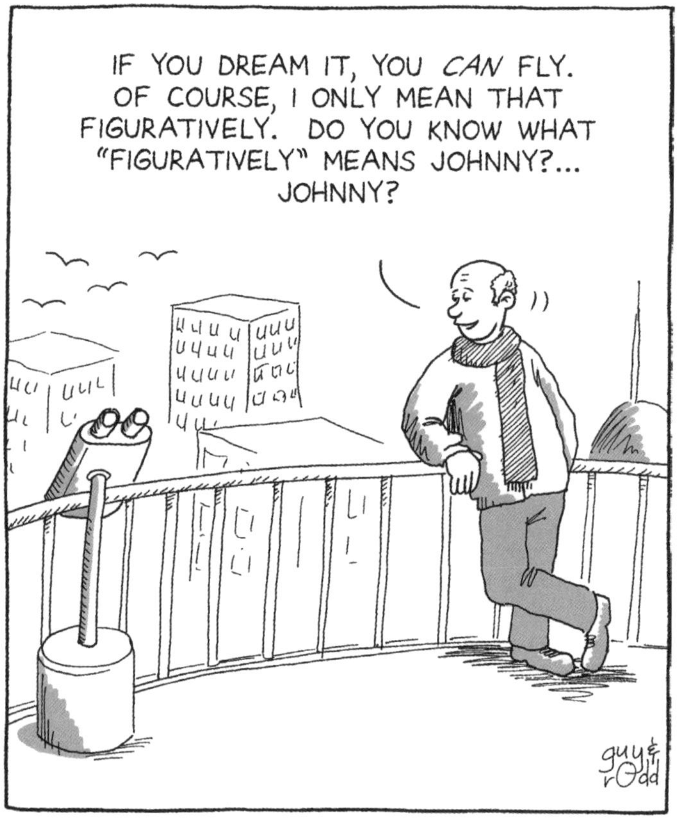
IF YOU DREAM IT, YOU *CAN* FLY. OF COURSE, I ONLY MEAN THAT FIGURATIVELY. DO YOU KNOW WHAT "FIGURATIVELY" MEANS JOHNNY?... JOHNNY?
guy & rOdd

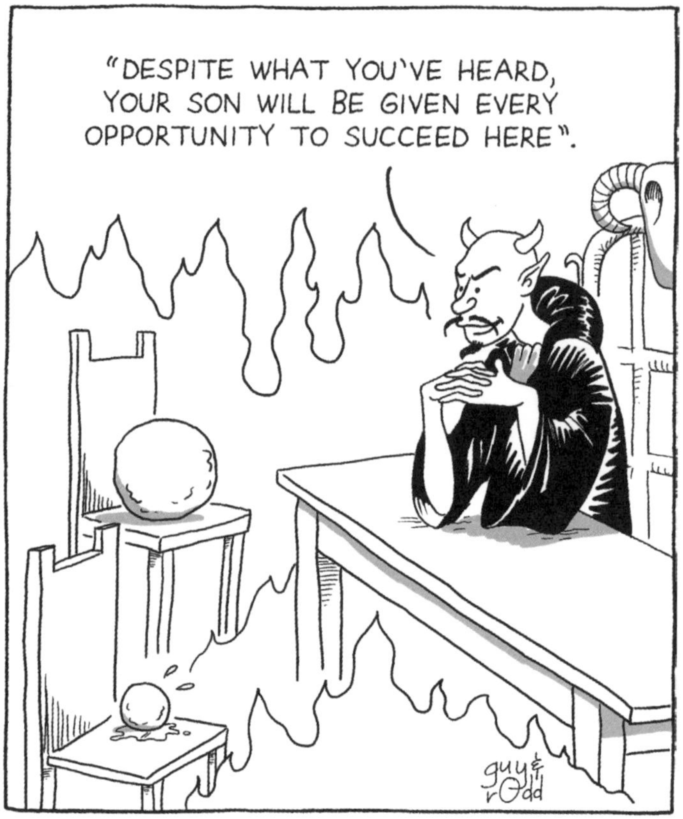
"DESPITE WHAT YOU'VE HEARD, YOUR SON WILL BE GIVEN EVERY OPPORTUNITY TO SUCCEED HERE".
guy & rOdd

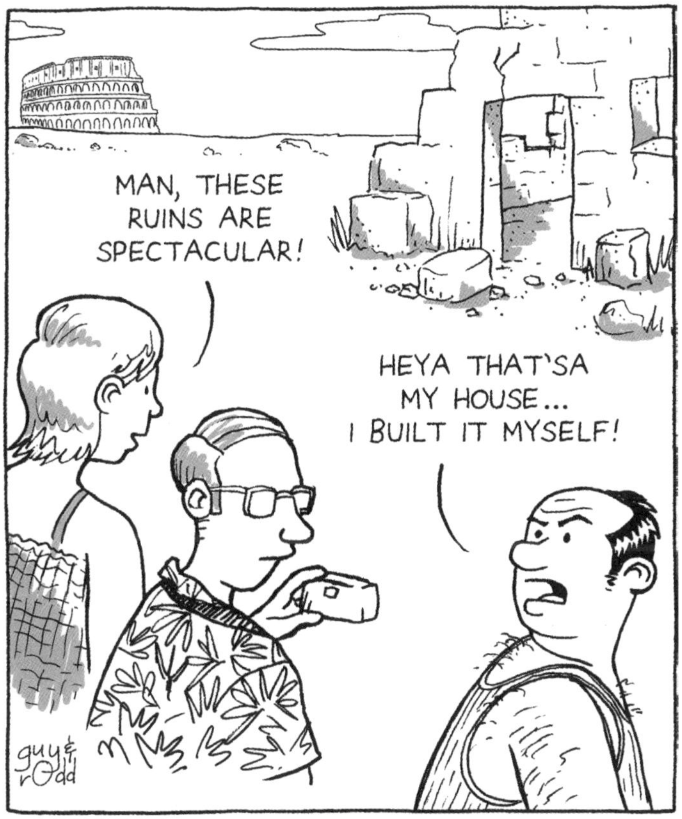
MAN, THESE RUINS ARE SPECTACULAR!
HEYA THAT'SA MY HOUSE... I BUILT IT MYSELF!
guy & rOdd

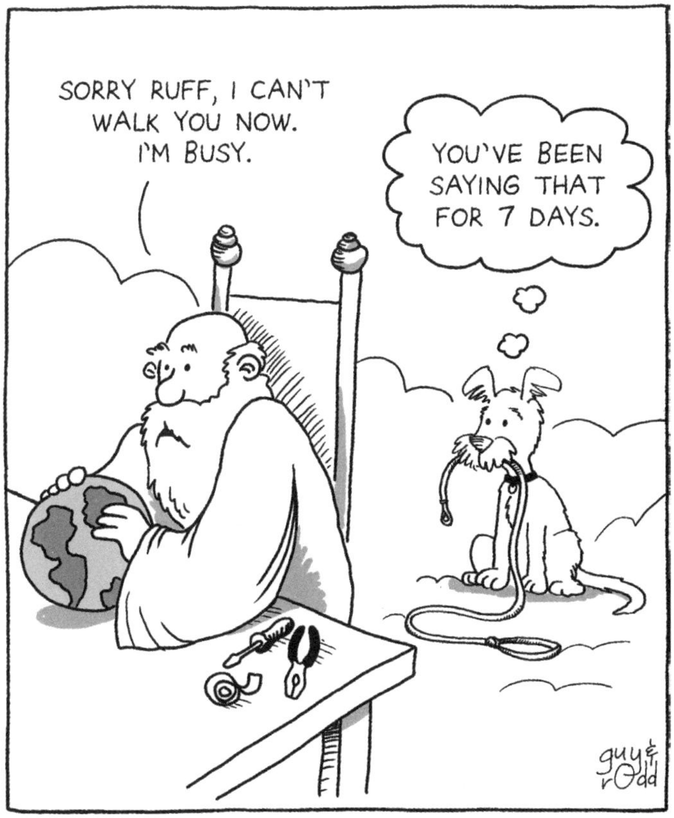
SORRY RUFF, I CAN'T WALK YOU NOW. I'M BUSY.
YOU'VE BEEN SAYING THAT FOR 7 DAYS.
guy & rOdd

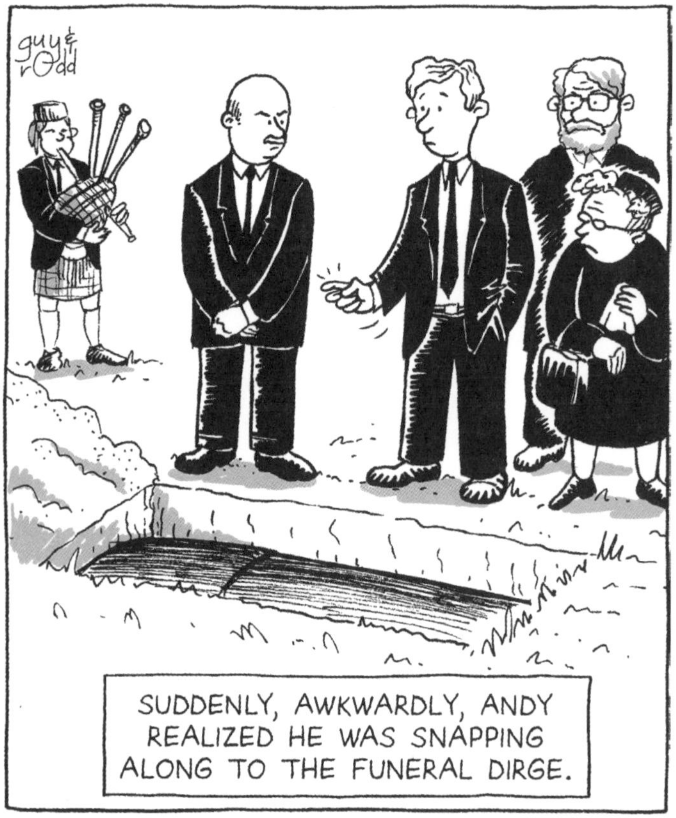
guy & rodd
SUDDENLY, AWKWARDLY, ANDY REALIZED HE WAS SNAPPING ALONG TO THE FUNERAL DIRGE.

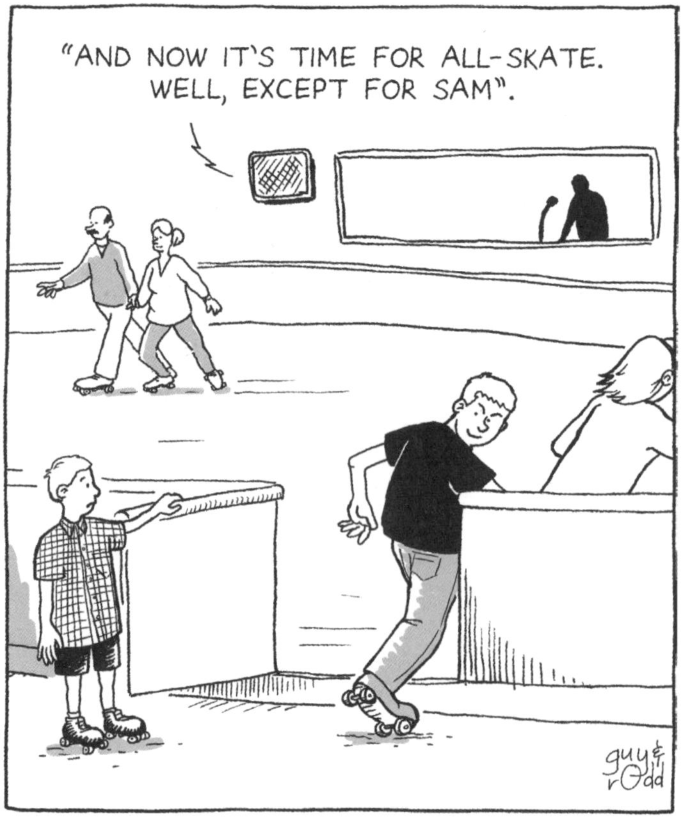
"AND NOW IT'S TIME FOR ALL-SKATE. WELL, EXCEPT FOR SAM".
guy & rodd

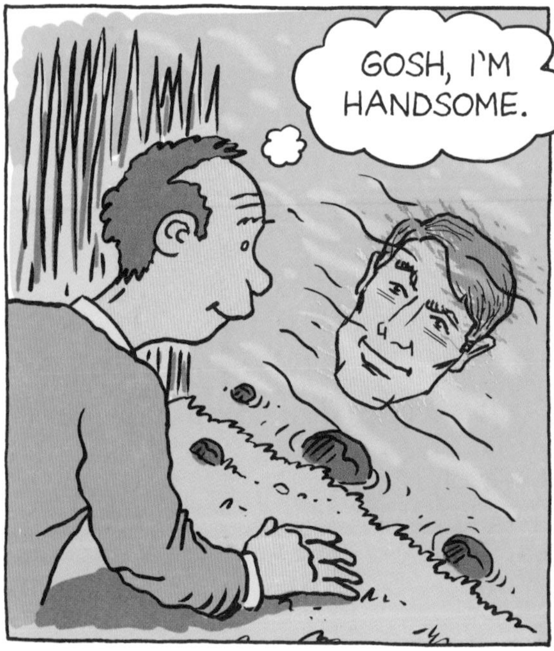
GOSH, I'M HANDSOME.

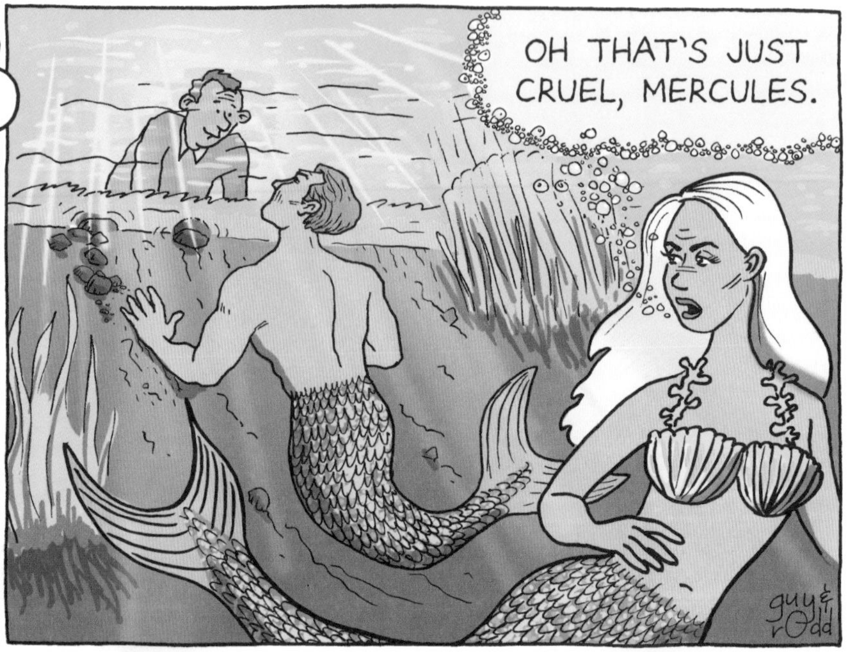
OH THAT'S JUST CRUEL, MERCULES.
guy & rodd

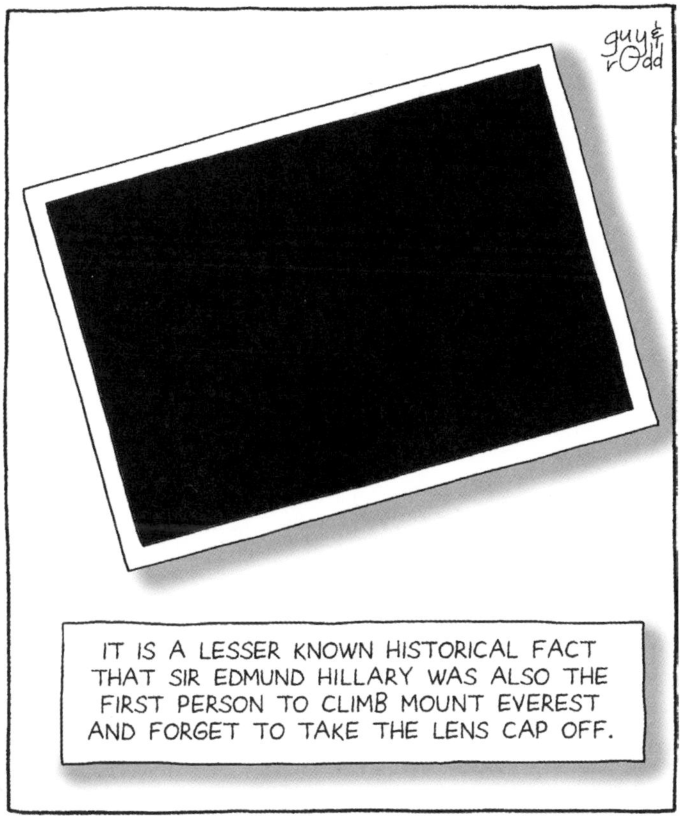
IT IS A LESSER KNOWN HISTORICAL FACT THAT SIR EDMUND HILLARY WAS ALSO THE FIRST PERSON TO CLIMB MOUNT EVEREST AND FORGET TO TAKE THE LENS CAP OFF.

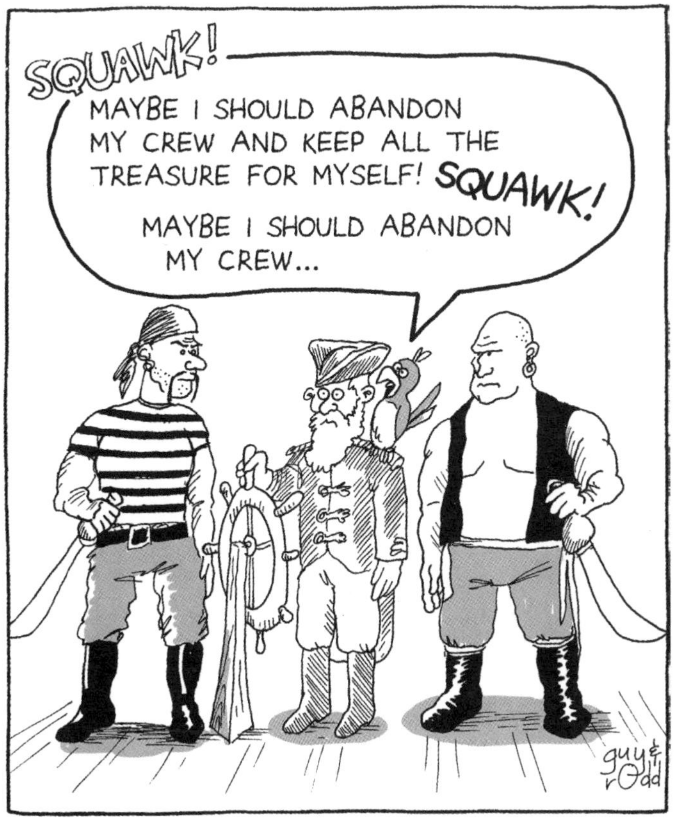
SQUAWK!
MAYBE I SHOULD ABANDON MY CREW AND KEEP ALL THE TREASURE FOR MYSELF! SQUAWK!
MAYBE I SHOULD ABANDON MY CREW...

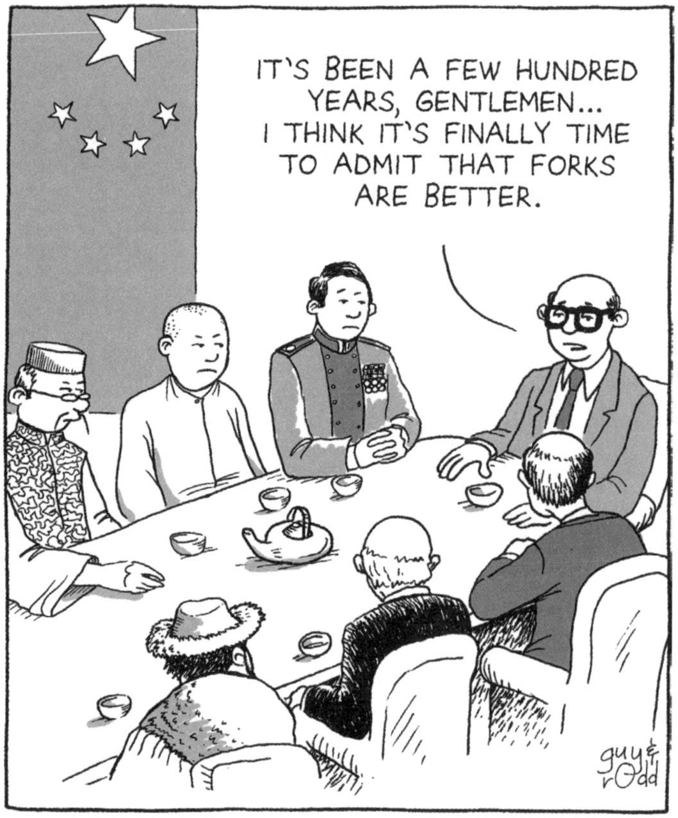
IT'S BEEN A FEW HUNDRED YEARS, GENTLEMEN... I THINK IT'S FINALLY TIME TO ADMIT THAT FORKS ARE BETTER.
guy & rOdd

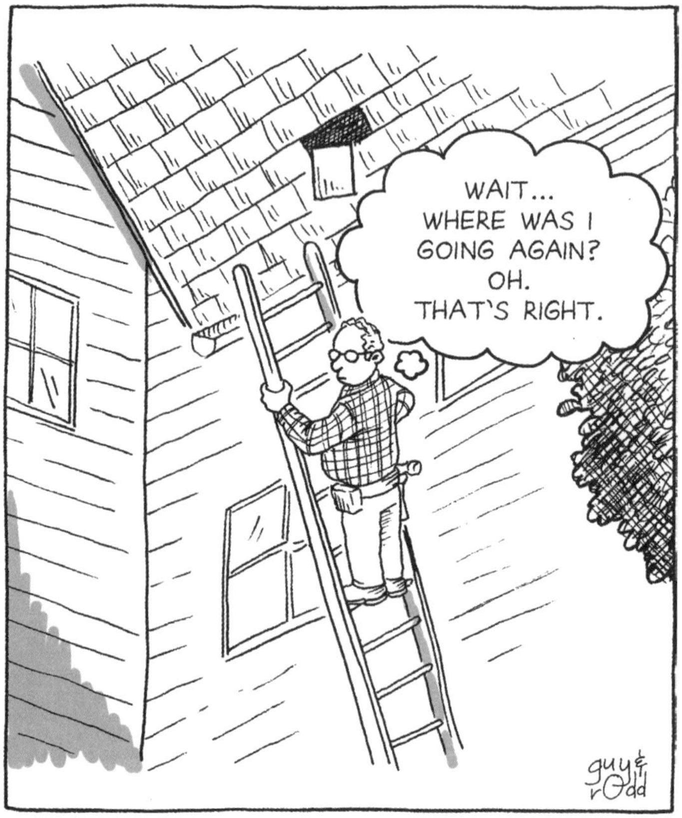
WAIT... WHERE WAS I GOING AGAIN? OH. THAT'S RIGHT.
guy & rOdd

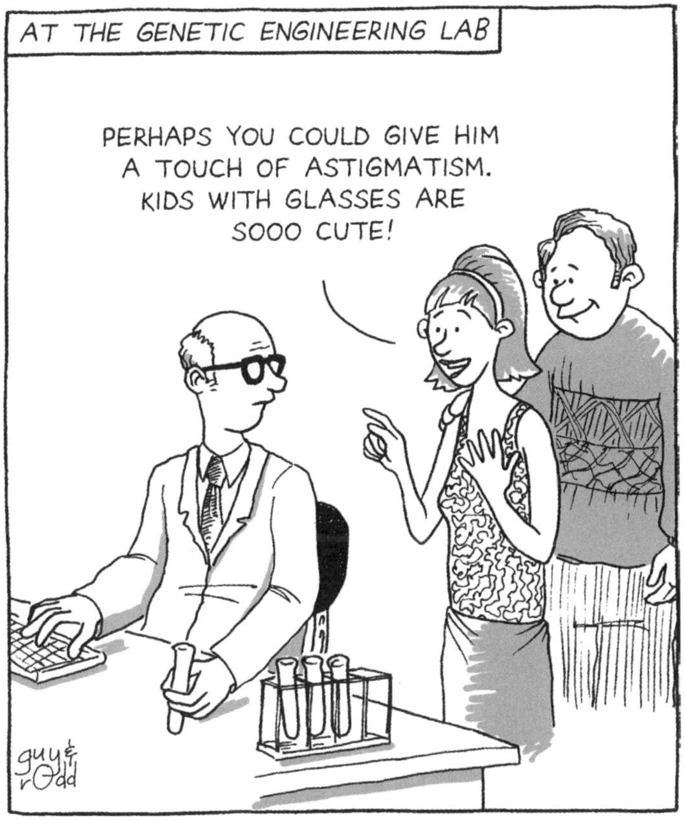
AT THE GENETIC ENGINEERING LAB
PERHAPS YOU COULD GIVE HIM A TOUCH OF ASTIGMATISM. KIDS WITH GLASSES ARE SOOO CUTE!
guy & rOdd

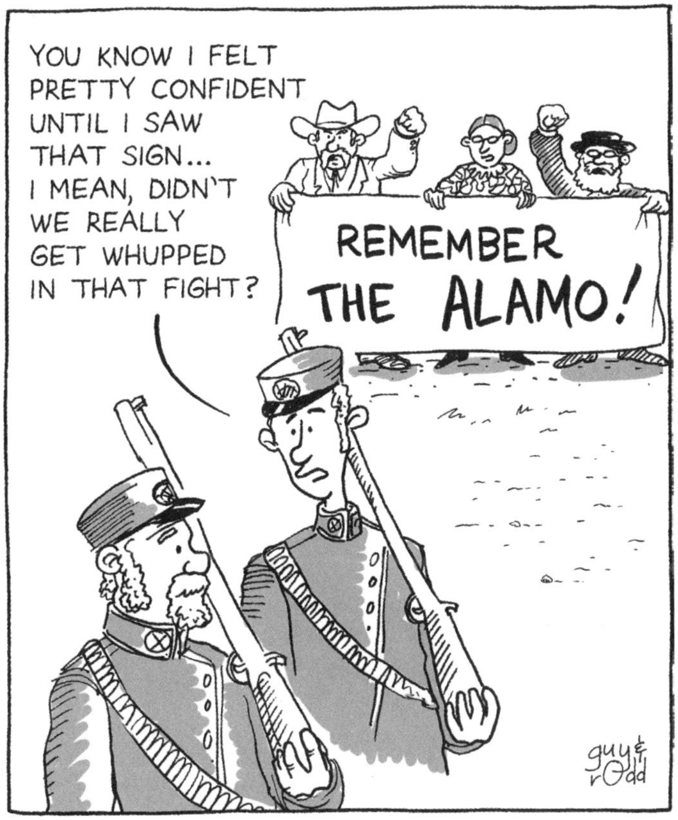
YOU KNOW I FELT PRETTY CONFIDENT UNTIL I SAW THAT SIGN... I MEAN, DIDN'T WE REALLY GET WHUPPED IN THAT FIGHT?
REMEMBER THE ALAMO!
guy & rOdd

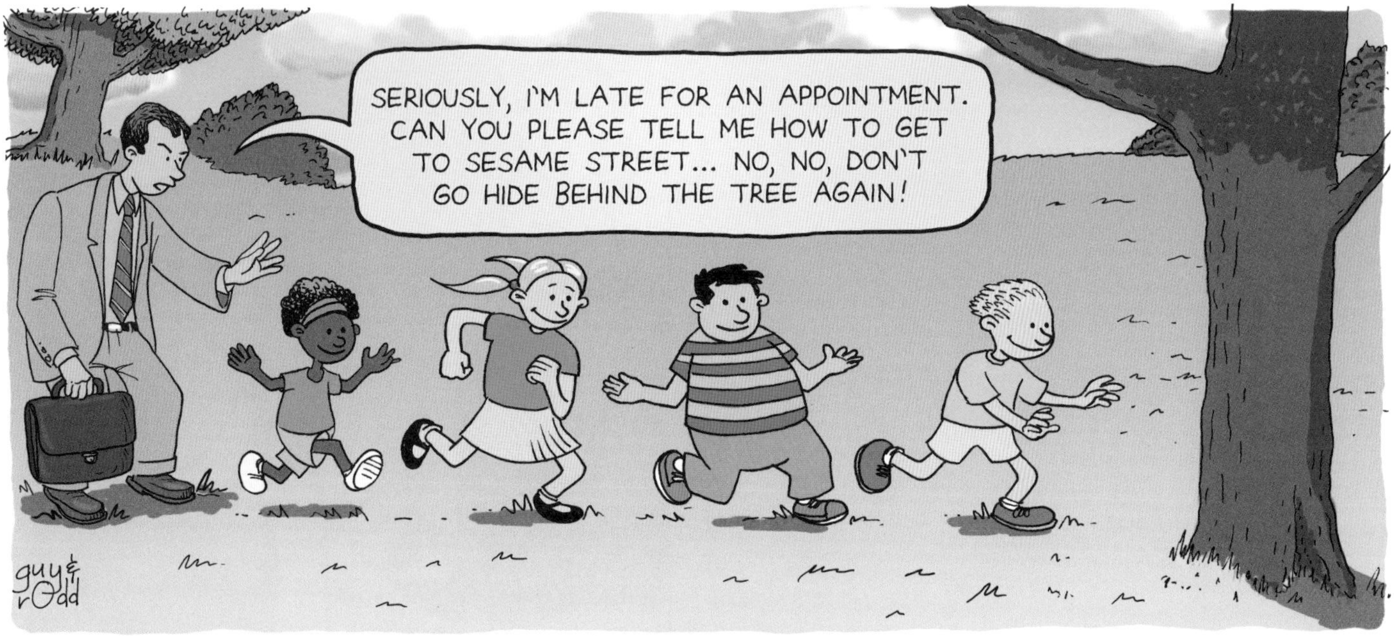
SERIOUSLY, I'M LATE FOR AN APPOINTMENT. CAN YOU PLEASE TELL ME HOW TO GET TO SESAME STREET... NO, NO, DON'T GO HIDE BEHIND THE TREE AGAIN!
guy & rOdd

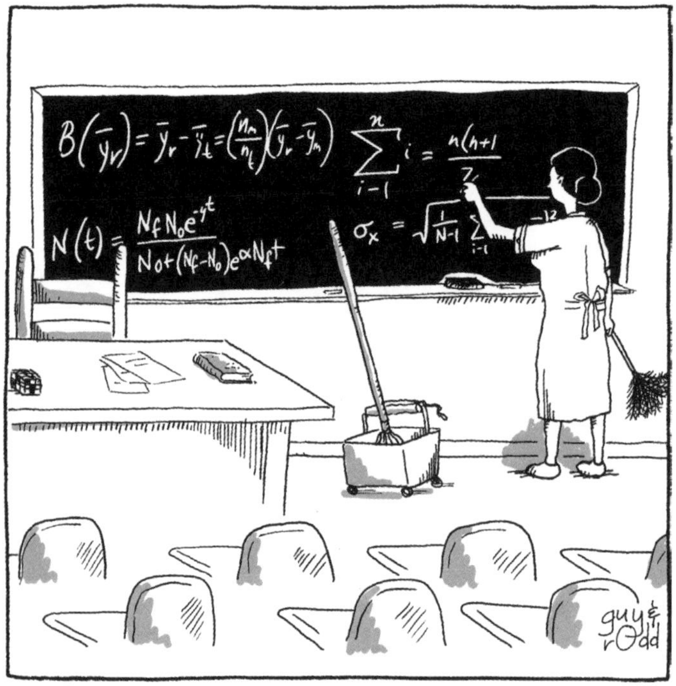
guy & rOdd

BECAUSE SHE'D ALWAYS HAD A CRUSH ON THE HANDSOME BUT STUPID PROFESSOR, SOMETIMES AT NIGHT SHE'D FIX SOME OF HIS MORE OBVIOUS COMPUTATIONAL ERRORS.

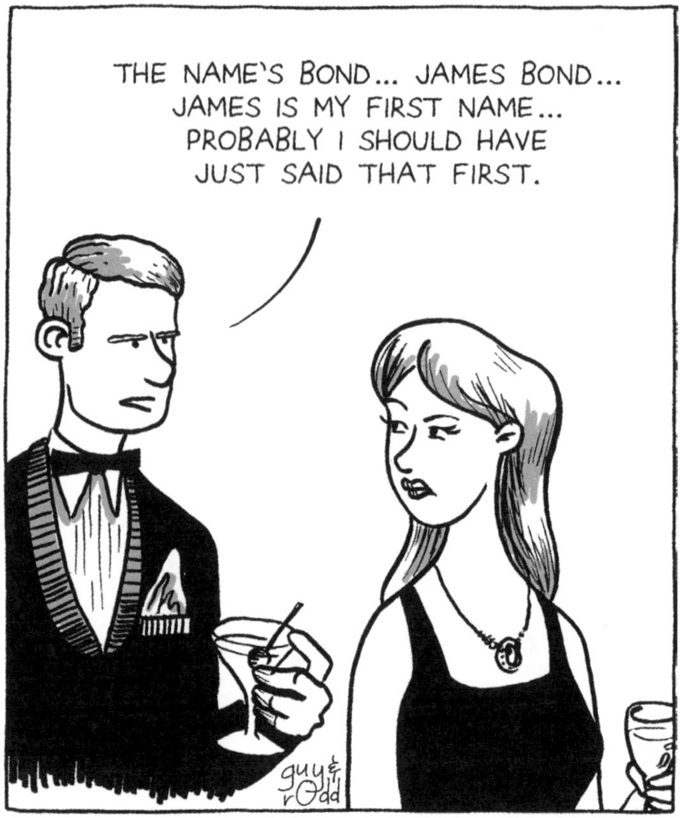
THE NAME'S BOND... JAMES BOND... JAMES IS MY FIRST NAME... PROBABLY I SHOULD HAVE JUST SAID THAT FIRST.
guy & rOdd

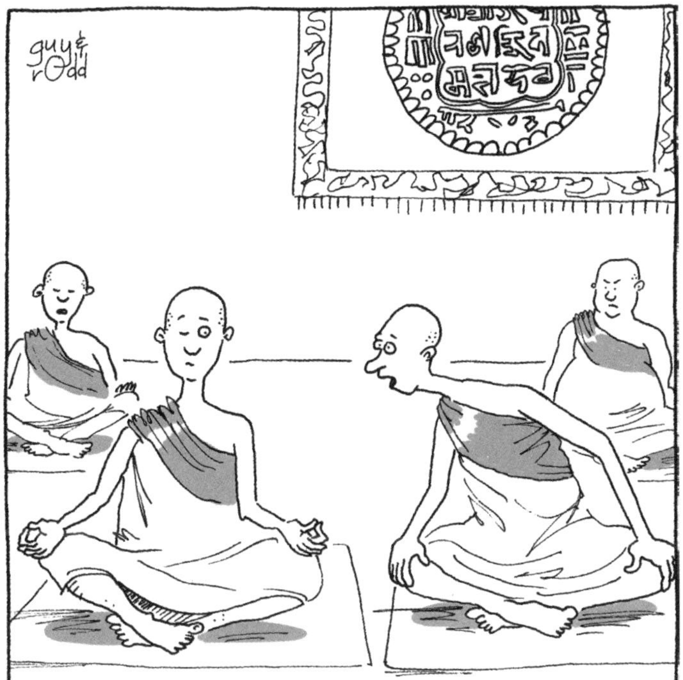
guy & rOdd

"PSST! I JUST REALIZED SOMETHING... I'M HELLA BORED".

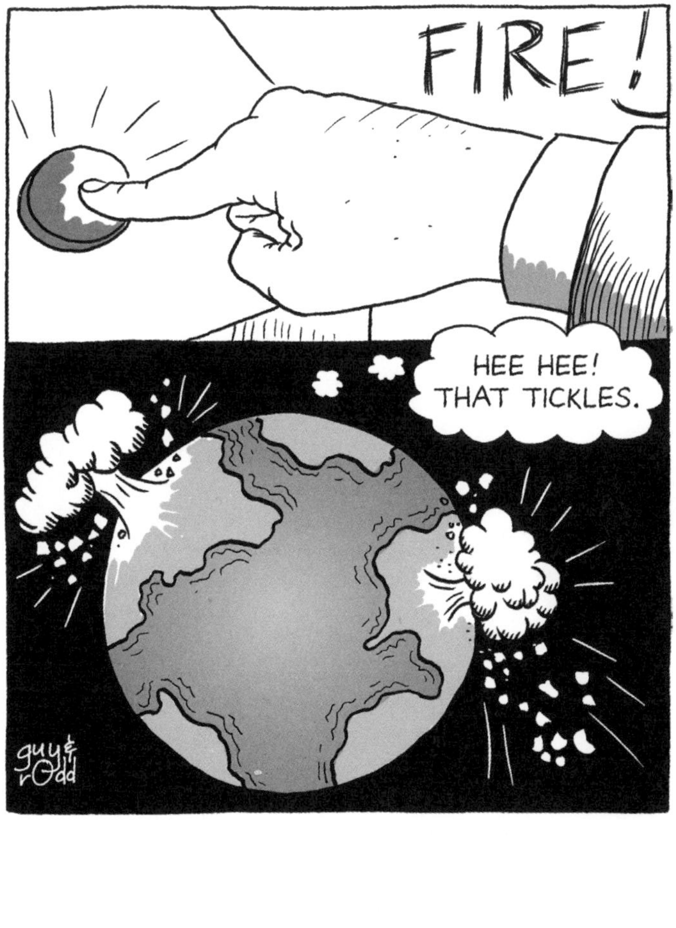
FIRE!
HEE HEE! THAT TICKLES.
guy & rOdd

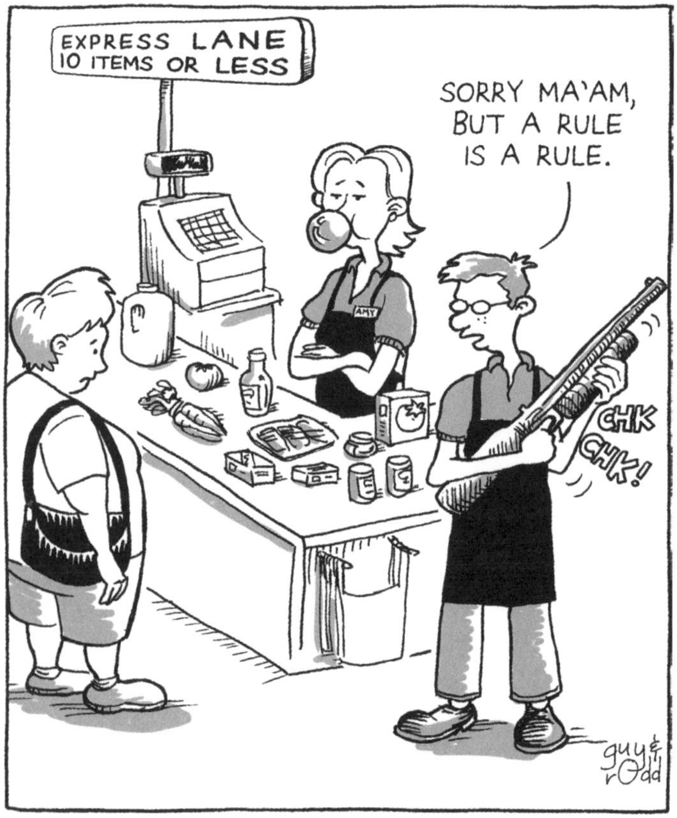
EXPRESS LANE
10 ITEMS OR LESS
AMY
SORRY MA'AM, BUT A RULE IS A RULE.
CHK
CHK!
guy & rOdd

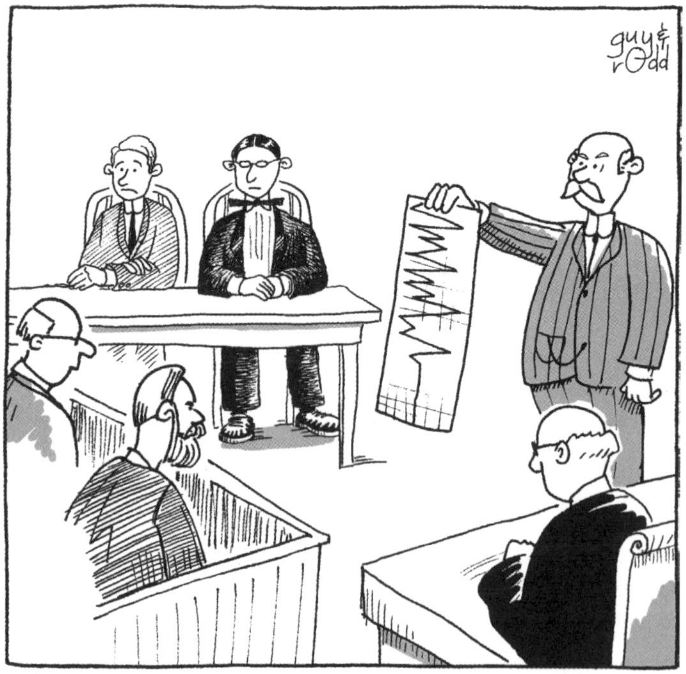
guy & rOdd

AT THE END OF THE DAY, ALL JOHN HENRY BARNSBY WAS GUILTY OF WAS TAKING A LIE DETECTOR TEST DURING THE GREAT SAN FRANCISCO EARTHQUAKE OF 1906.

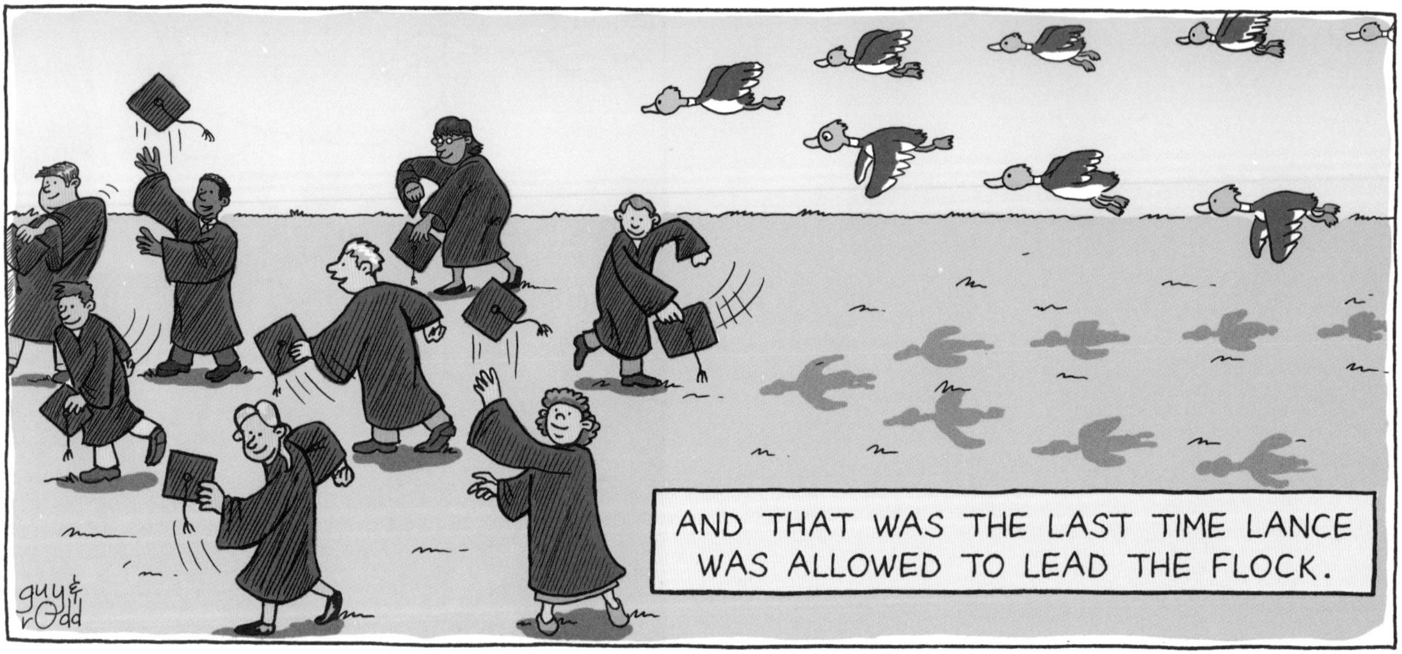
AND THAT WAS THE LAST TIME LANCE WAS ALLOWED TO LEAD THE FLOCK.
guy & rOdd

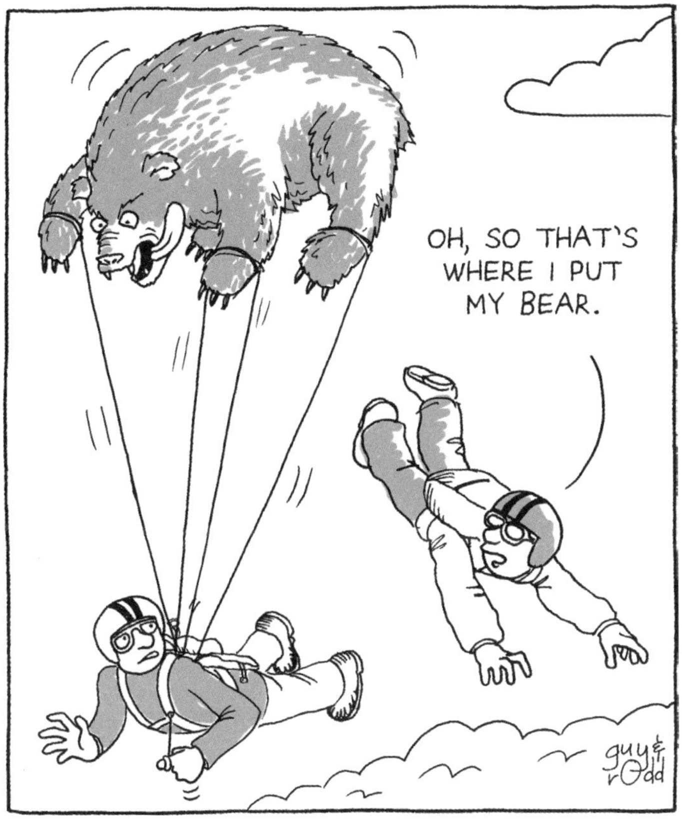
OH, SO THAT'S WHERE I PUT MY BEAR.
guy & rOdd

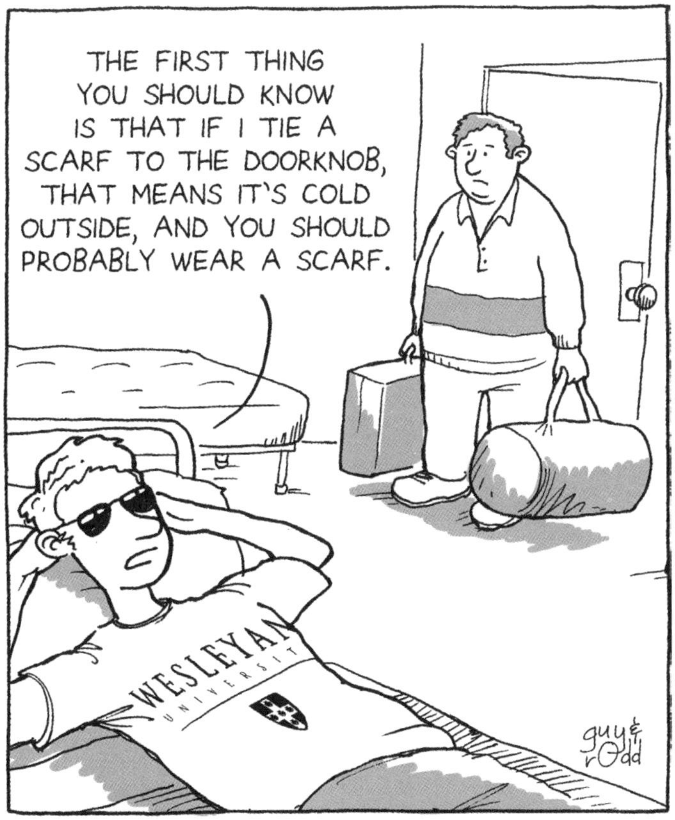
THE FIRST THING YOU SHOULD KNOW IS THAT IF I TIE A SCARF TO THE DOORKNOB, THAT MEANS IT'S COLD OUTSIDE, AND YOU SHOULD PROBABLY WEAR A SCARF.
WESLEYAN UNIVERSITY
guy & rOdd

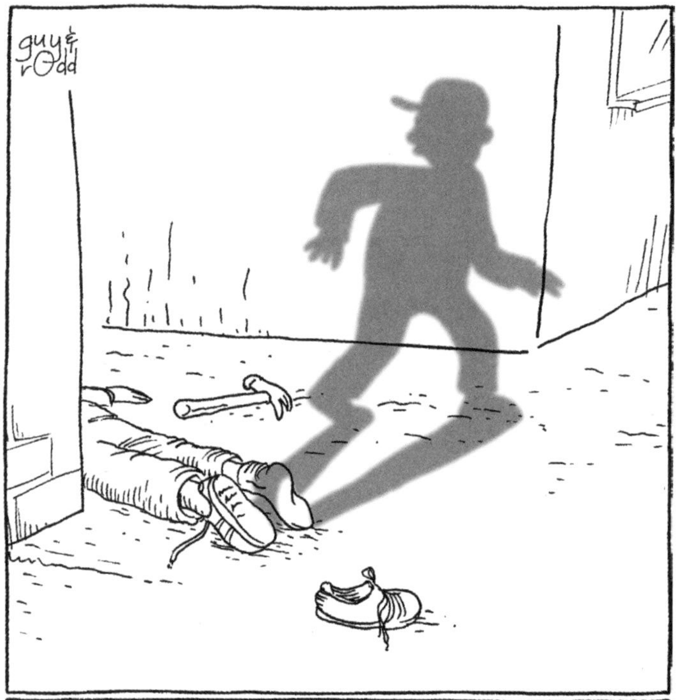

EVERYBODY MADE FUN OF JOSH FOR BEING AFRAID OF HIS SHADOW, BUT LATER THAT DAY, THEY WOULD ALL BE SORRY.

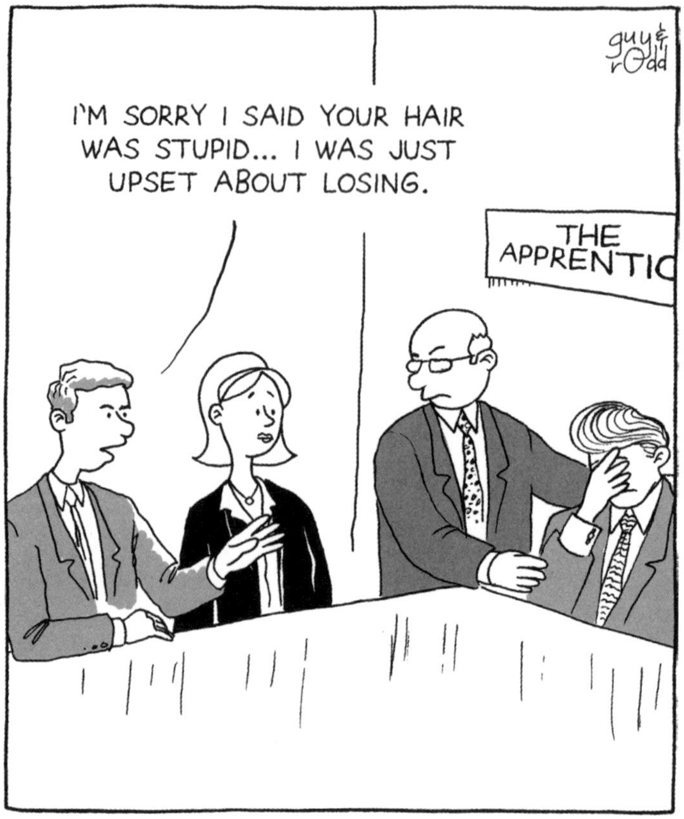
I'M SORRY I SAID YOUR HAIR WAS STUPID... I WAS JUST UPSET ABOUT LOSING.
THE APPRENTIC

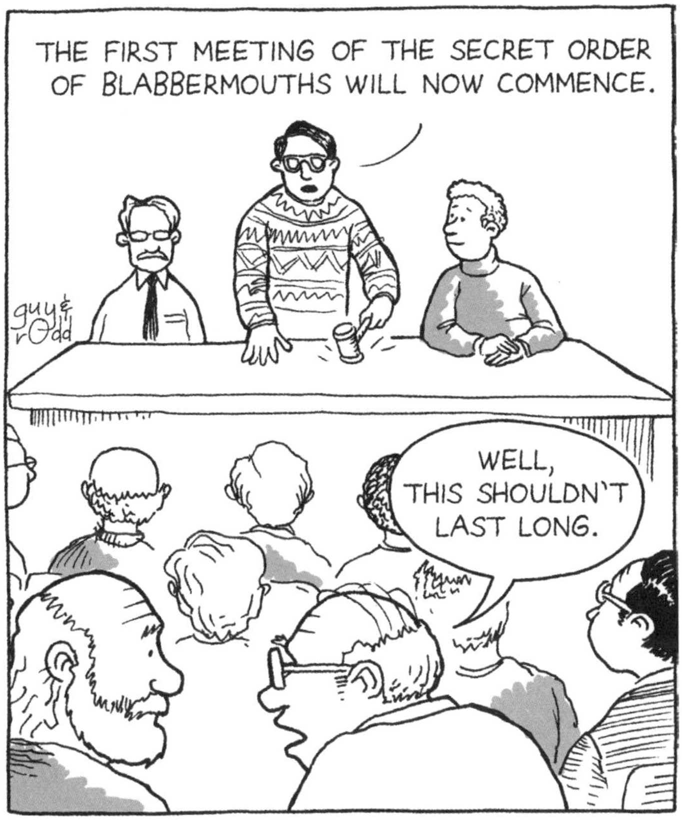
THE FIRST MEETING OF THE SECRET ORDER OF BLABBERMOUTHS WILL NOW COMMENCE.
WELL, THIS SHOULDN'T LAST LONG.
guy & rOdd

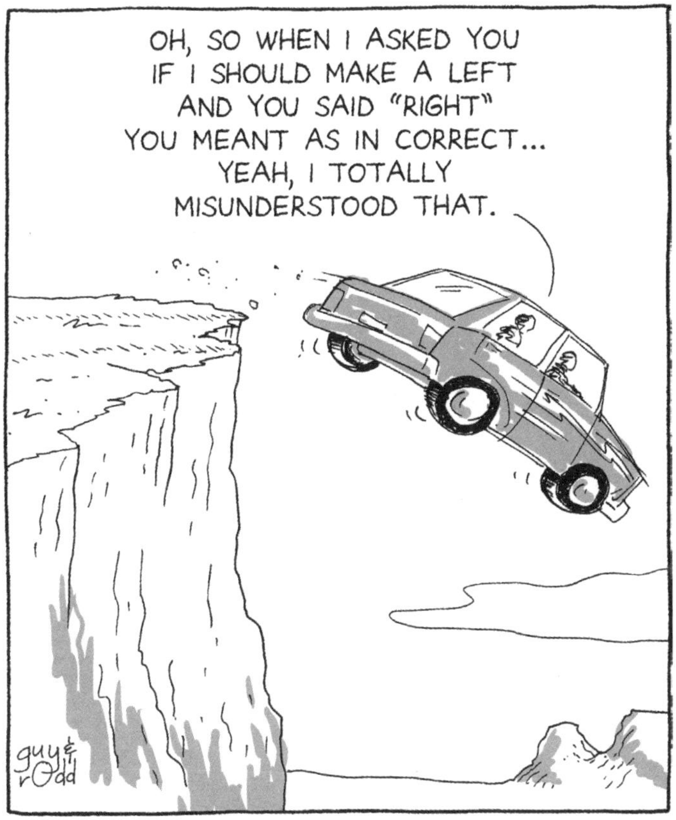
OH, SO WHEN I ASKED YOU IF I SHOULD MAKE A LEFT AND YOU SAID "RIGHT" YOU MEANT AS IN CORRECT... YEAH, I TOTALLY MISUNDERSTOOD THAT.
guy & rOdd

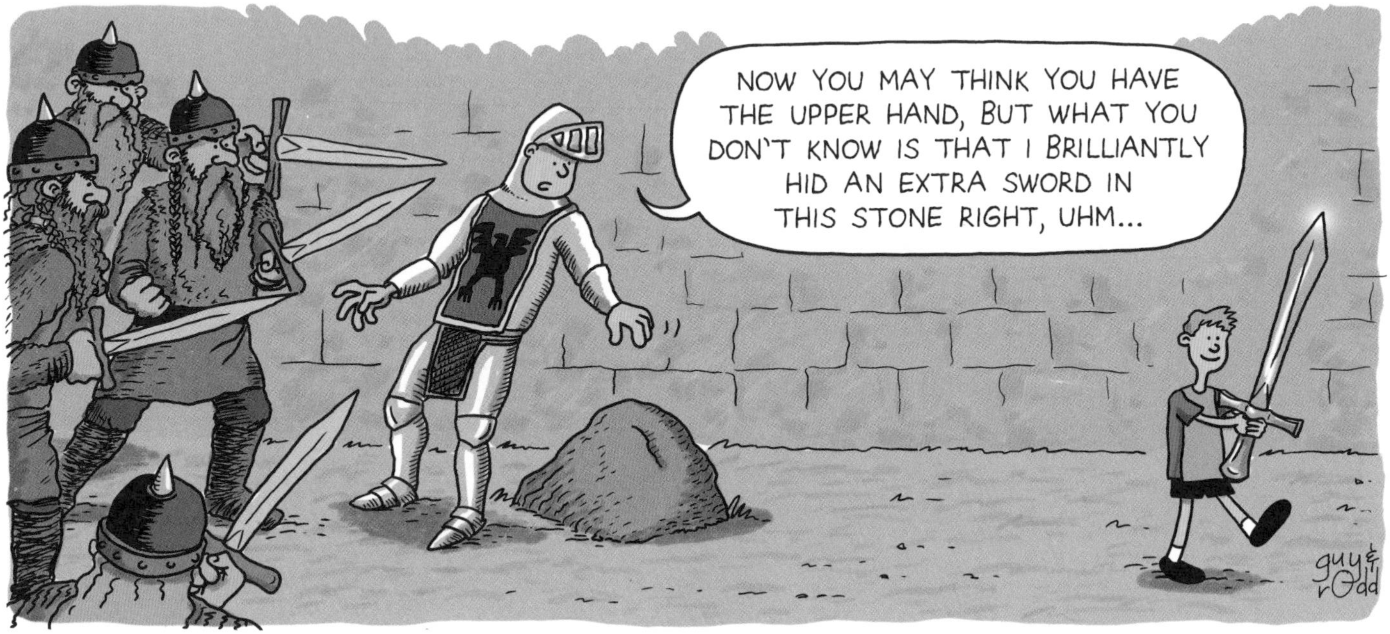
NOW YOU MAY THINK YOU HAVE THE UPPER HAND, BUT WHAT YOU DON'T KNOW IS THAT I BRILLIANTLY HID AN EXTRA SWORD IN THIS STONE RIGHT, UHM...
guy & rOdd

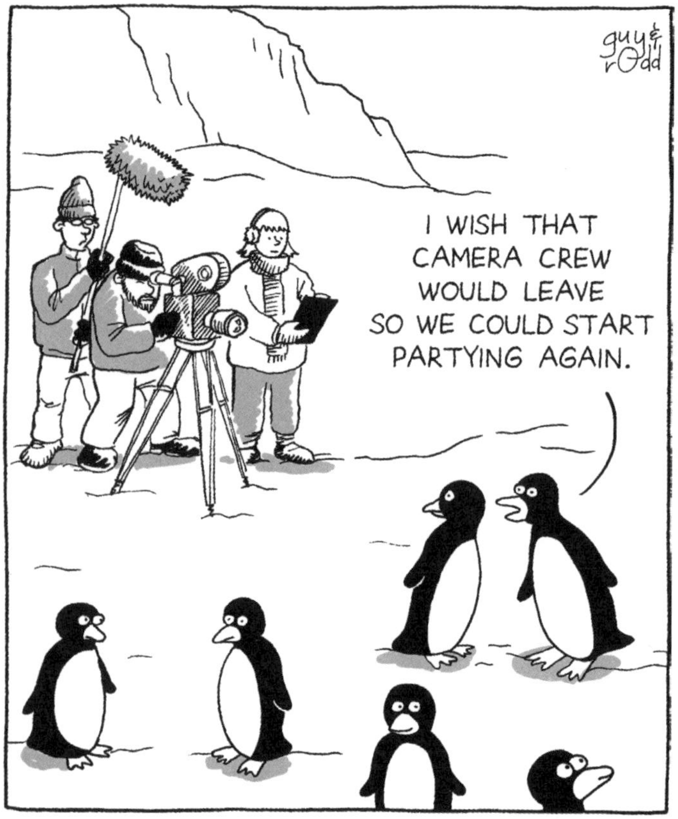
guy & rOdd
I WISH THAT CAMERA CREW WOULD LEAVE SO WE COULD START PARTYING AGAIN.

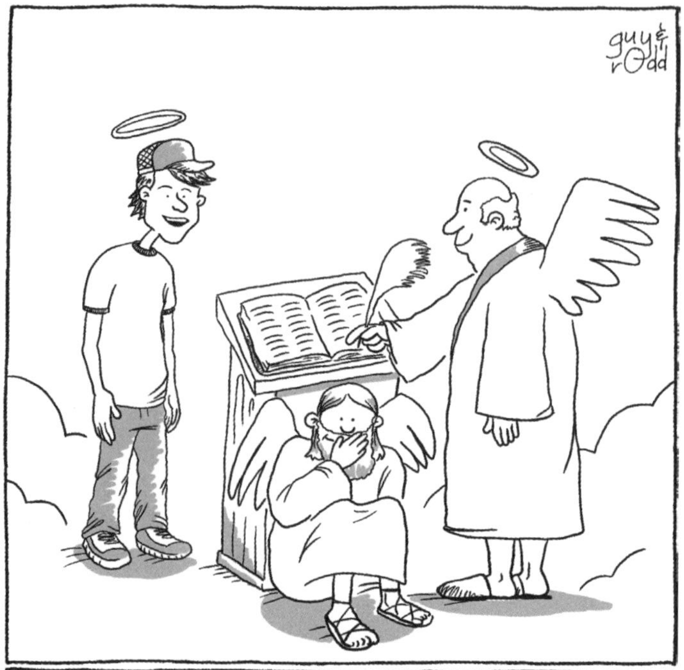
guy & rOdd

BECAUSE HE HAD DONE SOME SHADY THINGS IN LIFE, ASHTON WAS SURPRISED BY THE WARM RECEPTION HE RECEIVED IN HEAVEN. THEN JESUS POPPED OUT AND YELLED "PUNK'D"!

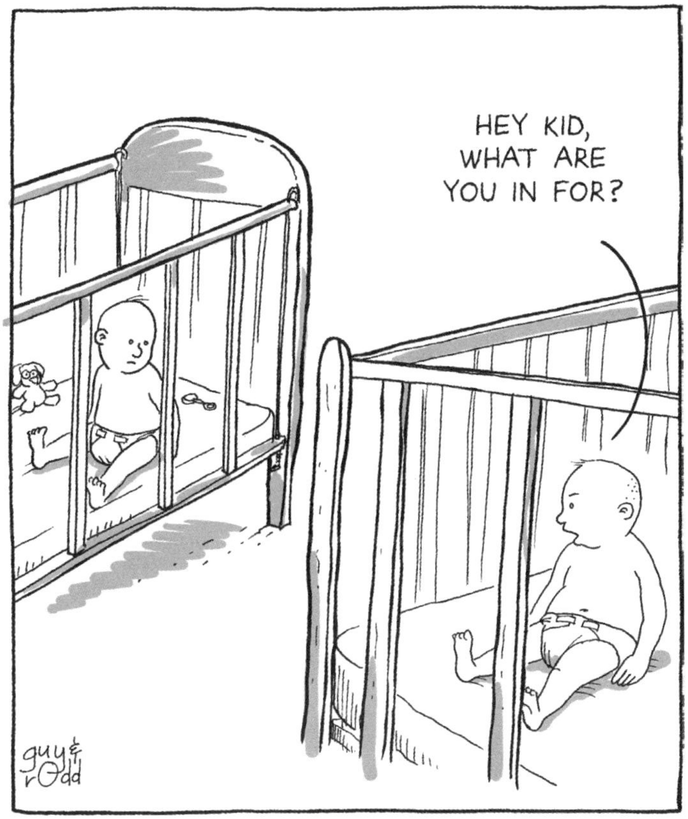
HEY KID,
WHAT ARE
YOU IN FOR?
guy & rOdd

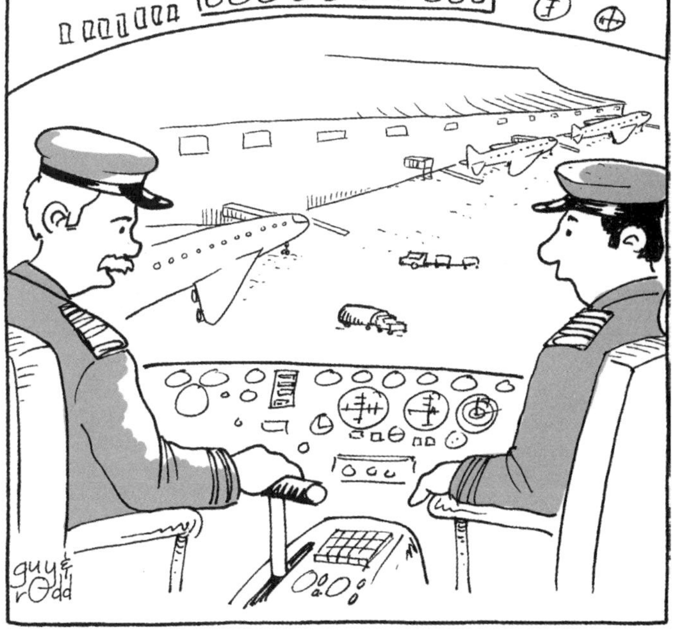
guy & rOdd

"WOULD YOU MIND SWITCHING SEATS WITH ME... I'M ACTUALLY TERRIBLE AT PARALLEL PARKING".

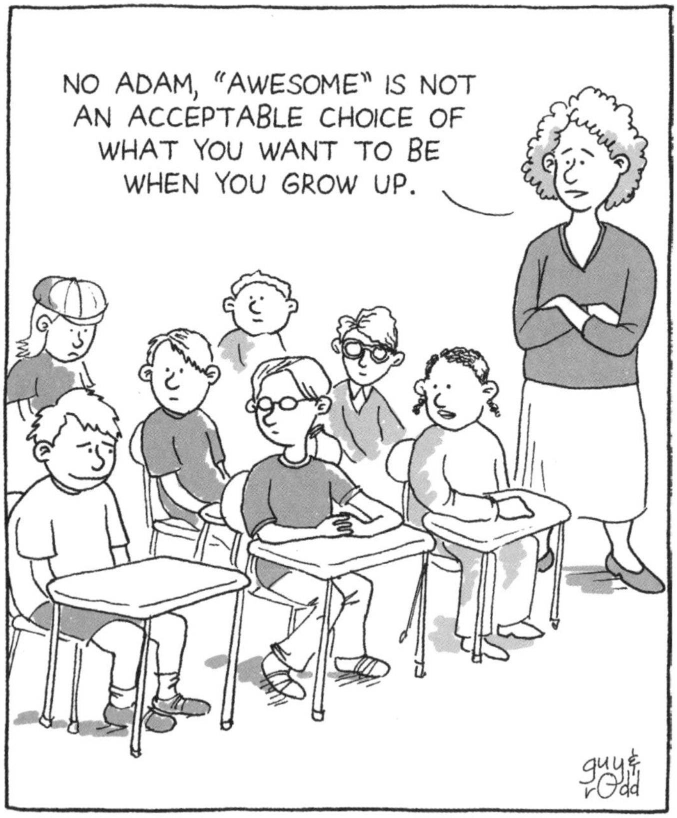
NO ADAM, "AWESOME" IS NOT AN ACCEPTABLE CHOICE OF WHAT YOU WANT TO BE WHEN YOU GROW UP.
guy & rOdd

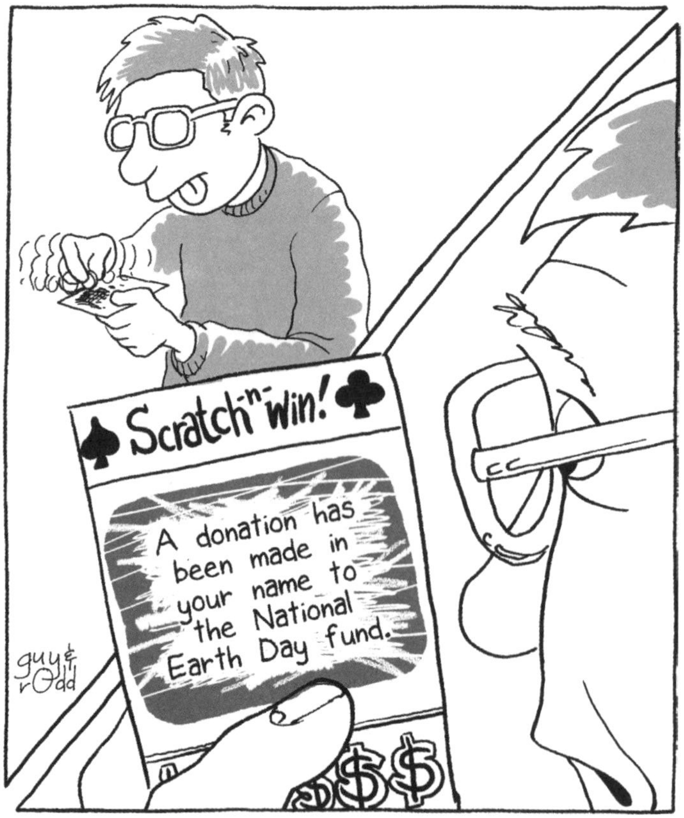
Scratch-n-win!
A donation has been made in your name to the National Earth Day fund.
guy & rOdd

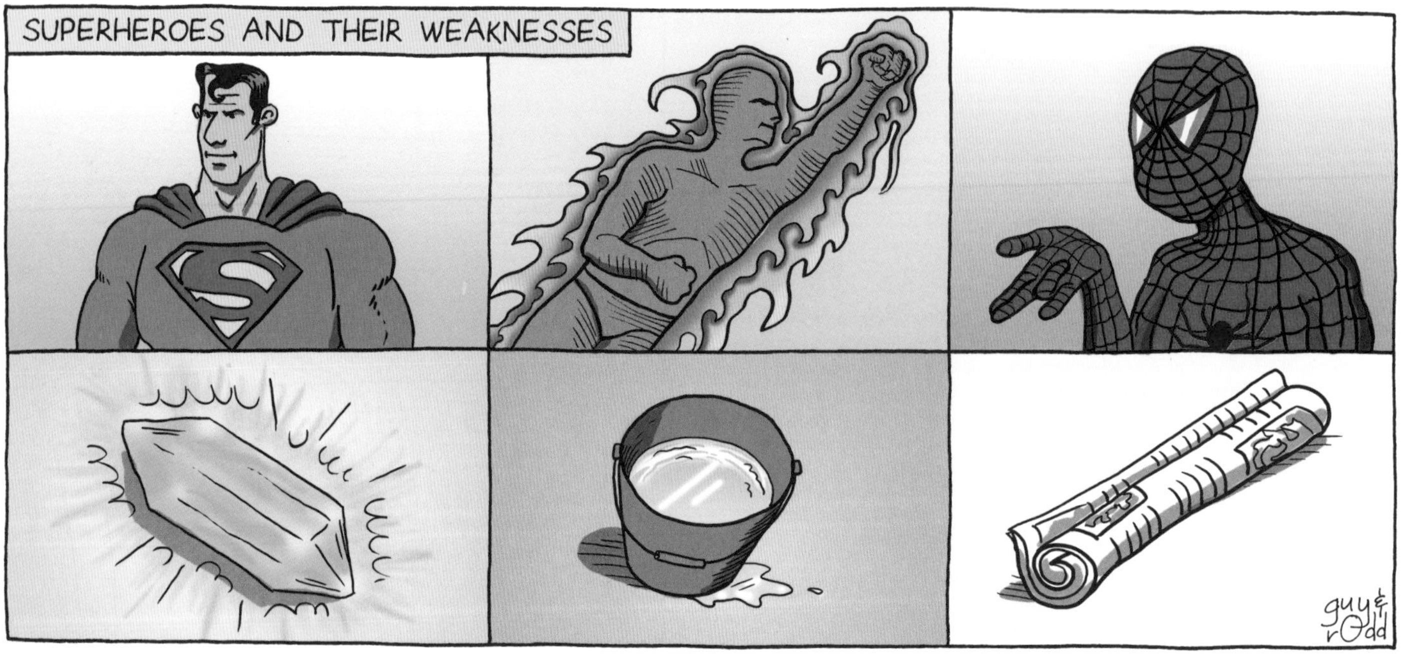
SUPERHEROES AND THEIR WEAKNESSES
guy & rOdd

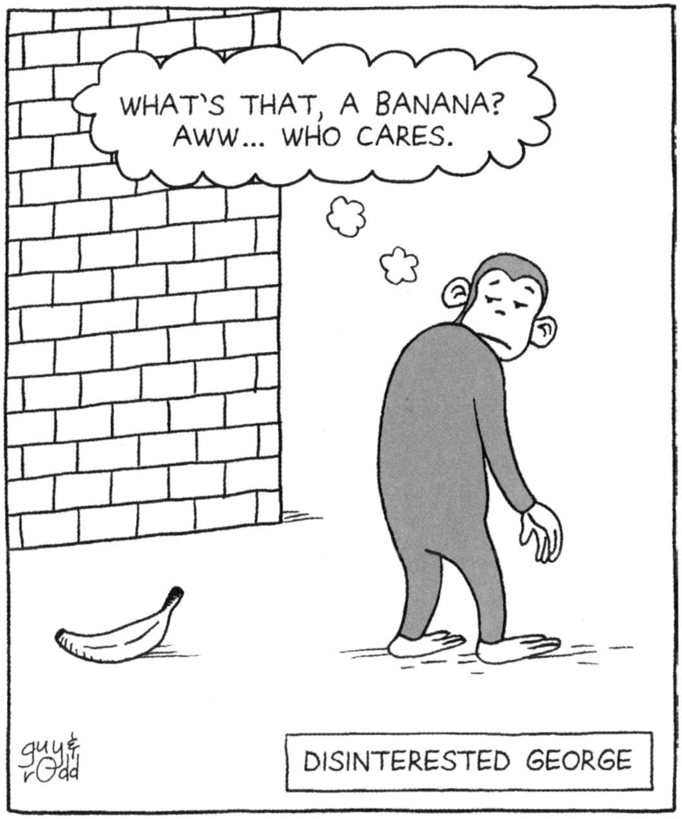
WHAT'S THAT, A BANANA?
AWW... WHO CARES.
guy & rOdd
DISINTERESTED GEORGE

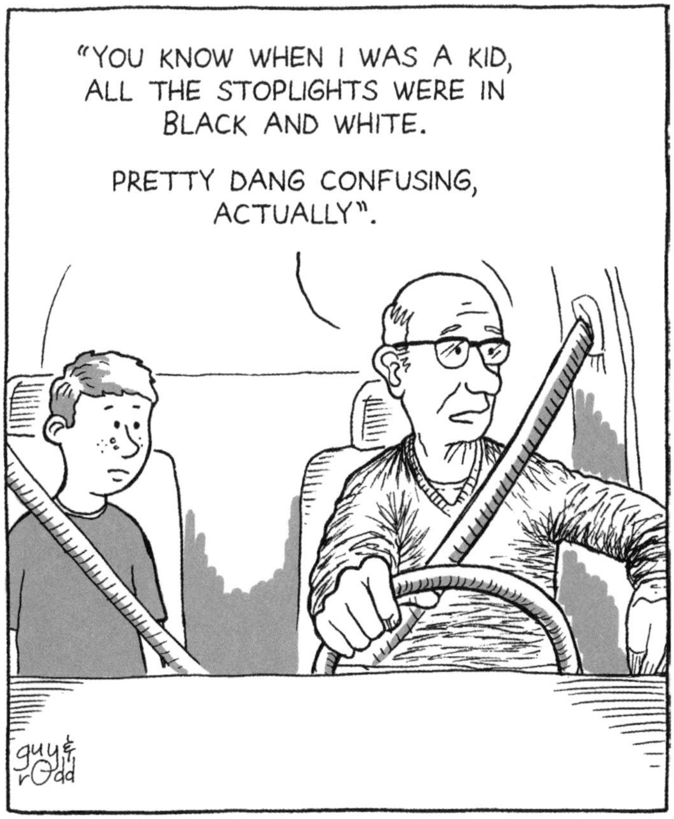
"YOU KNOW WHEN I WAS A KID, ALL THE STOPLIGHTS WERE IN BLACK AND WHITE.
PRETTY DANG CONFUSING, ACTUALLY".
guy & rOdd

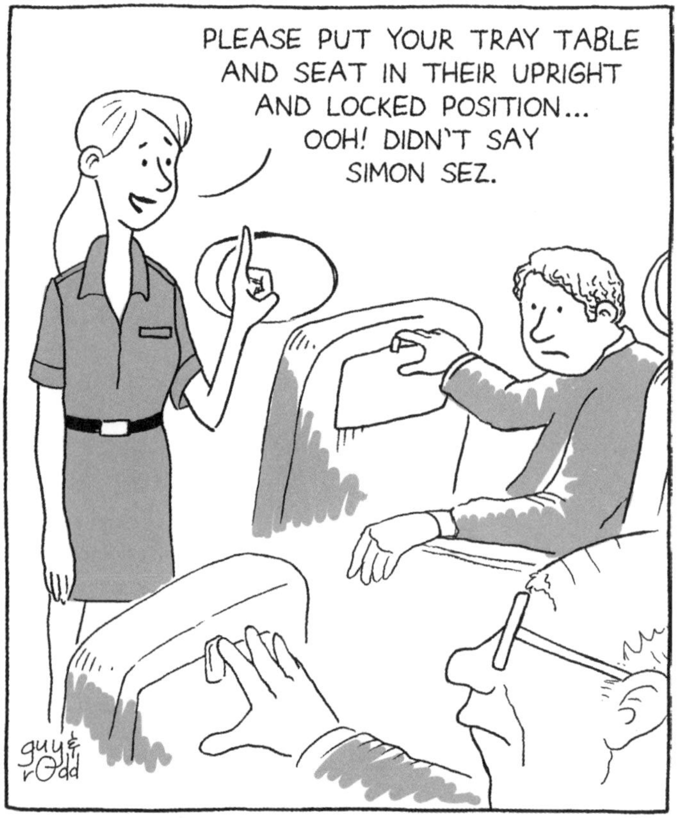
PLEASE PUT YOUR TRAY TABLE AND SEAT IN THEIR UPRIGHT AND LOCKED POSITION... OOH! DIDN'T SAY SIMON SEZ.
guy & rOdd

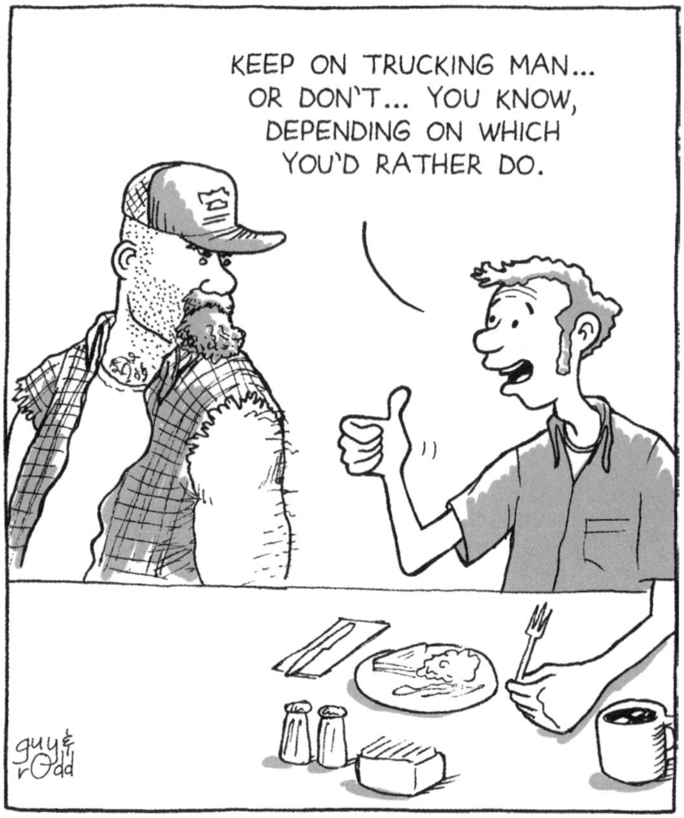
KEEP ON TRUCKING MAN... OR DON'T... YOU KNOW, DEPENDING ON WHICH YOU'D RATHER DO.
guy & rOdd

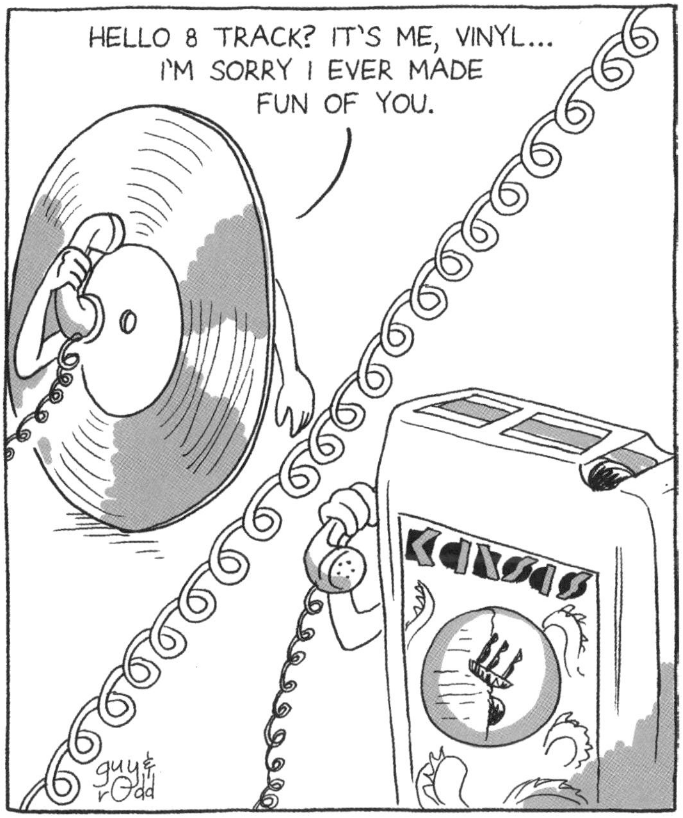
HELLO 8 TRACK? IT'S ME, VINYL... I'M SORRY I EVER MADE FUN OF YOU.

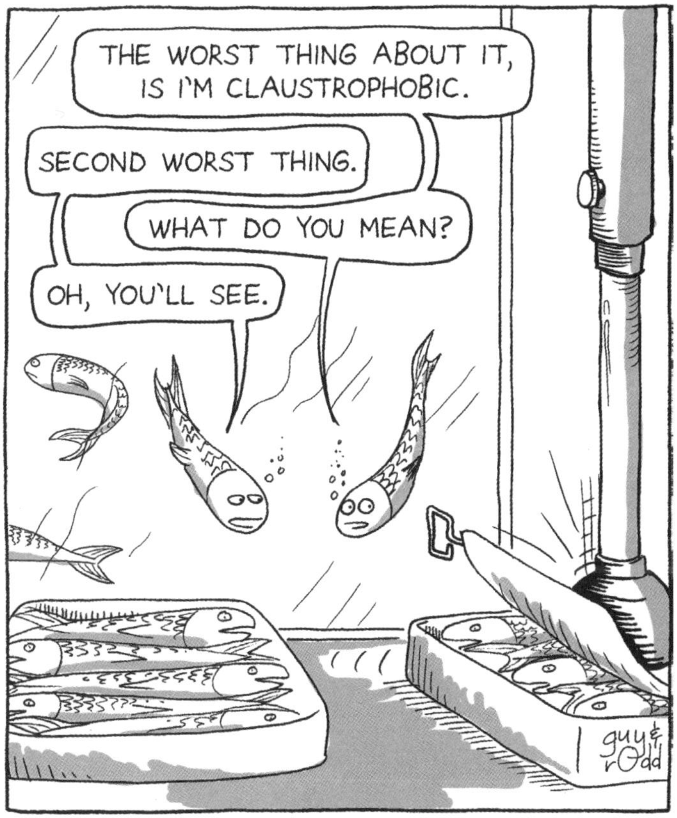
THE WORST THING ABOUT IT, IS I'M CLAUSTROPHOBIC.
SECOND WORST THING.
WHAT DO YOU MEAN?
OH, YOU'LL SEE.

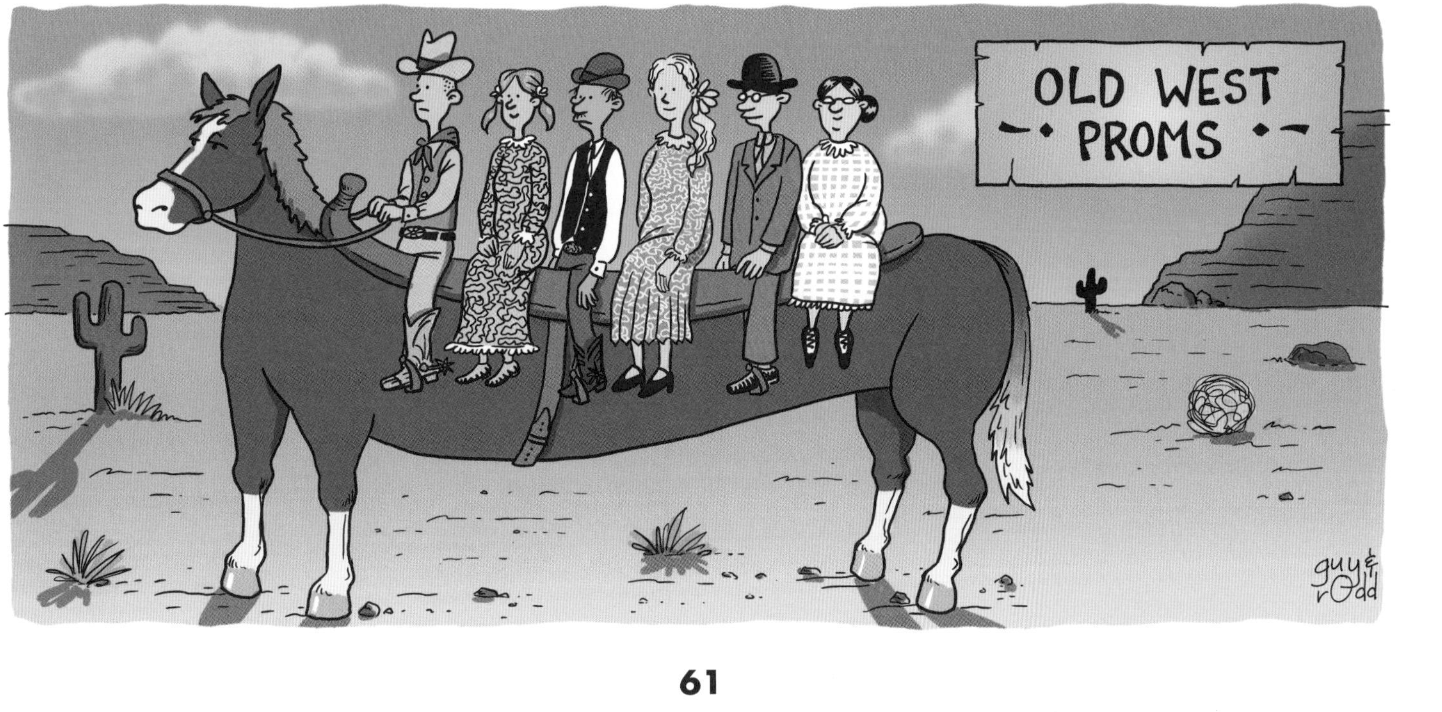
OLD WEST PROMS

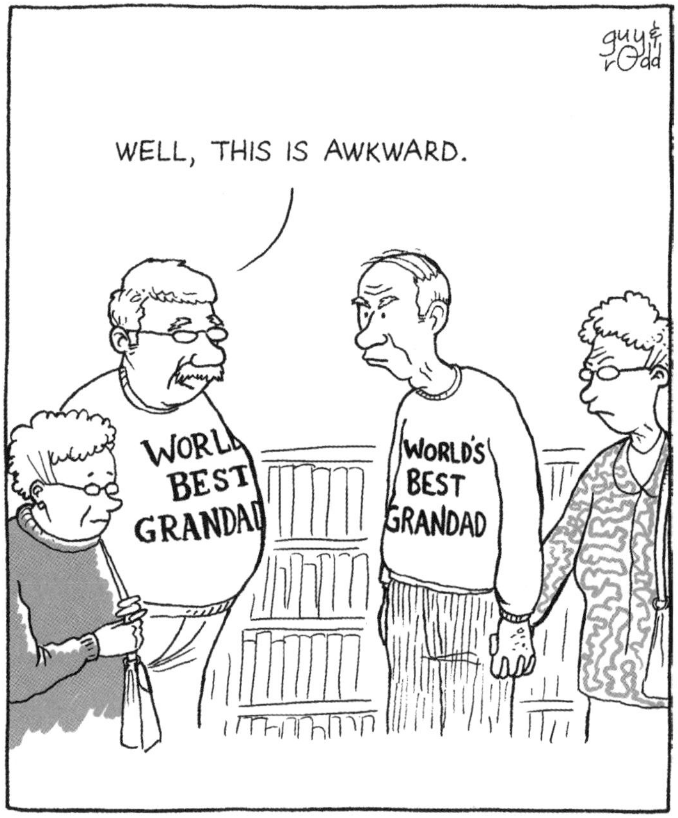
guy & rOdd
WELL, THIS IS AWKWARD.
WORLD'S BEST GRANDAD
WORLD'S BEST GRANDAD

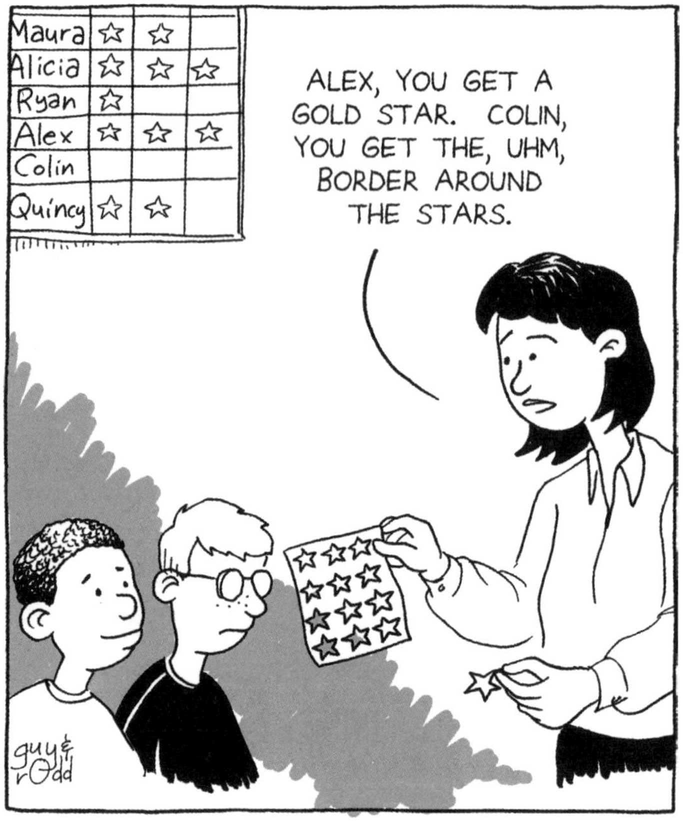
Maura
Alicia
Ryan
Alex
Colin
Quincy
ALEX, YOU GET A GOLD STAR. COLIN, YOU GET THE, UHM, BORDER AROUND THE STARS.
guy & rOdd

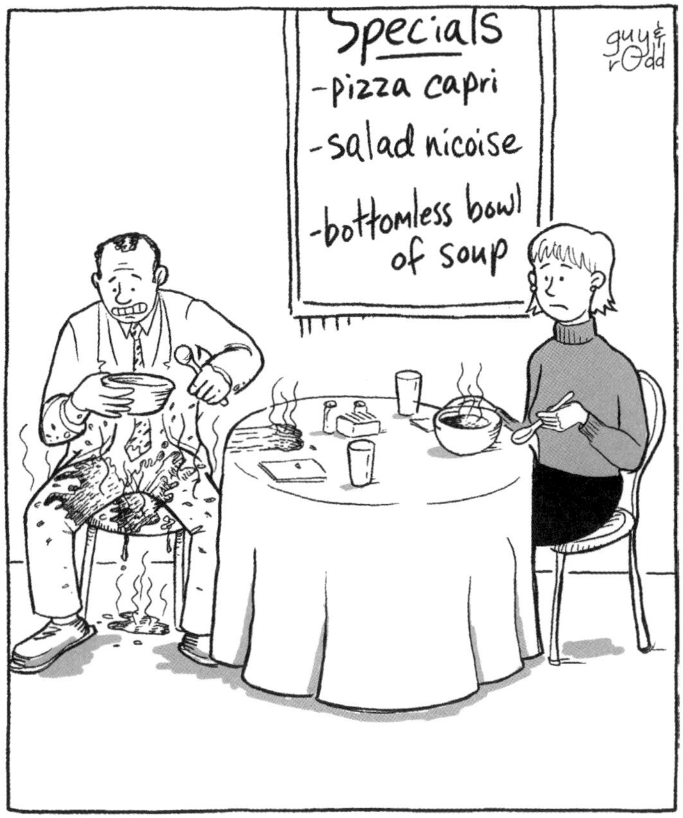
Specials
-pizza capri
-salad nicoise
-bottomless bowl of soup
guy & rOdd

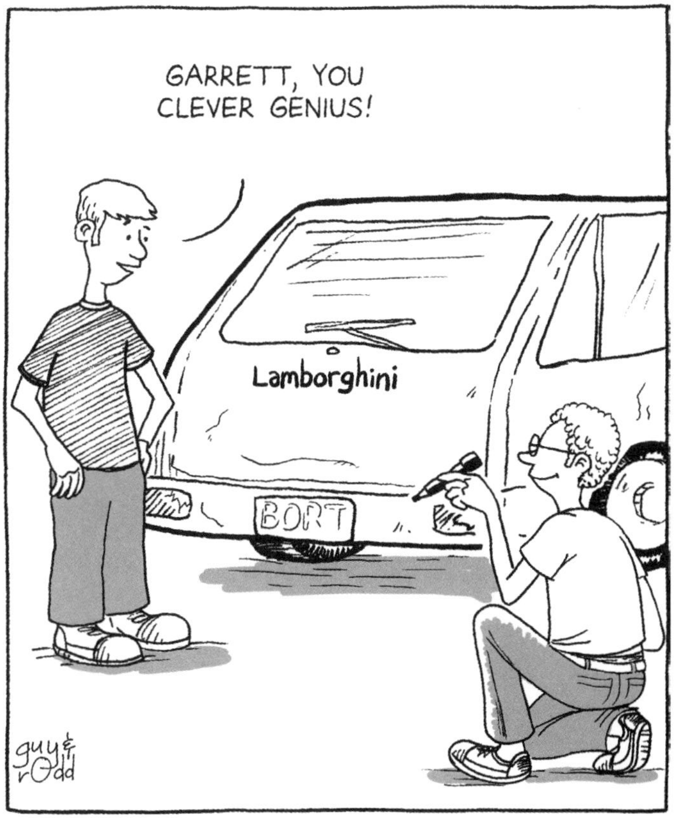
GARRETT, YOU CLEVER GENIUS!
Lamborghini
BORT
guy & rOdd

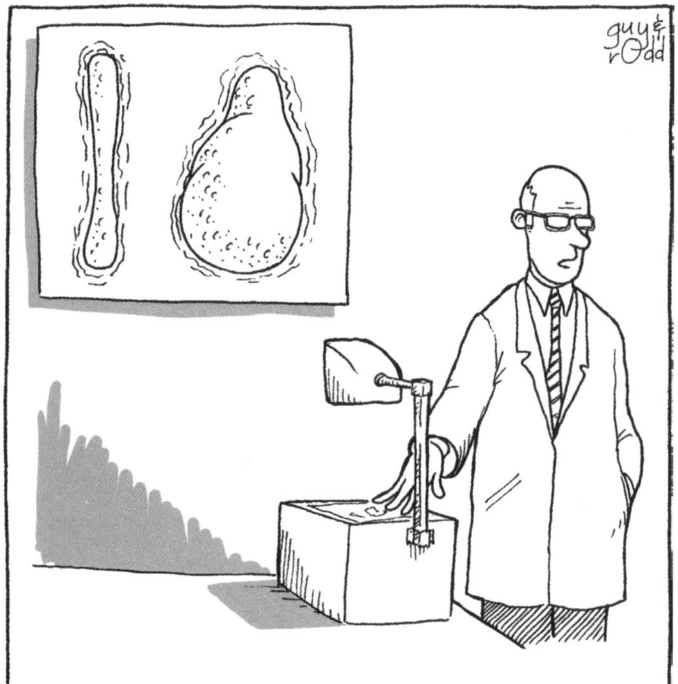

"WE'VE ISOLATED THE OBESITY GENE DOWN TO ONE OF THESE TWO".

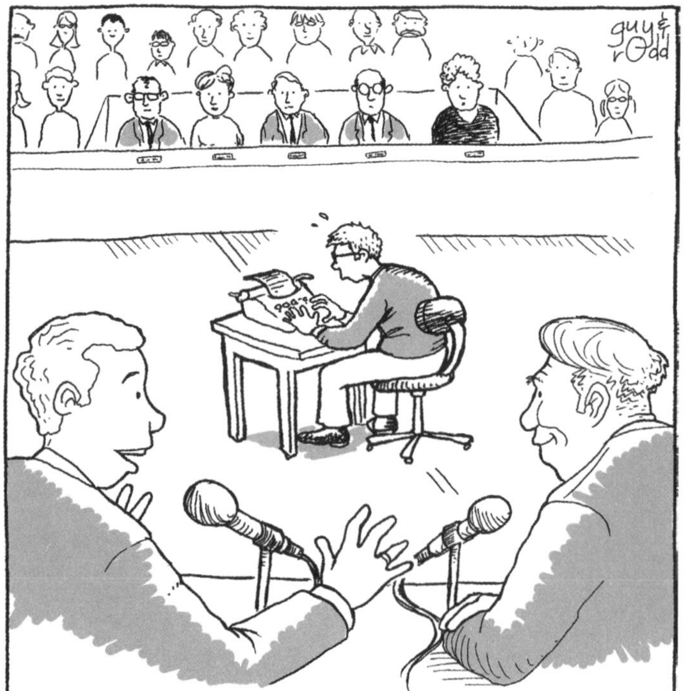

"OH MAN, HE JUST NAILED THAT TRIPLE ENTENDRE... THAT ALL BUT GUARANTEES HIM A MEDAL".

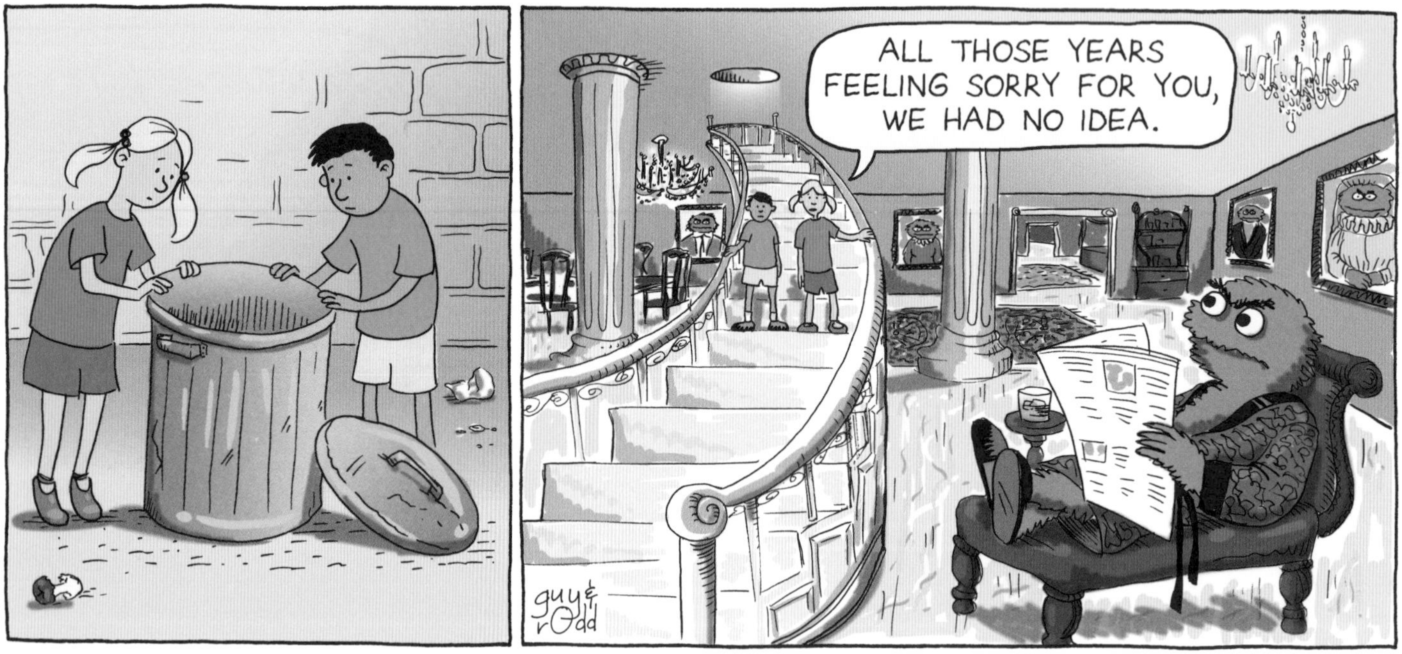
ALL THOSE YEARS FEELING SORRY FOR YOU, WE HAD NO IDEA.

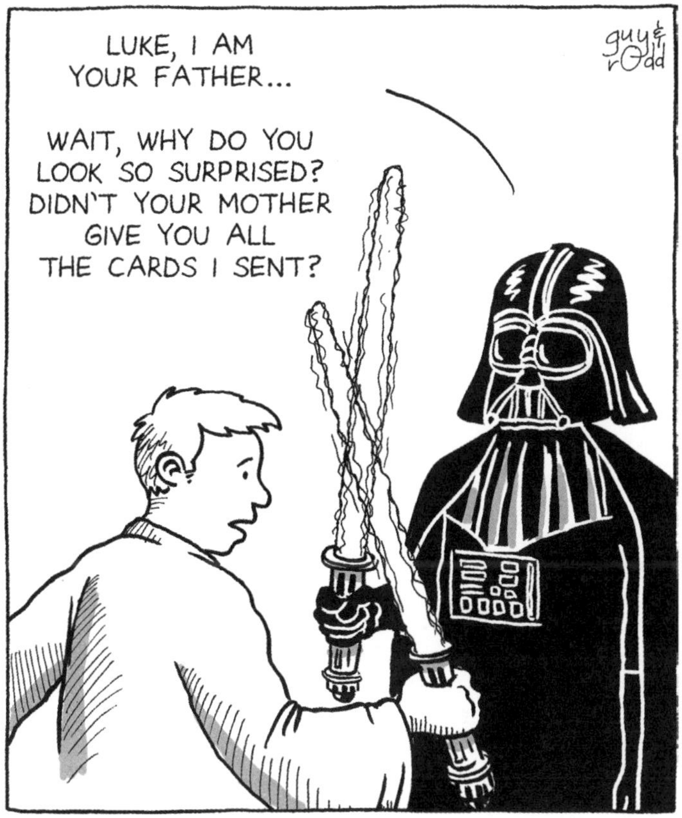
LUKE, I AM
YOUR FATHER...
WAIT, WHY DO YOU
LOOK SO SURPRISED?
DIDN'T YOUR MOTHER
GIVE YOU ALL
THE CARDS I SENT?
guy & rOdd

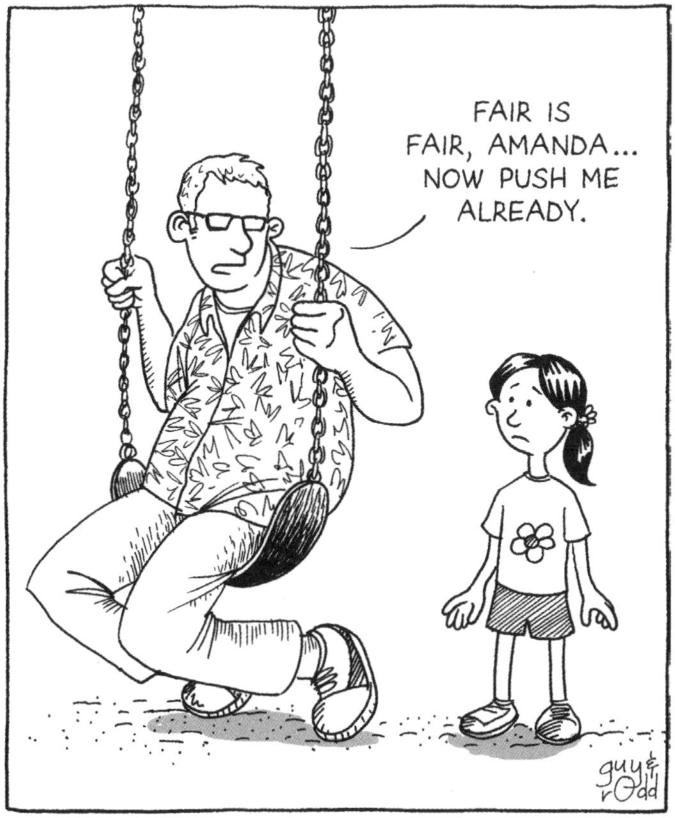
FAIR IS
FAIR, AMANDA...
NOW PUSH ME
ALREADY.
guy & rOdd

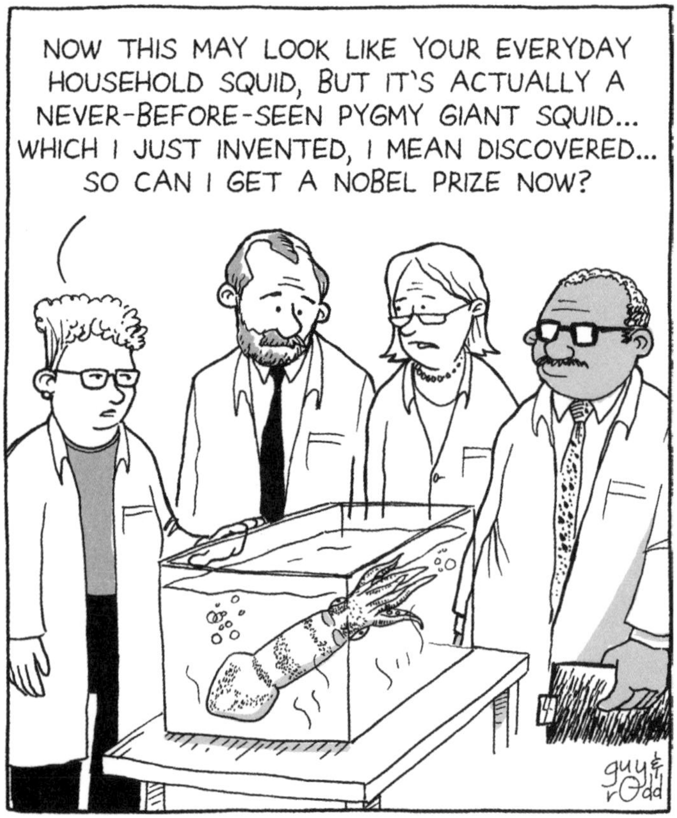
NOW THIS MAY LOOK LIKE YOUR EVERYDAY HOUSEHOLD SQUID, BUT IT'S ACTUALLY A NEVER-BEFORE-SEEN PYGMY GIANT SQUID... WHICH I JUST INVENTED, I MEAN DISCOVERED... SO CAN I GET A NOBEL PRIZE NOW?
guy & rOdd

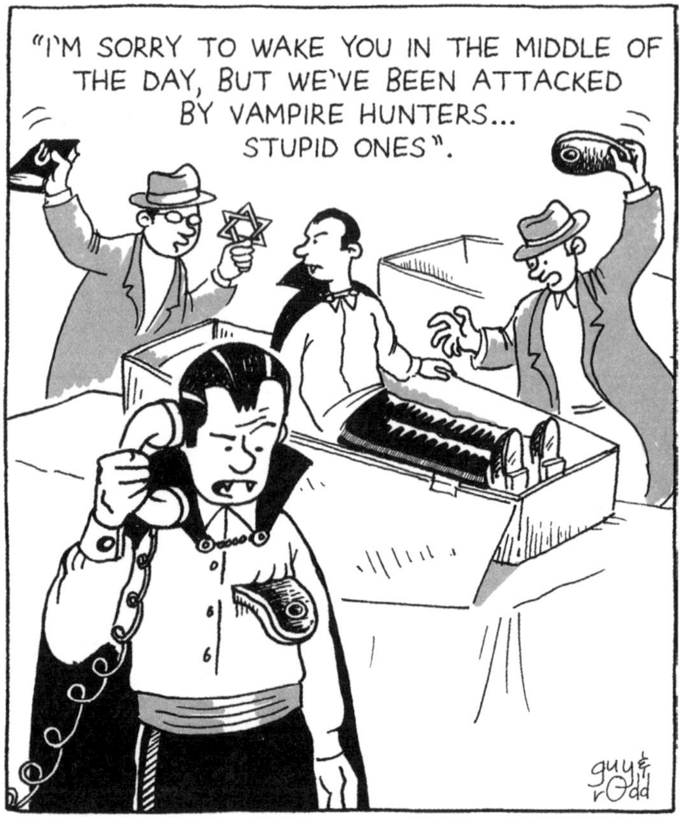
"I'M SORRY TO WAKE YOU IN THE MIDDLE OF THE DAY, BUT WE'VE BEEN ATTACKED BY VAMPIRE HUNTERS... STUPID ONES".
guy & rOdd

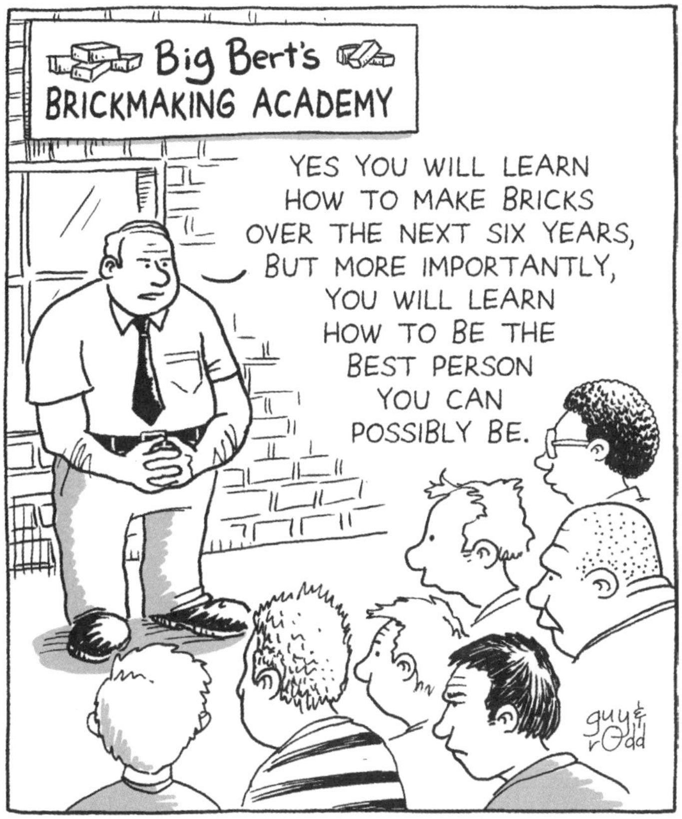
Big Bert's
BRICKMAKING ACADEMY
YES YOU WILL LEARN HOW TO MAKE BRICKS OVER THE NEXT SIX YEARS, BUT MORE IMPORTANTLY, YOU WILL LEARN HOW TO BE THE BEST PERSON YOU CAN POSSIBLY BE.
guy & rOdd

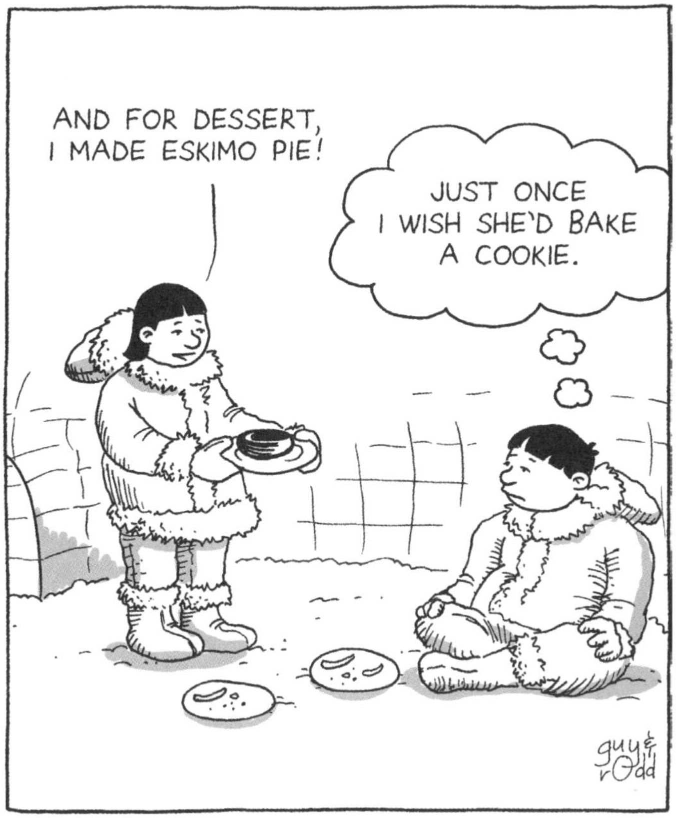
AND FOR DESSERT, I MADE ESKIMO PIE!
JUST ONCE I WISH SHE'D BAKE A COOKIE.
guy & rOdd

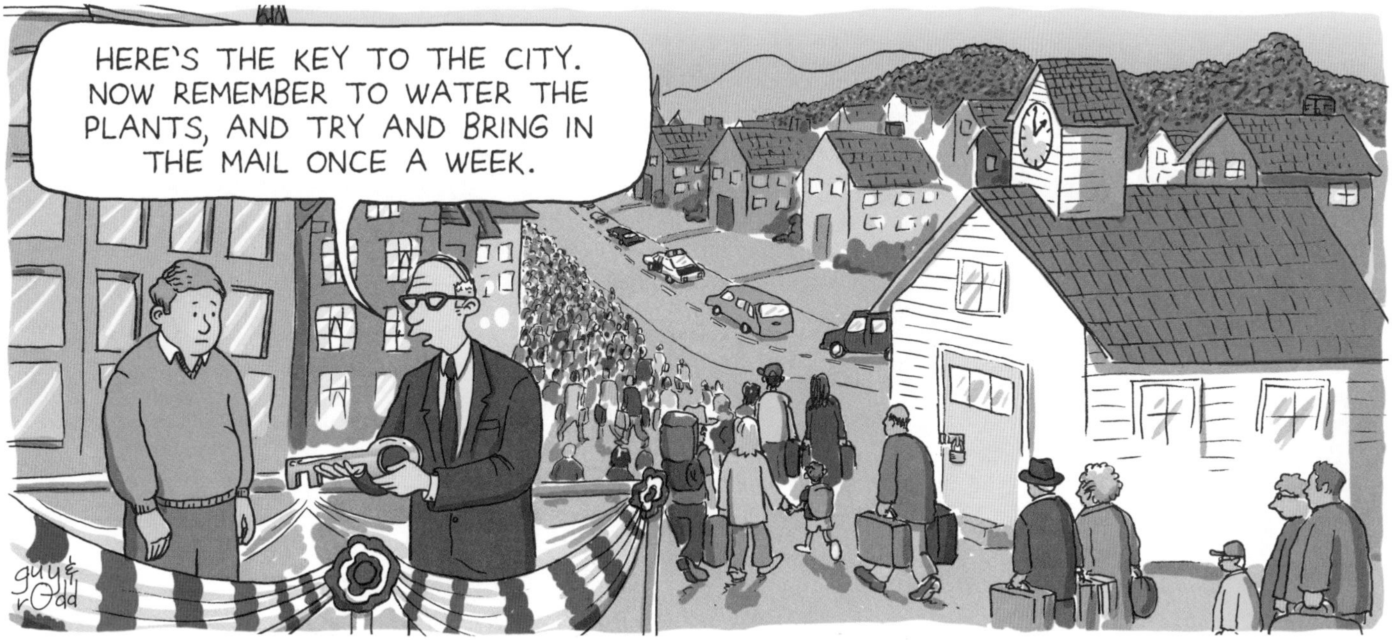
HERE'S THE KEY TO THE CITY. NOW REMEMBER TO WATER THE PLANTS, AND TRY AND BRING IN THE MAIL ONCE A WEEK.
guy & rOdd

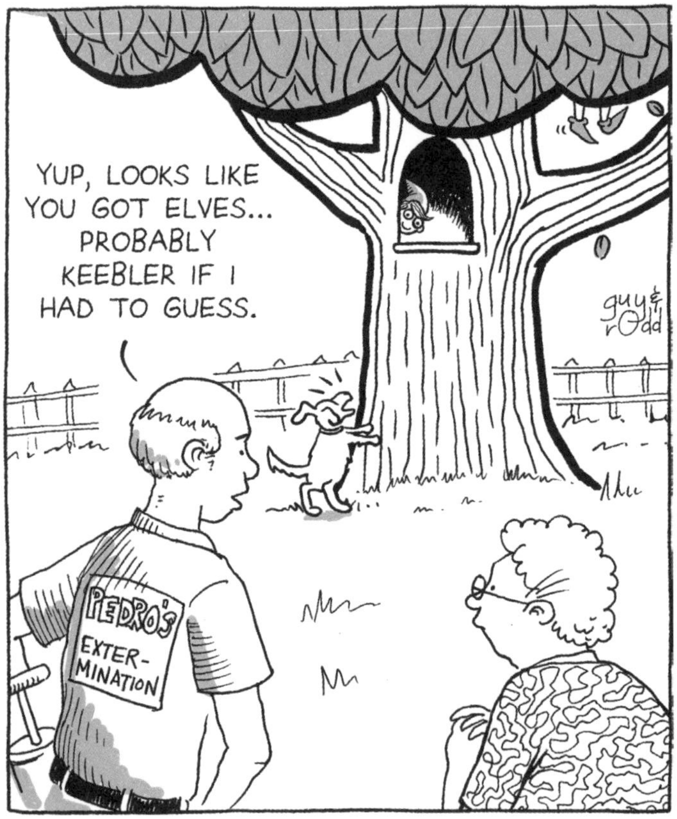
YUP, LOOKS LIKE YOU GOT ELVES... PROBABLY KEEBLER IF I HAD TO GUESS.
PEDRO'S EXTER-MINATION
guy & rodd

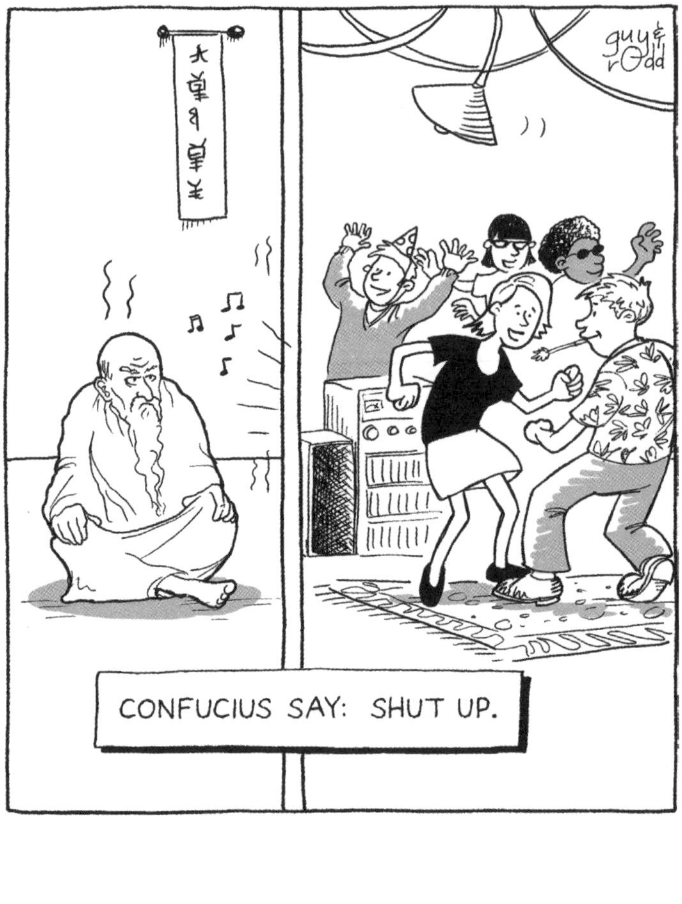
guy & rodd
CONFUCIUS SAY: SHUT UP.

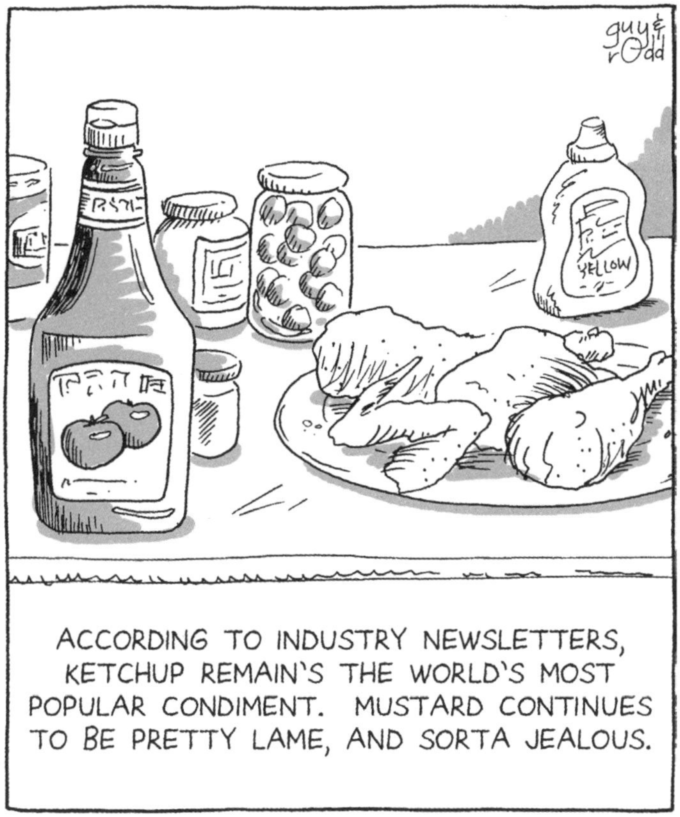
guy & rodd
ACCORDING TO INDUSTRY NEWSLETTERS, KETCHUP REMAIN'S THE WORLD'S MOST POPULAR CONDIMENT. MUSTARD CONTINUES TO BE PRETTY LAME, AND SORTA JEALOUS.

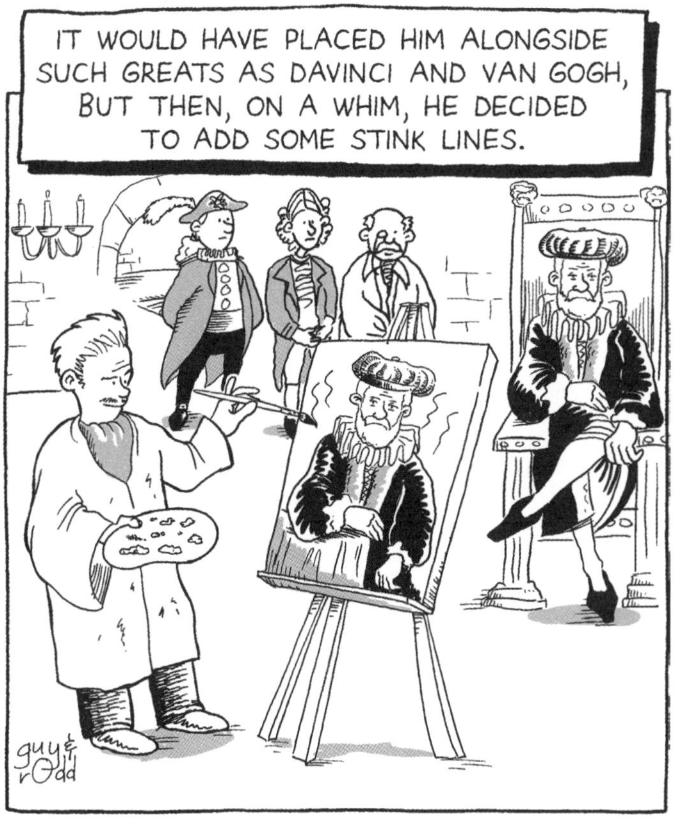
IT WOULD HAVE PLACED HIM ALONGSIDE SUCH GREATS AS DAVINCI AND VAN GOGH, BUT THEN, ON A WHIM, HE DECIDED TO ADD SOME STINK LINES.
guy & rodd

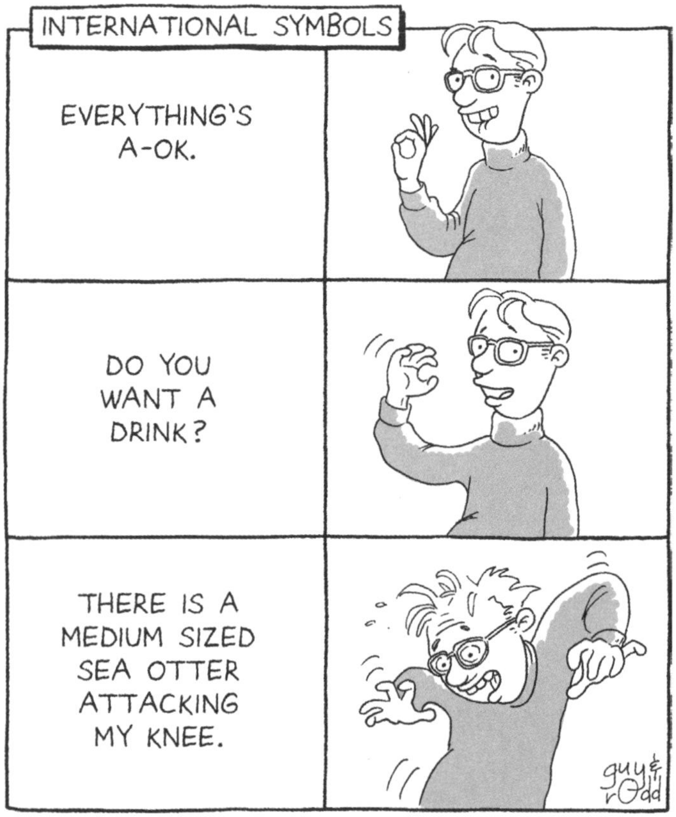
INTERNATIONAL SYMBOLS
EVERYTHING'S A-OK.
DO YOU WANT A DRINK?
THERE IS A MEDIUM SIZED SEA OTTER ATTACKING MY KNEE.
guy & rOdd

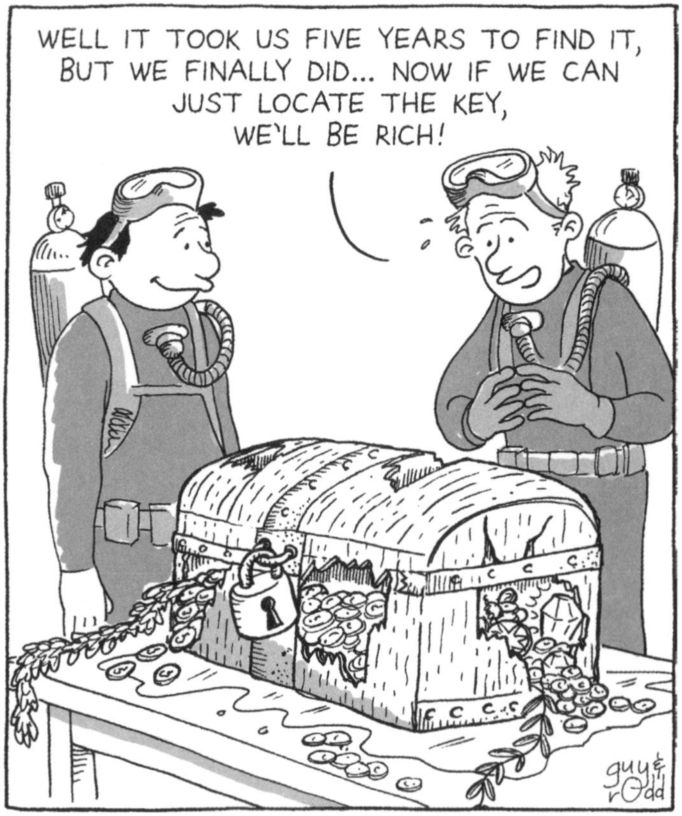
WELL IT TOOK US FIVE YEARS TO FIND IT, BUT WE FINALLY DID... NOW IF WE CAN JUST LOCATE THE KEY, WE'LL BE RICH!
guy & rOdd

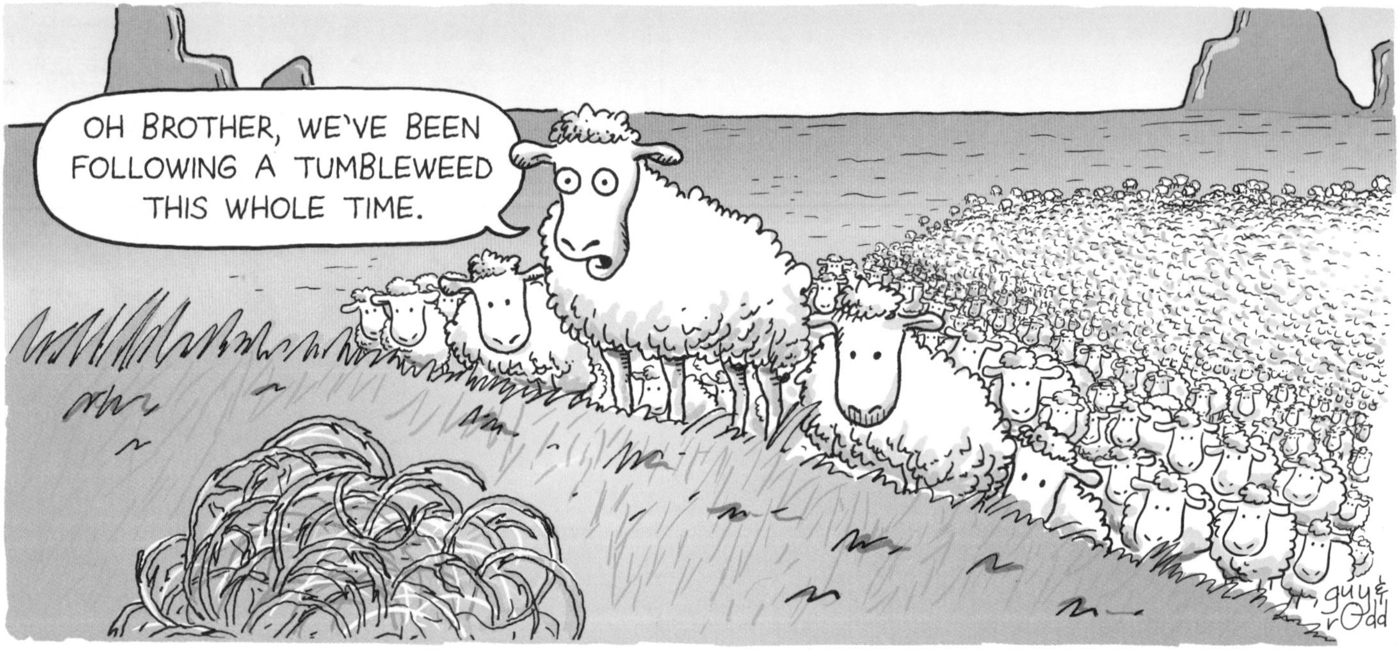
OH BROTHER, WE'VE BEEN FOLLOWING A TUMBLEWEED THIS WHOLE TIME.
guy & rOdd

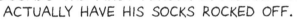

AND THEN, RIGHT IN THE MIDDLE OF A WARRANT/WINGER DOUBLE BILL, ROB MYERS BECOMES THE FIRST PERSON IN HISTORY TO ACTUALLY HAVE HIS SOCKS ROCKED OFF.

EXCUSE ME, COULD EVERYONE BE QUIET, I'M TRYING TO TALK ON MY CELL PHONE.

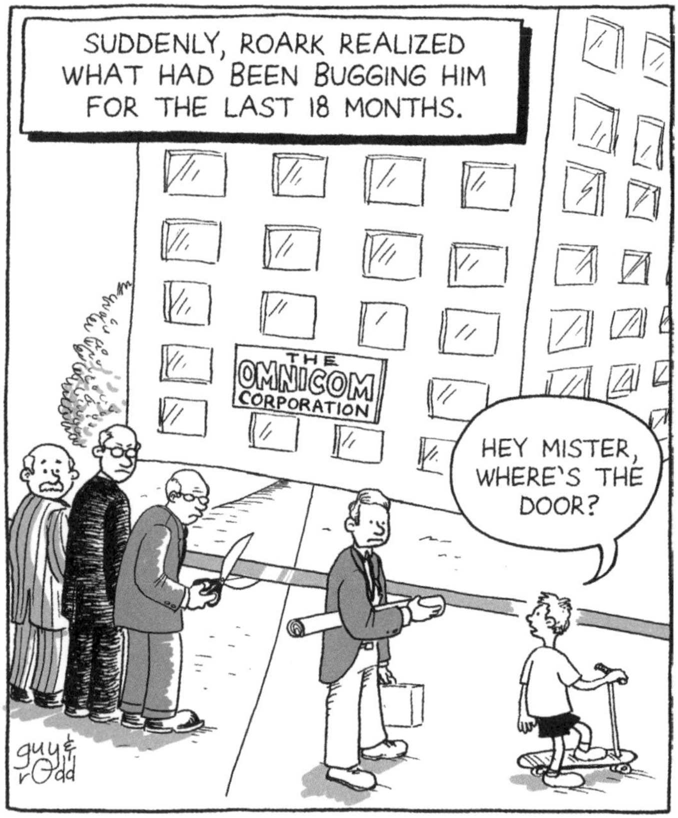
SUDDENLY, ROARK REALIZED WHAT HAD BEEN BUGGING HIM FOR THE LAST 18 MONTHS.
THE OMNICOM CORPORATION
HEY MISTER, WHERE'S THE DOOR?
guy & rOdd

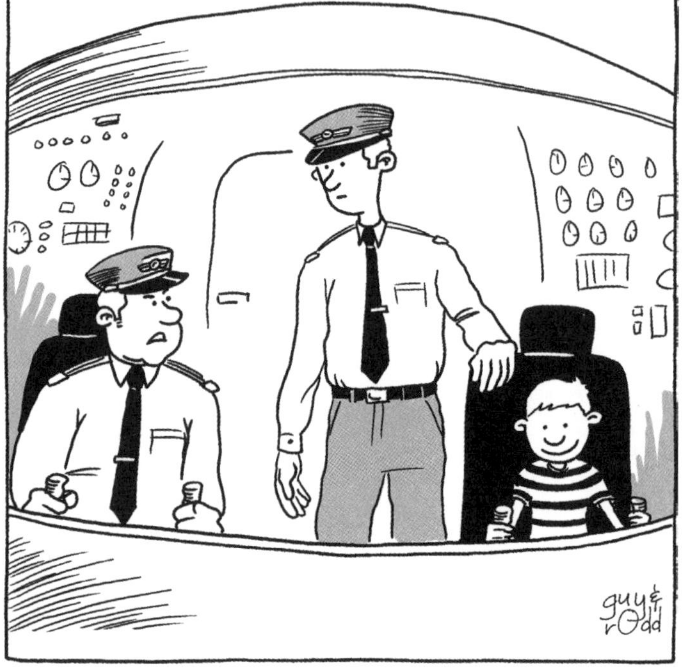
guy & rOdd

"YOU KNOW, JUST BECAUSE THEY ASK, DOESN'T MEAN YOU HAVE TO LET THEM FLY".

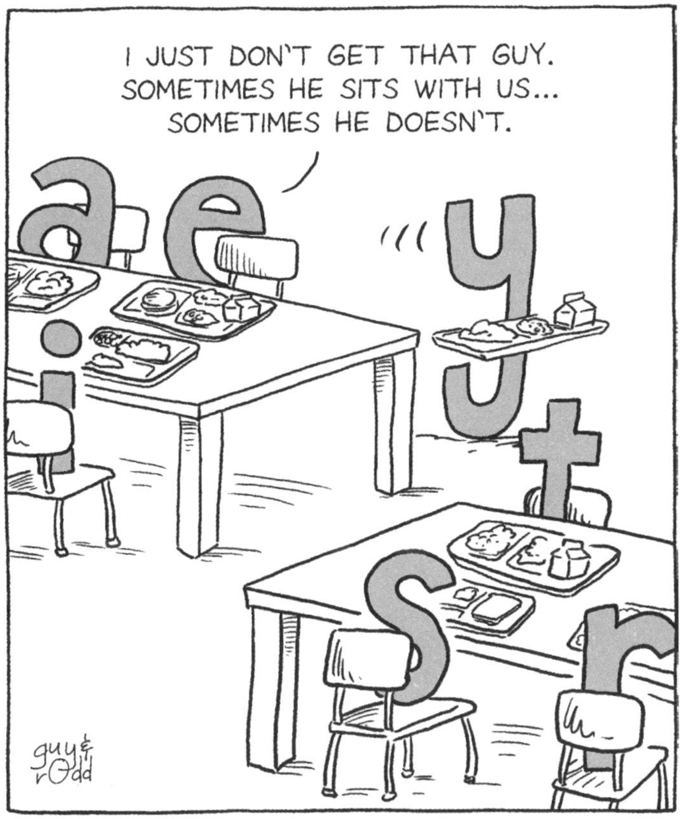
I JUST DON'T GET THAT GUY. SOMETIMES HE SITS WITH US... SOMETIMES HE DOESN'T.
guy & rOdd

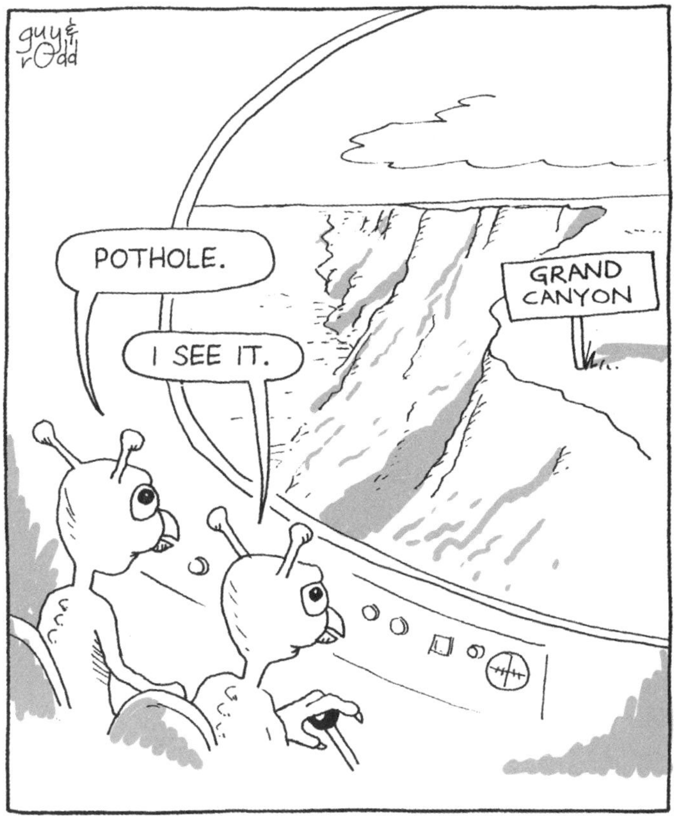
guy & rOdd
POTHOLE.
I SEE IT.
GRAND CANYON

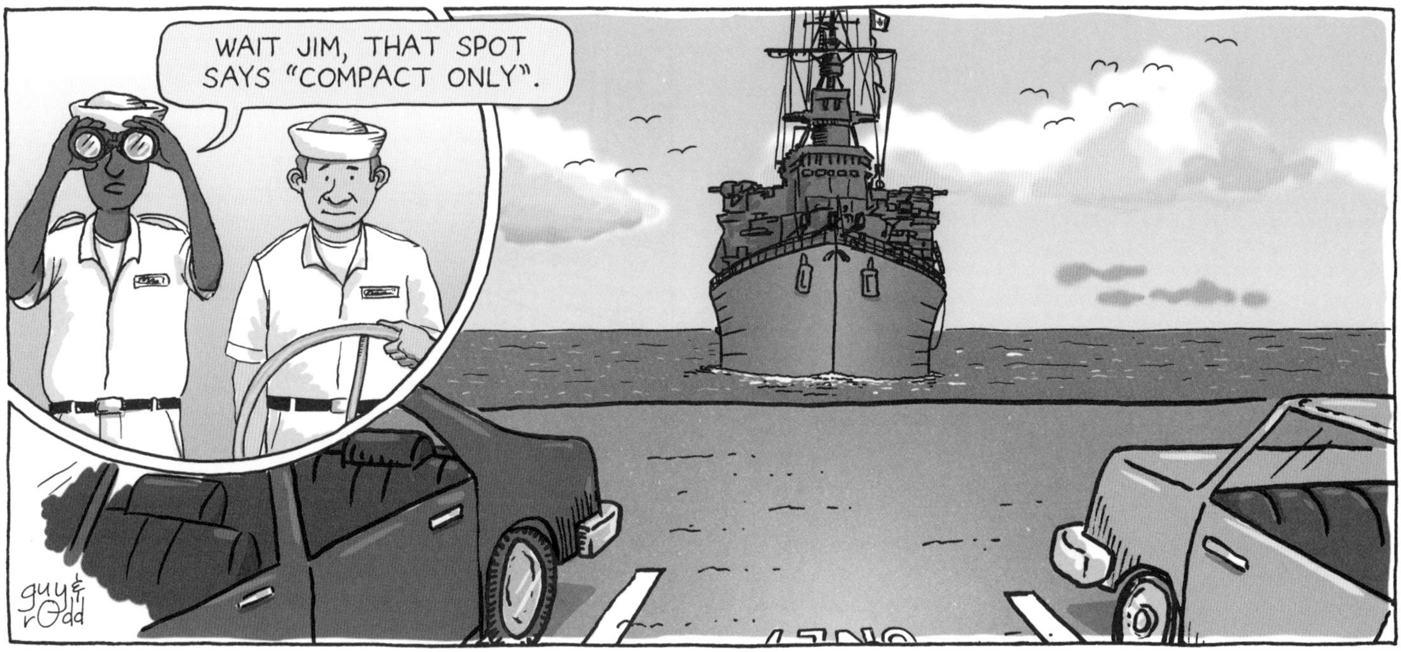
WAIT JIM, THAT SPOT SAYS "COMPACT ONLY".
guy & rOdd

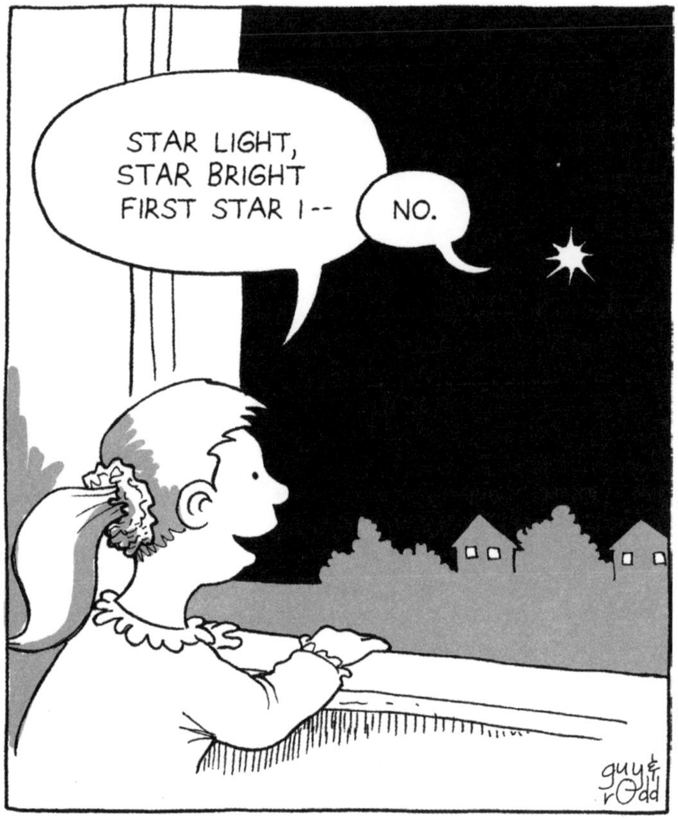
STAR LIGHT, STAR BRIGHT FIRST STAR I--
NO.
guy & rOdd

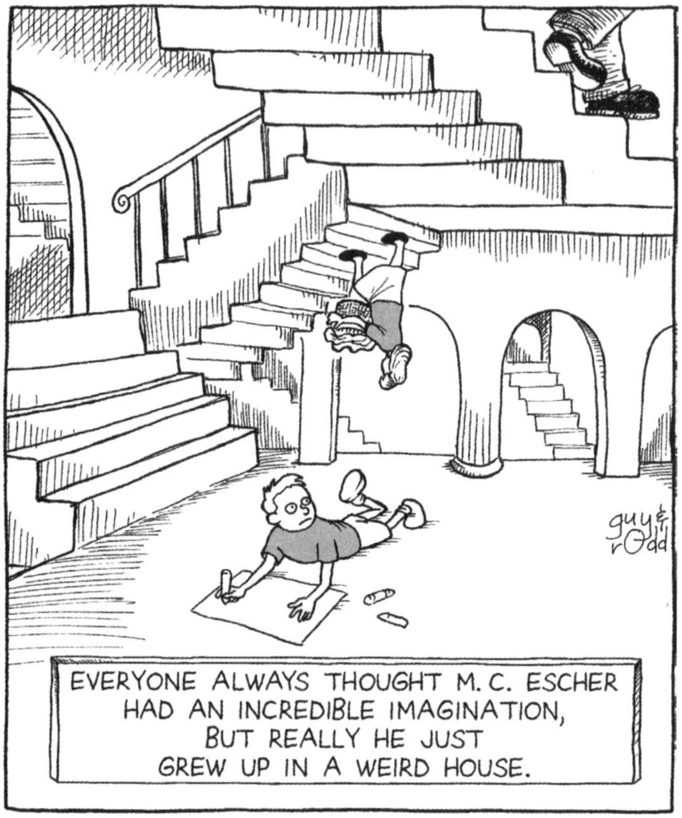
guy & rOdd
EVERYONE ALWAYS THOUGHT M. C. ESCHER HAD AN INCREDIBLE IMAGINATION, BUT REALLY HE JUST GREW UP IN A WEIRD HOUSE.

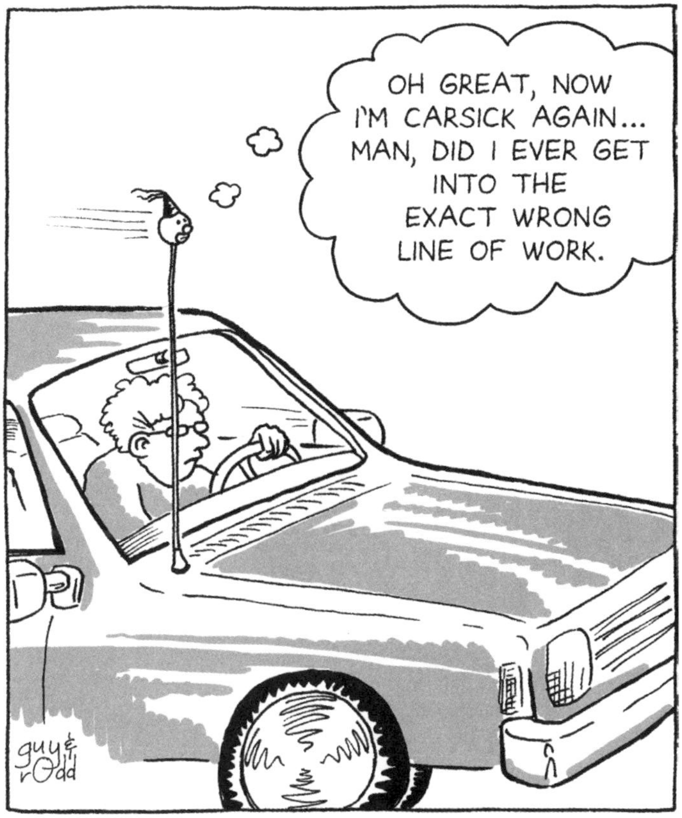
OH GREAT, NOW I'M CARSICK AGAIN... MAN, DID I EVER GET INTO THE EXACT WRONG LINE OF WORK.
guy & rOdd

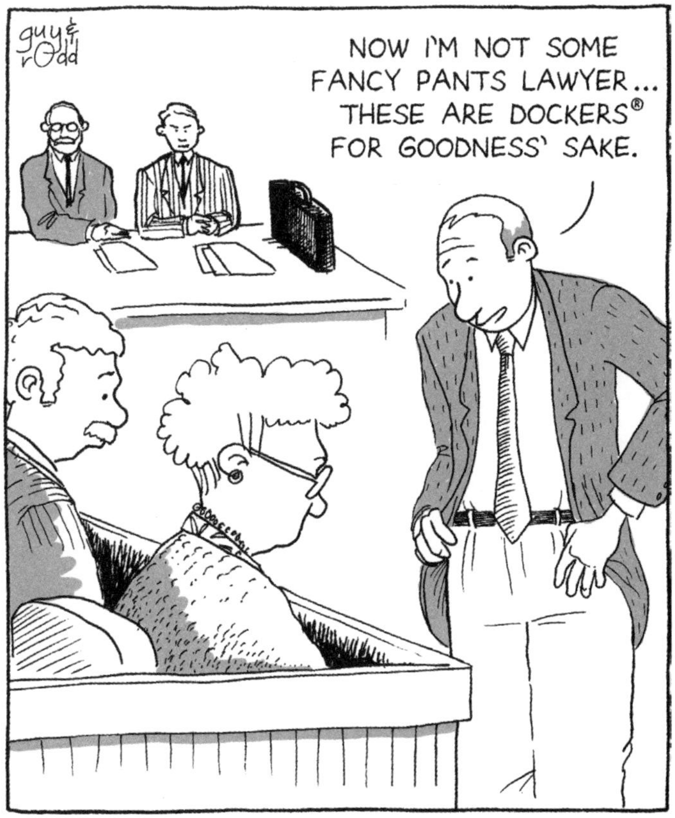
guy & rOdd
NOW I'M NOT SOME FANCY PANTS LAWYER... THESE ARE DOCKERS® FOR GOODNESS' SAKE.

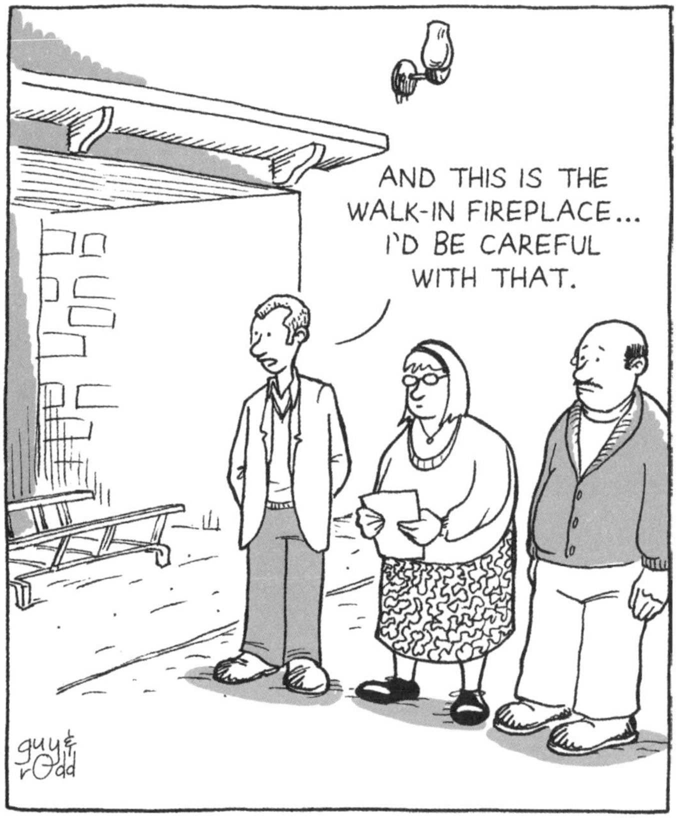
AND THIS IS THE WALK-IN FIREPLACE... I'D BE CAREFUL WITH THAT.

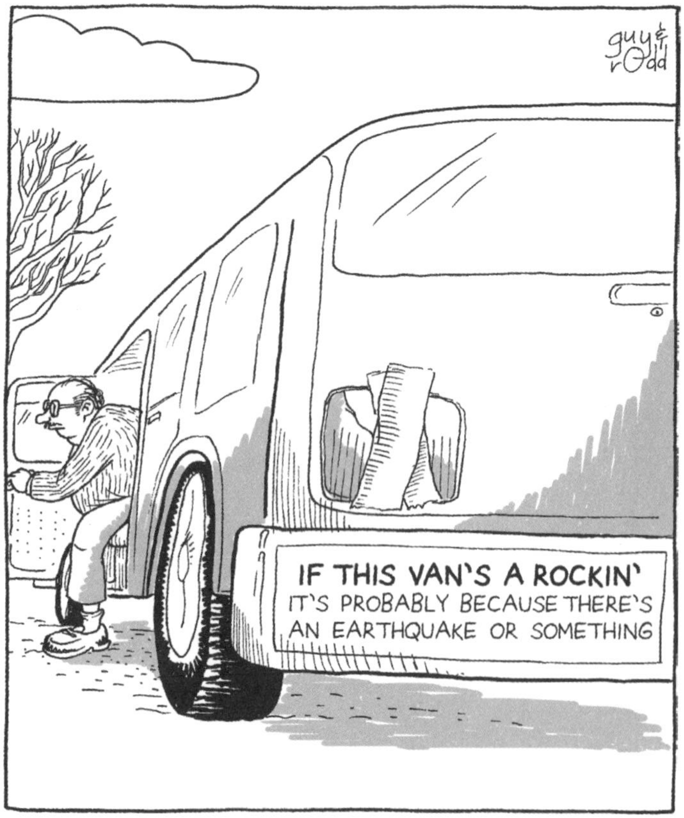
IF THIS VAN'S A ROCKIN'
IT'S PROBABLY BECAUSE THERE'S AN EARTHQUAKE OR SOMETHING

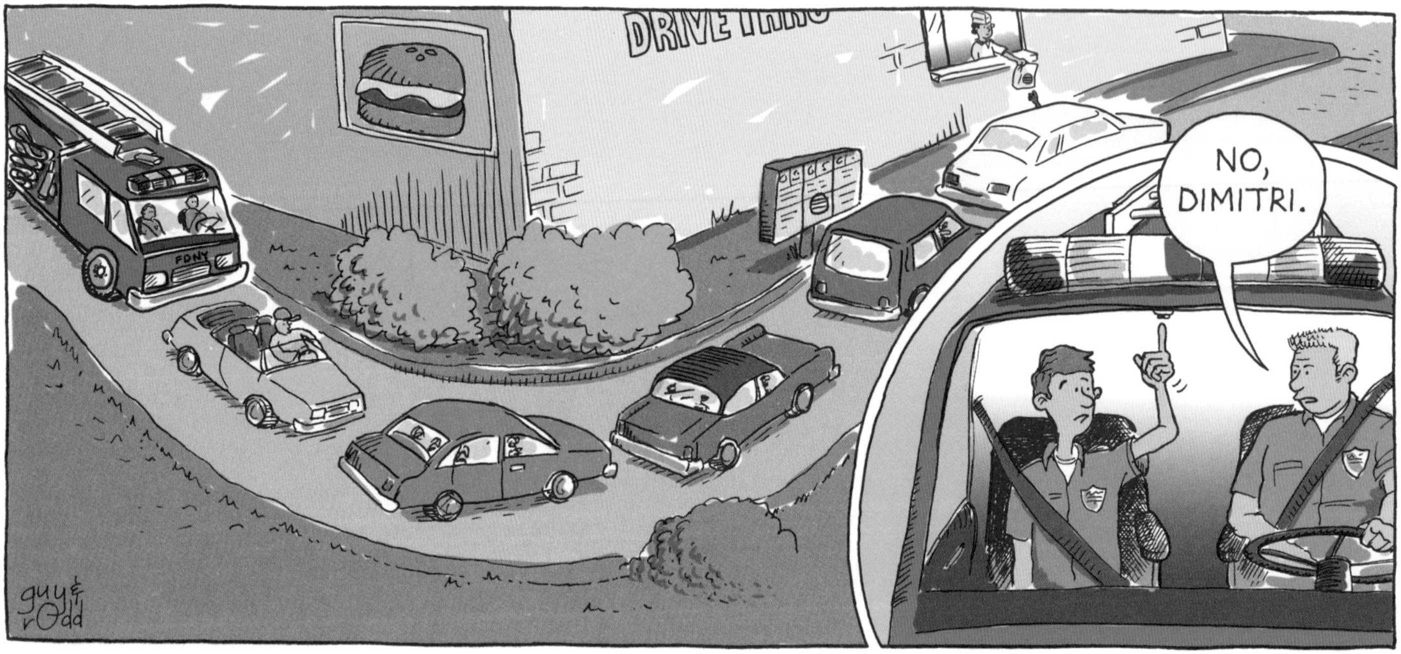
NO, DIMITRI.

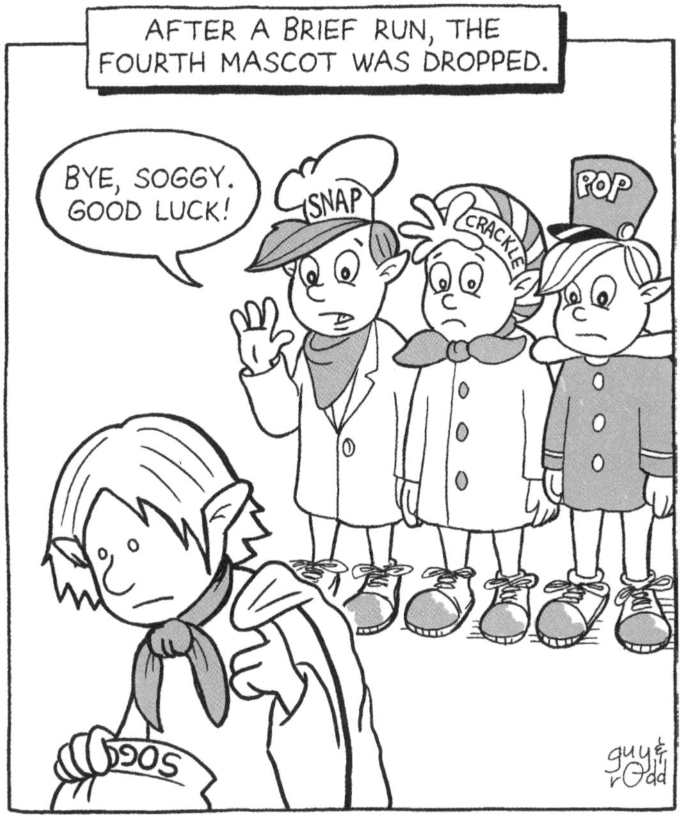
AFTER A BRIEF RUN, THE FOURTH MASCOT WAS DROPPED.
BYE, SOGGY. GOOD LUCK!
SNAP
CRACKLE
POP
guy & rOdd

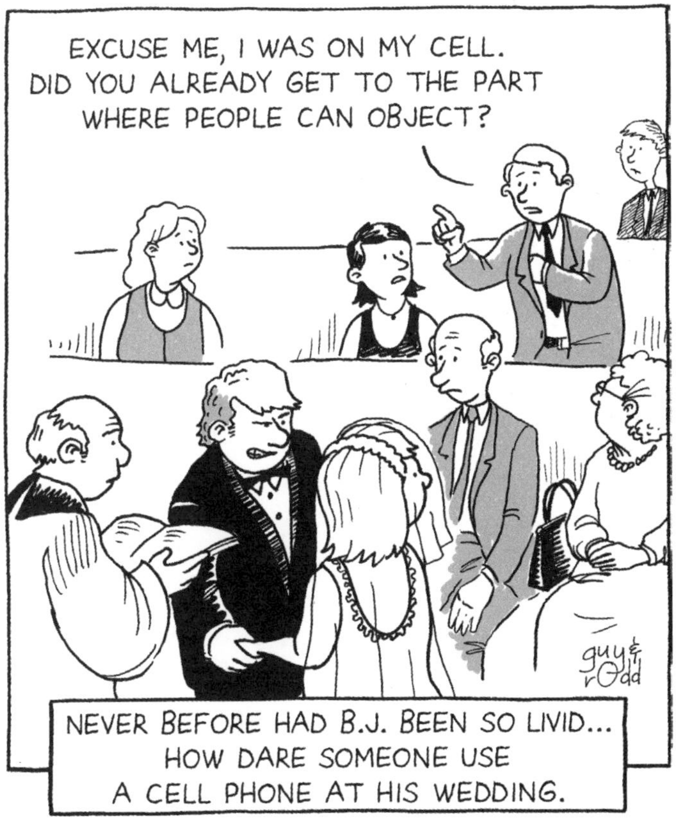
EXCUSE ME, I WAS ON MY CELL. DID YOU ALREADY GET TO THE PART WHERE PEOPLE CAN OBJECT?
guy & rOdd
NEVER BEFORE HAD B.J. BEEN SO LIVID... HOW DARE SOMEONE USE A CELL PHONE AT HIS WEDDING.

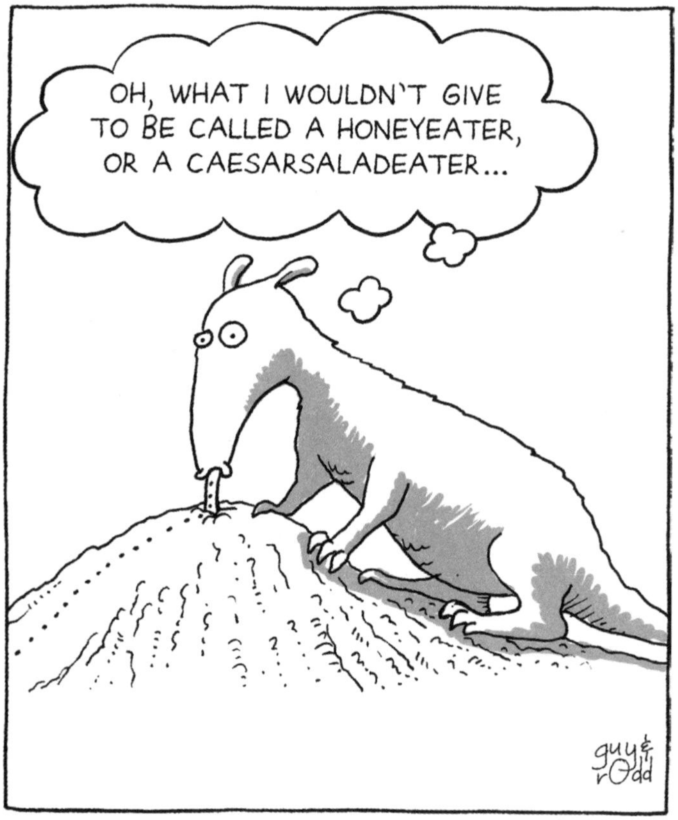
OH, WHAT I WOULDN'T GIVE TO BE CALLED A HONEYEATER, OR A CAESARSALADEATER...
guy & rOdd

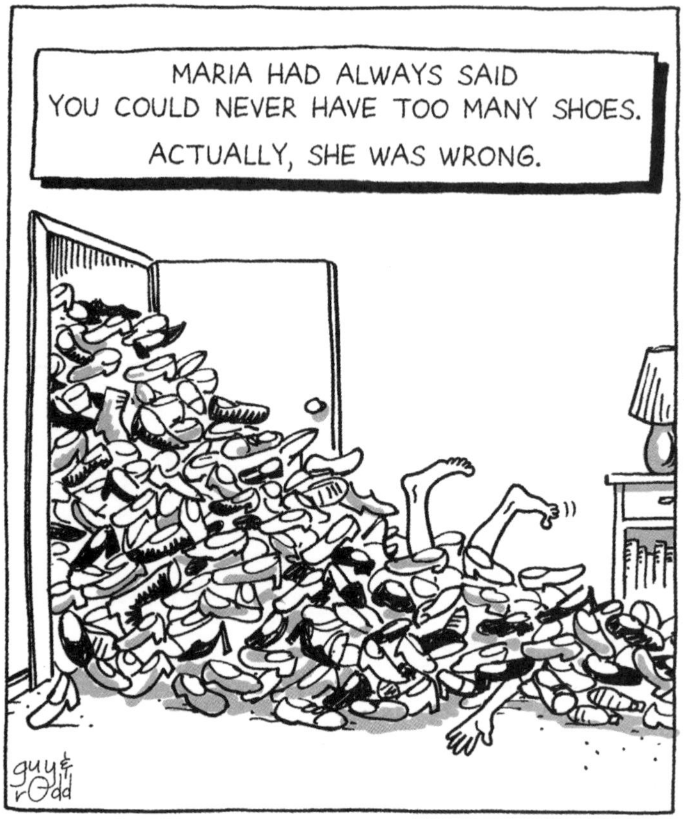
MARIA HAD ALWAYS SAID YOU COULD NEVER HAVE TOO MANY SHOES.
ACTUALLY, SHE WAS WRONG.
guy & rOdd

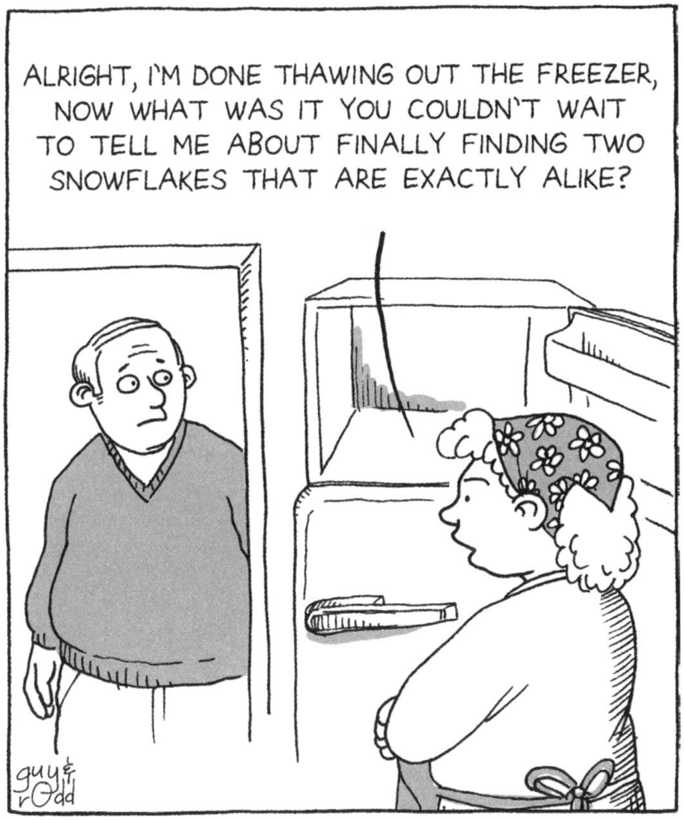
ALRIGHT, I'M DONE THAWING OUT THE FREEZER, NOW WHAT WAS IT YOU COULDN'T WAIT TO TELL ME ABOUT FINALLY FINDING TWO SNOWFLAKES THAT ARE EXACTLY ALIKE?

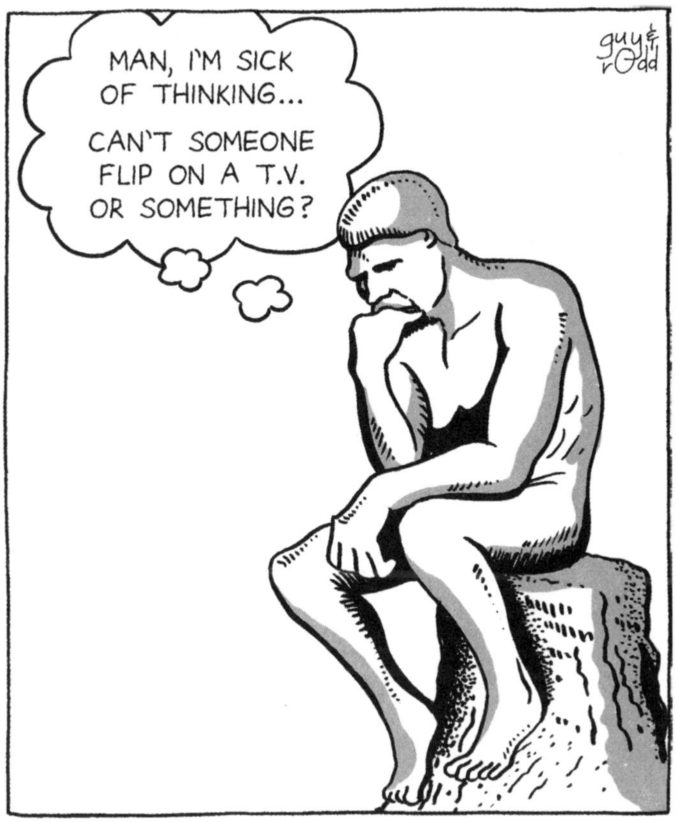
MAN, I'M SICK OF THINKING...
CAN'T SOMEONE FLIP ON A T.V. OR SOMETHING?

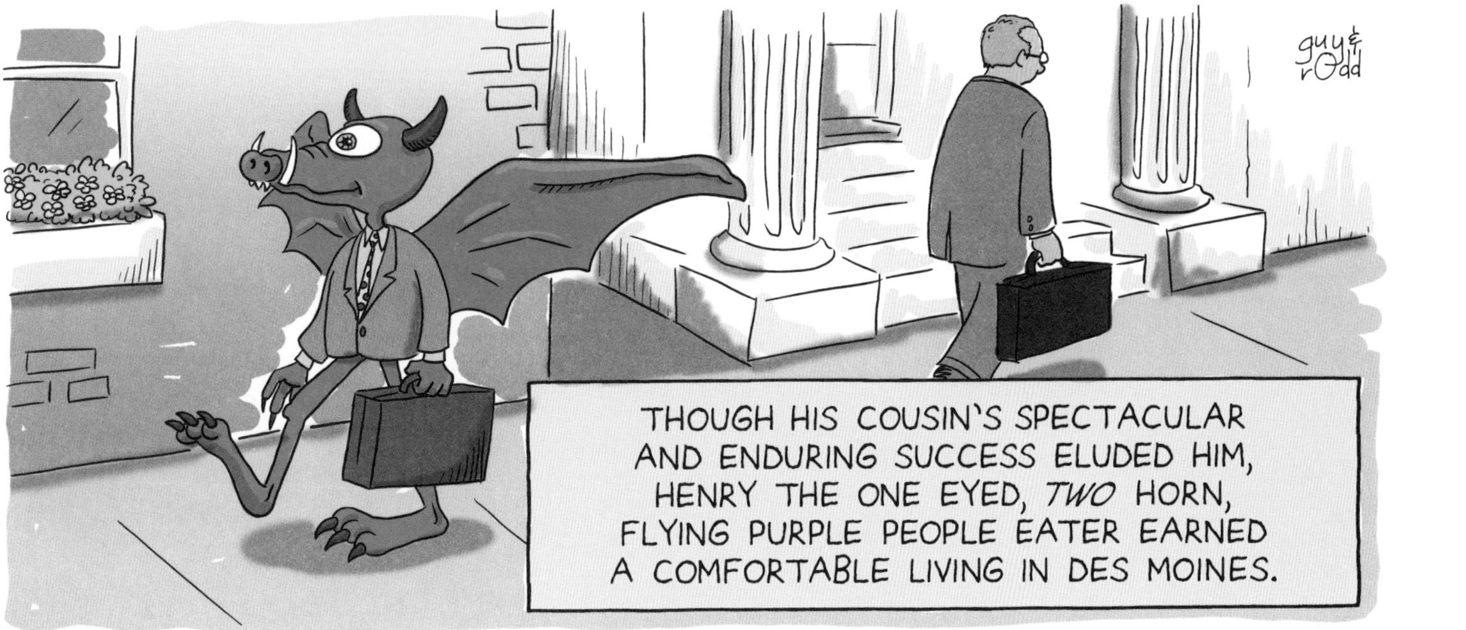
THOUGH HIS COUSIN'S SPECTACULAR AND ENDURING SUCCESS ELUDED HIM, HENRY THE ONE EYED, *TWO* HORN, FLYING PURPLE PEOPLE EATER EARNED A COMFORTABLE LIVING IN DES MOINES.

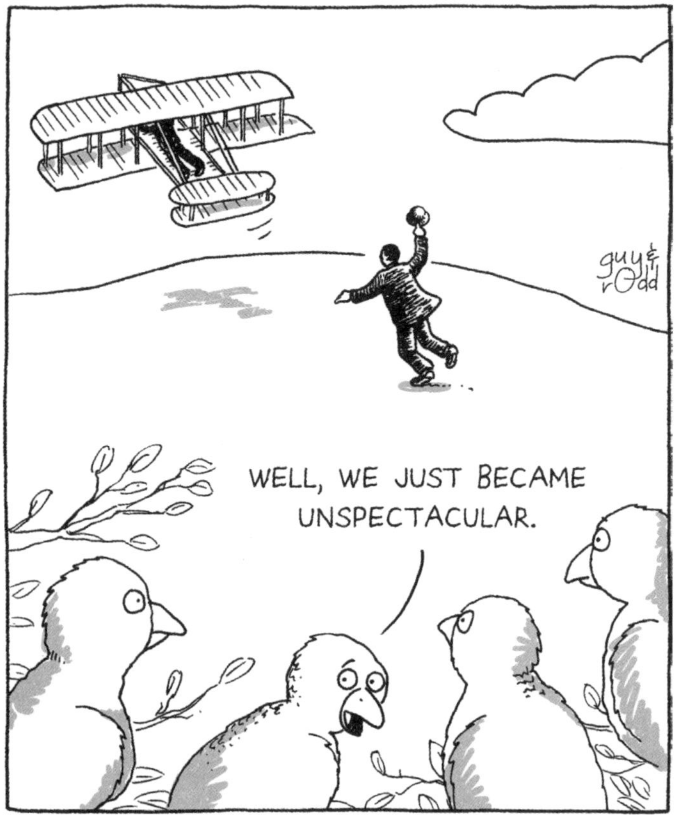
WELL, WE JUST BECAME UNSPECTACULAR.

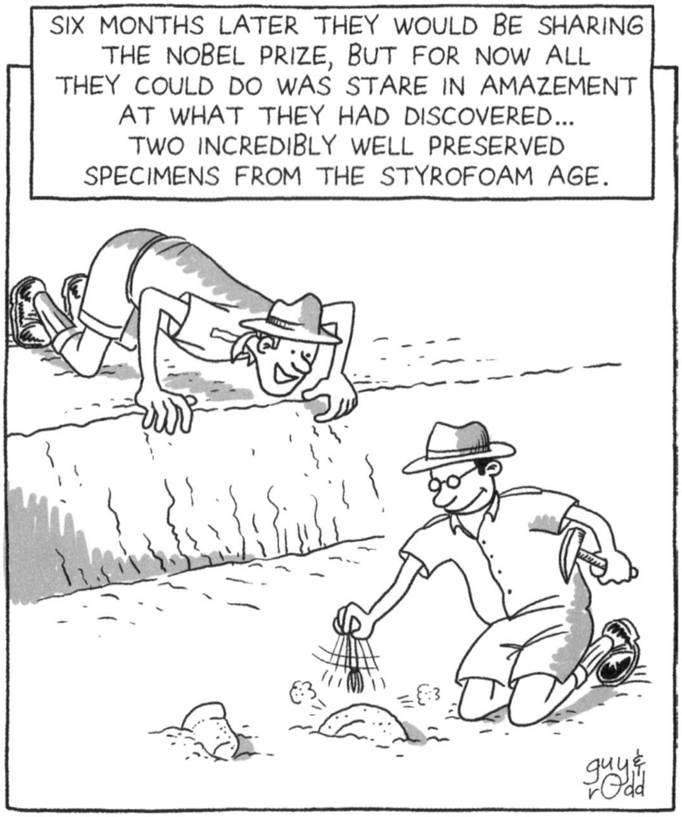
SIX MONTHS LATER THEY WOULD BE SHARING THE NOBEL PRIZE, BUT FOR NOW ALL THEY COULD DO WAS STARE IN AMAZEMENT AT WHAT THEY HAD DISCOVERED...
TWO INCREDIBLY WELL PRESERVED SPECIMENS FROM THE STYROFOAM AGE.

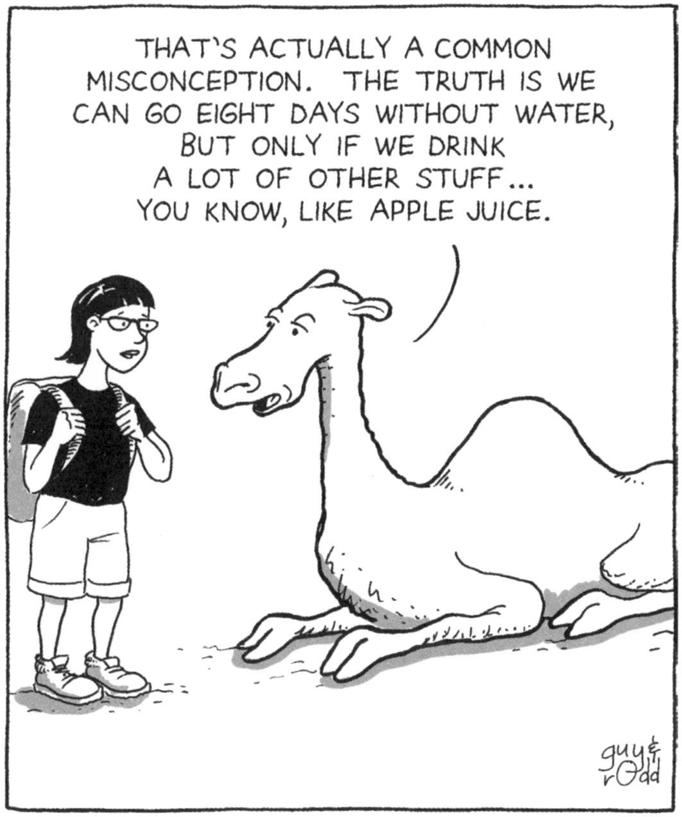
THAT'S ACTUALLY A COMMON MISCONCEPTION. THE TRUTH IS WE CAN GO EIGHT DAYS WITHOUT WATER, BUT ONLY IF WE DRINK A LOT OF OTHER STUFF... YOU KNOW, LIKE APPLE JUICE.
guy & rOdd

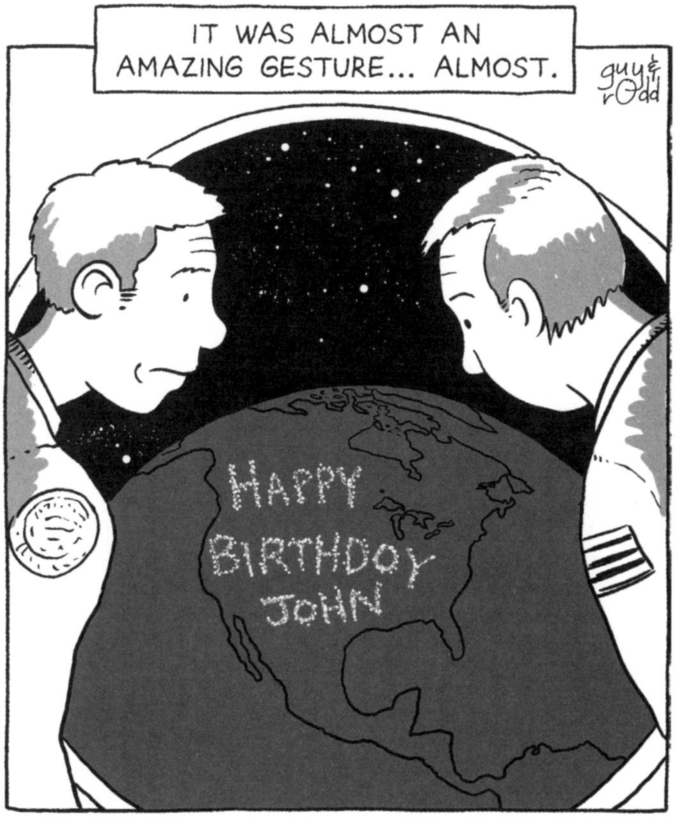
IT WAS ALMOST AN AMAZING GESTURE... ALMOST.
guy & rOdd
HAPPY
BIRTHDAY
JOHN

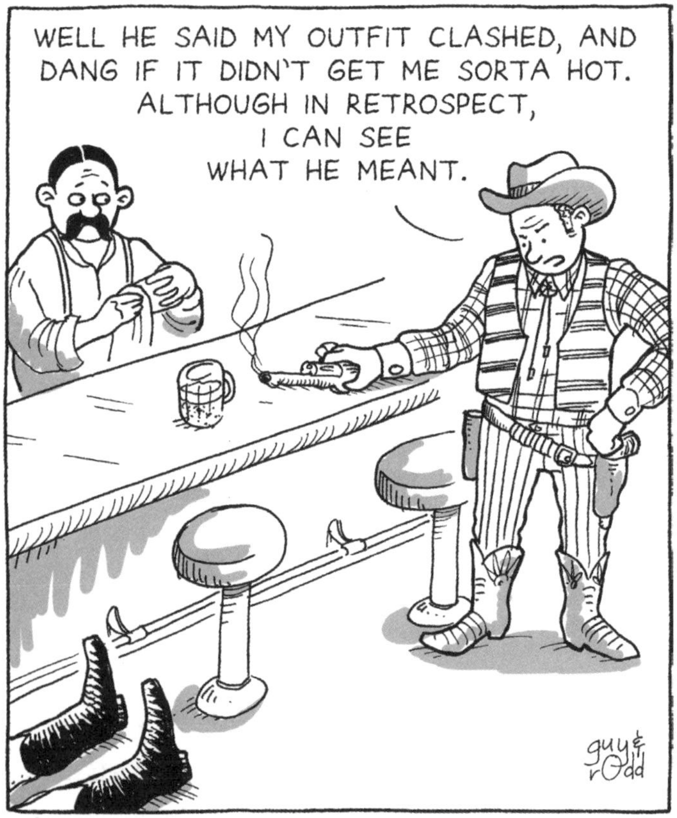
WELL HE SAID MY OUTFIT CLASHED, AND DANG IF IT DIDN'T GET ME SORTA HOT. ALTHOUGH IN RETROSPECT, I CAN SEE WHAT HE MEANT.
guy & rodd

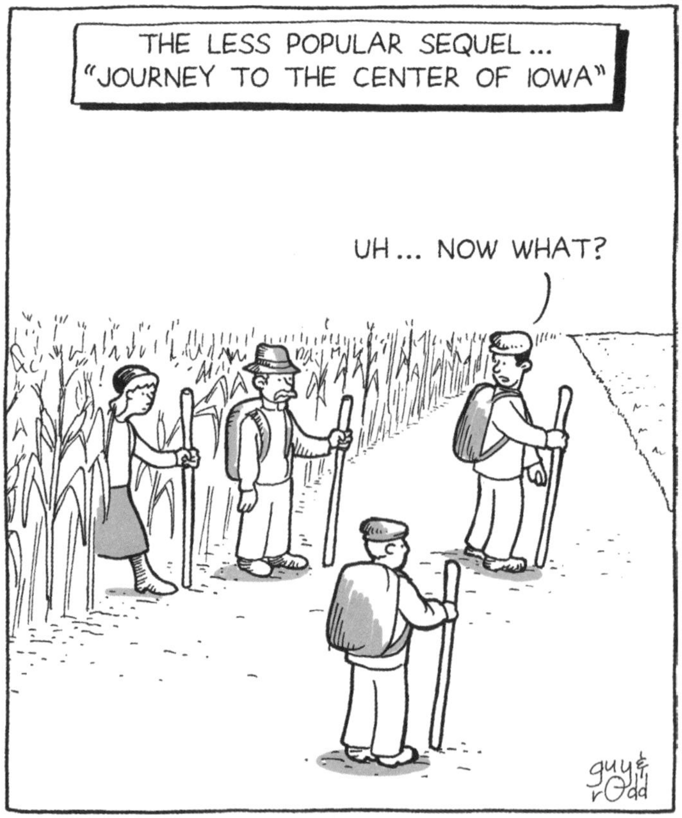
THE LESS POPULAR SEQUEL ... "JOURNEY TO THE CENTER OF IOWA"
UH ... NOW WHAT?
guy & rodd

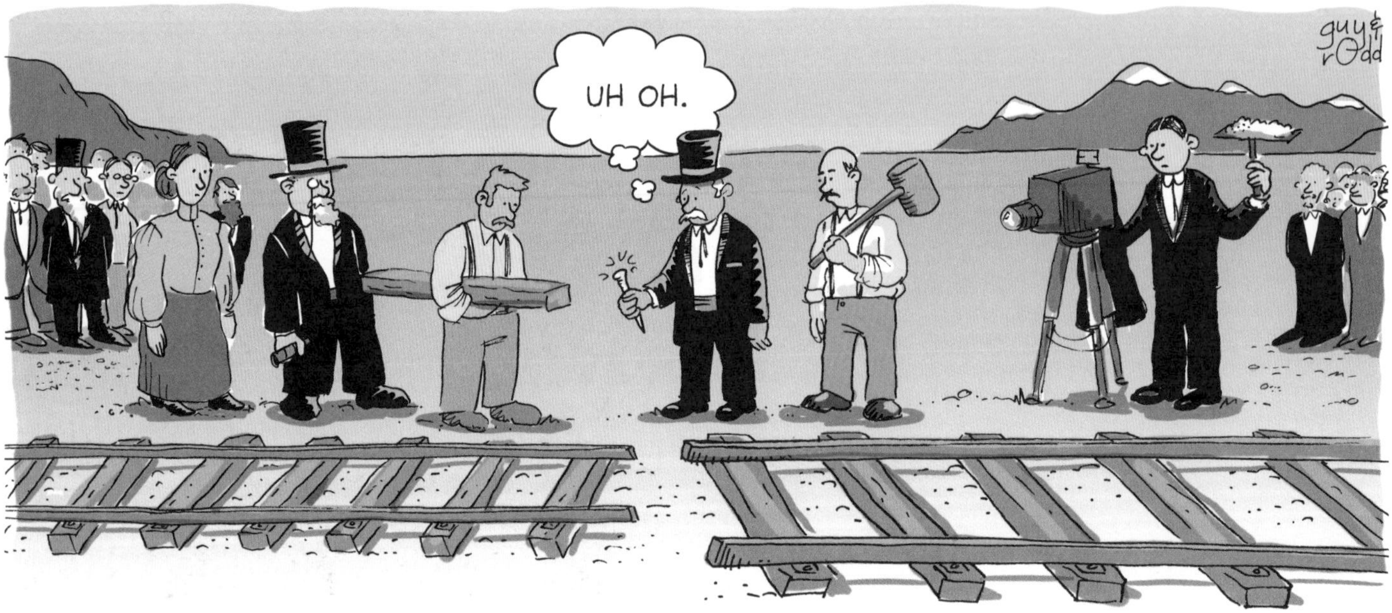
UH OH.
guy & rodd

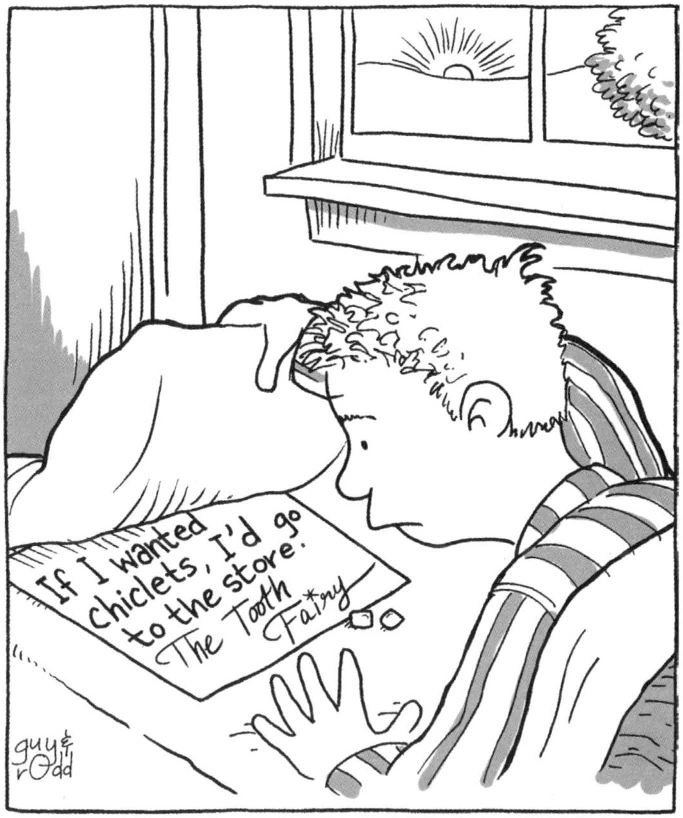
If I wanted chiclets, I'd go to the store.
The Tooth Fairy
guy & rOdd

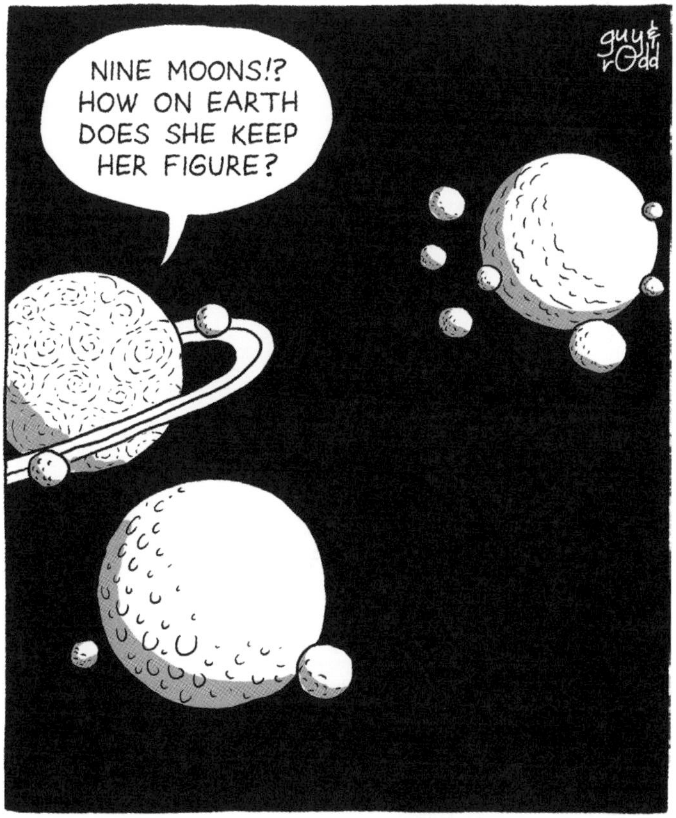
guy & rOdd
NINE MOONS!? HOW ON EARTH DOES SHE KEEP HER FIGURE?

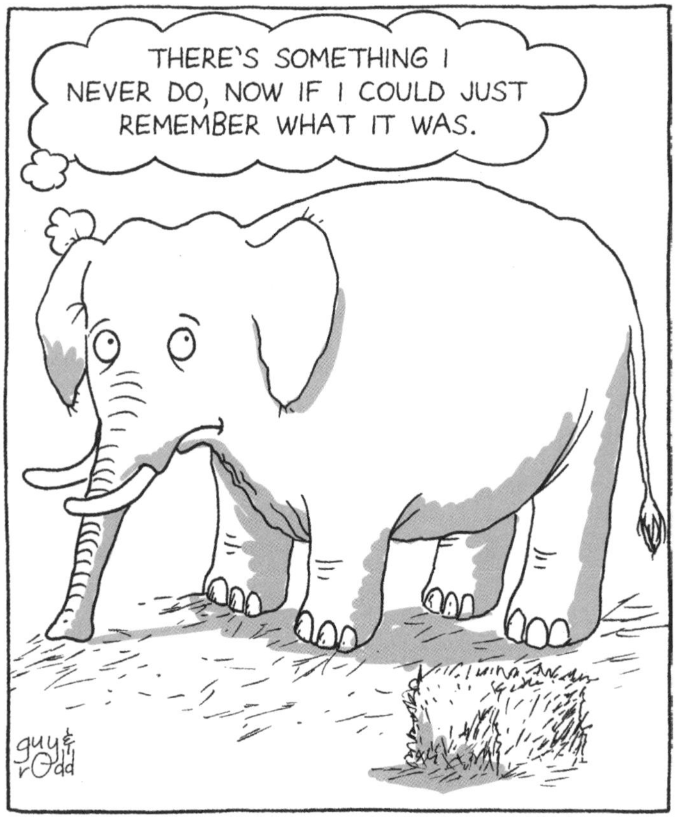
THERE'S SOMETHING I NEVER DO, NOW IF I COULD JUST REMEMBER WHAT IT WAS.
guy & rodd

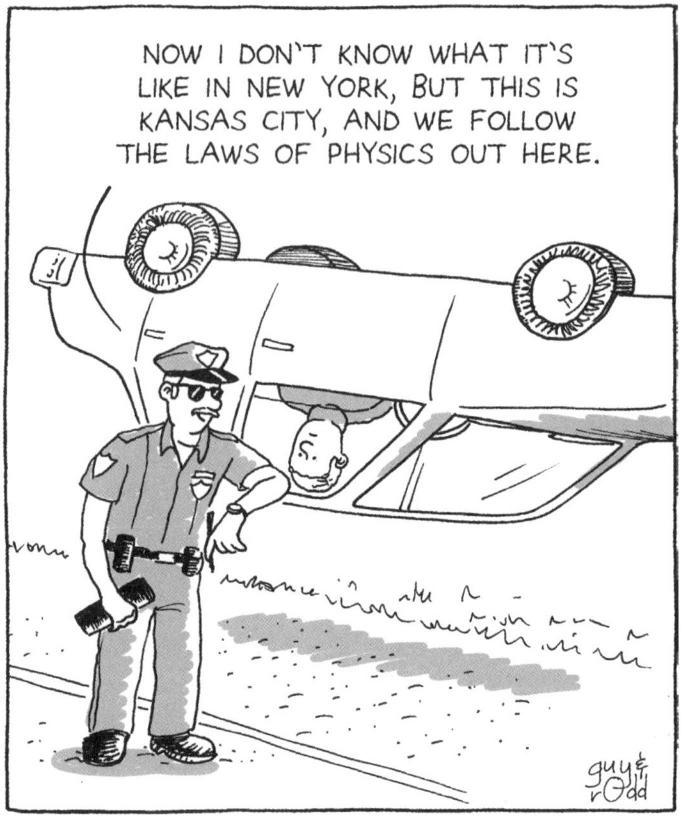
NOW I DON'T KNOW WHAT IT'S LIKE IN NEW YORK, BUT THIS IS KANSAS CITY, AND WE FOLLOW THE LAWS OF PHYSICS OUT HERE.
guy & rodd

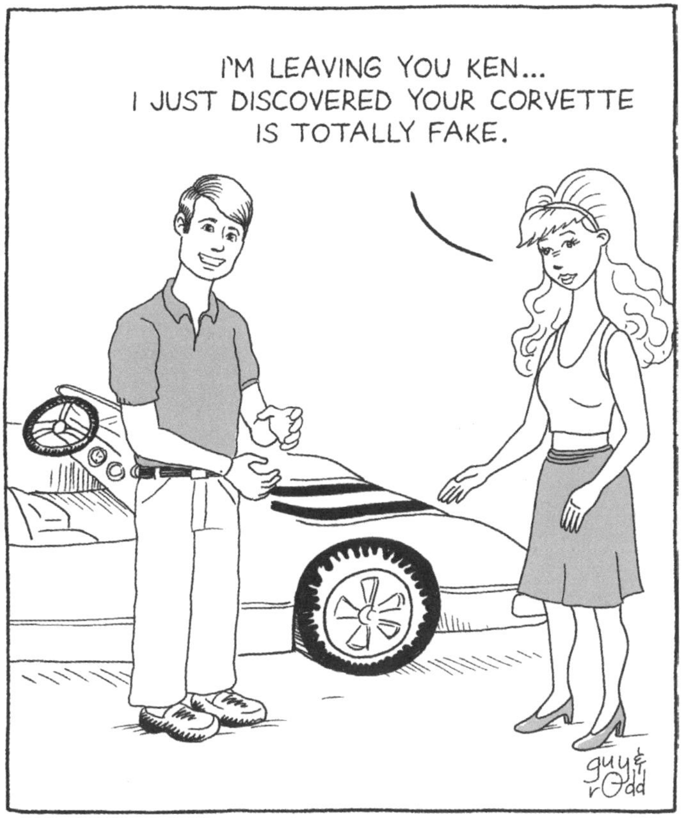
I'M LEAVING YOU KEN...
I JUST DISCOVERED YOUR CORVETTE
IS TOTALLY FAKE.
guy & rOdd

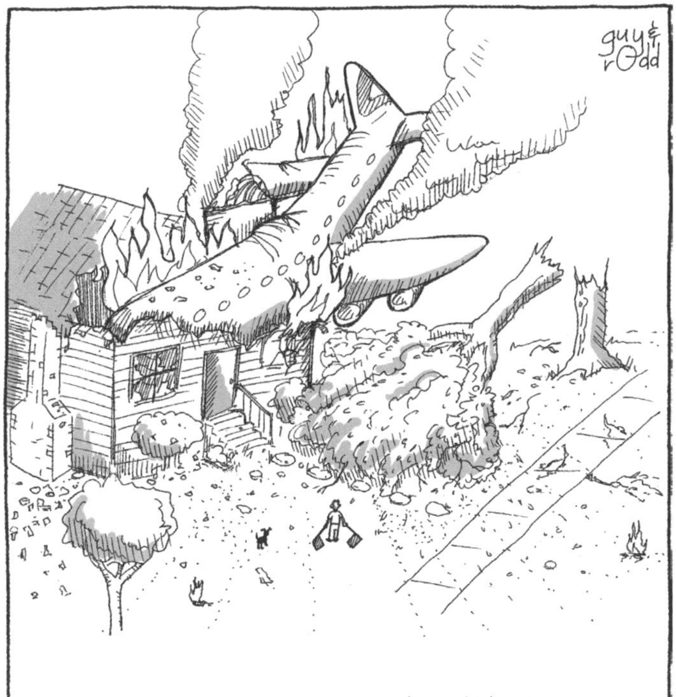
guy & rOdd

STEVE WAS INNOCENTLY PLAYING WITH
HIS FLAGS WHEN, ALL OF A SUDDEN,
SOMETHING TERRIBLE HAPPENED.

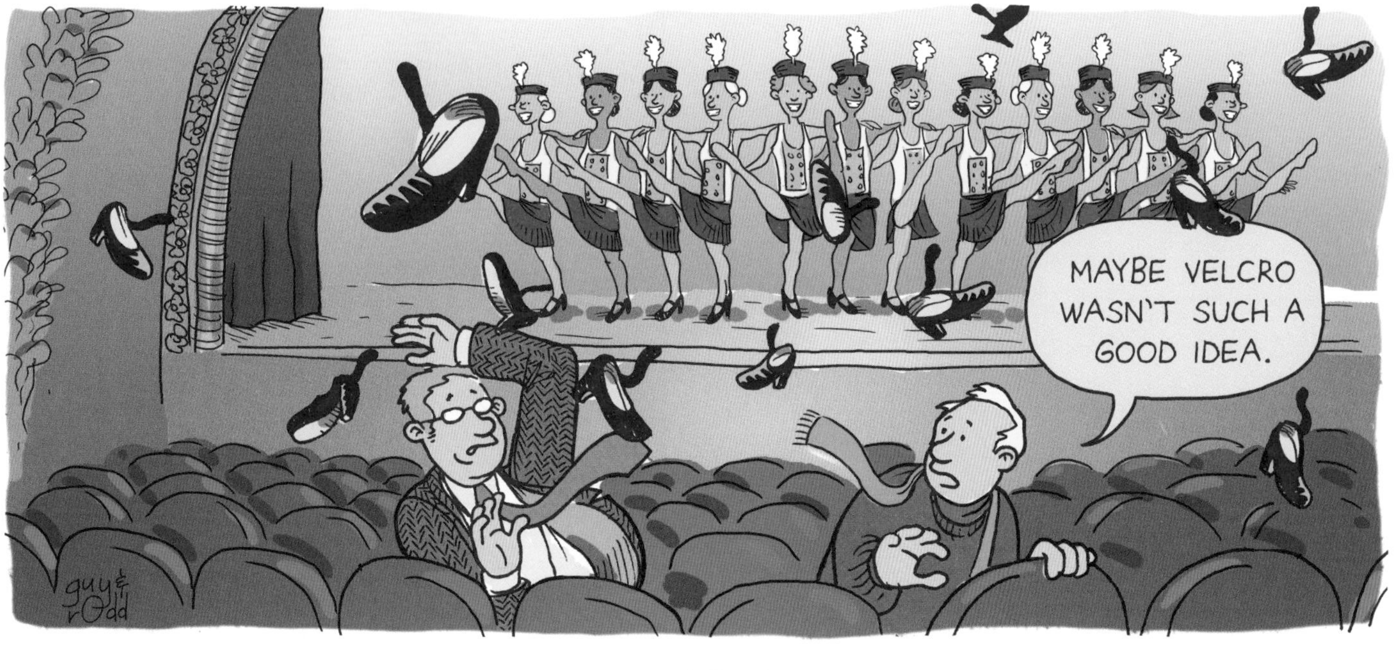
MAYBE VELCRO
WASN'T SUCH A
GOOD IDEA.
guy & rOdd

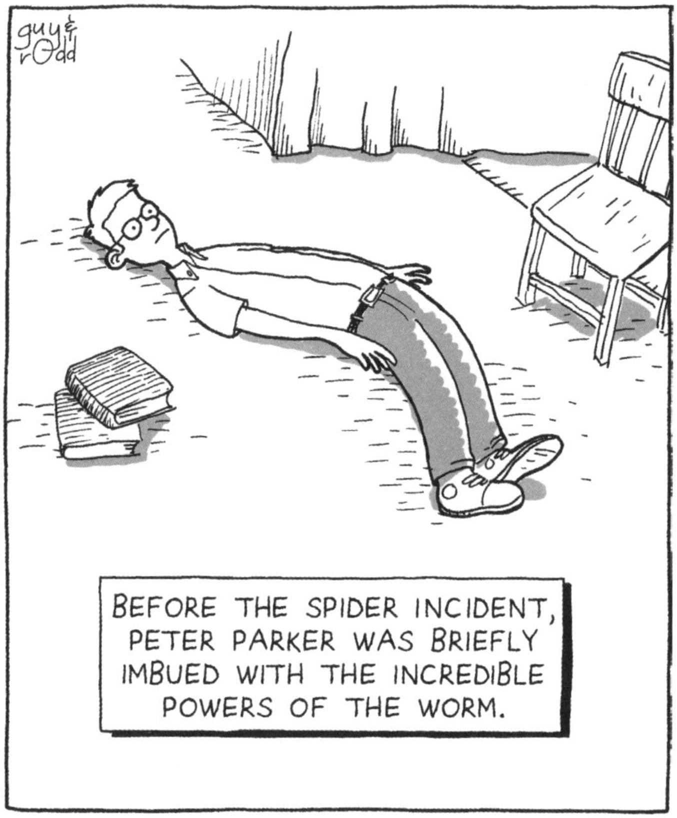
guy & rodd
BEFORE THE SPIDER INCIDENT, PETER PARKER WAS BRIEFLY IMBUED WITH THE INCREDIBLE POWERS OF THE WORM.

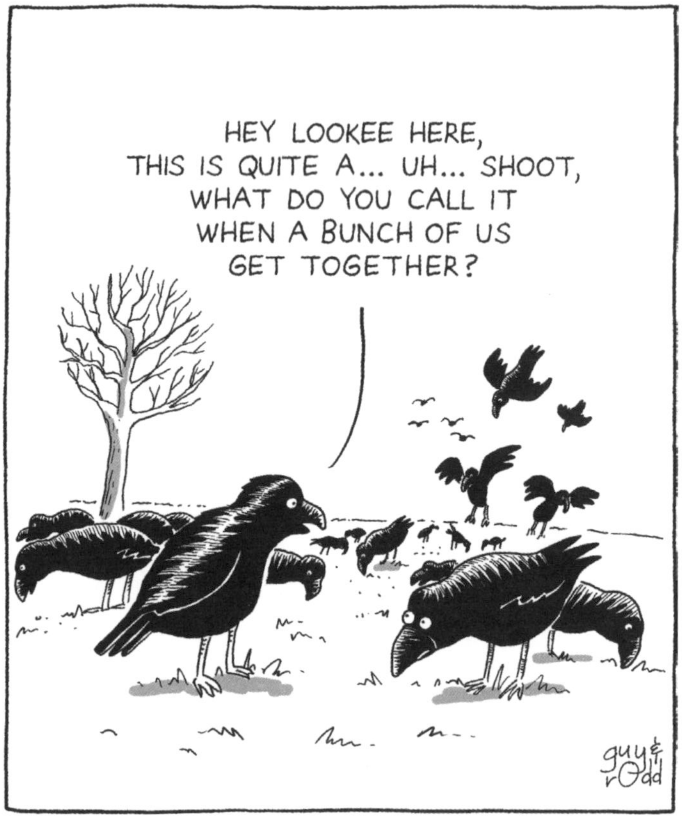
HEY LOOKEE HERE, THIS IS QUITE A... UH... SHOOT, WHAT DO YOU CALL IT WHEN A BUNCH OF US GET TOGETHER?
guy & rodd

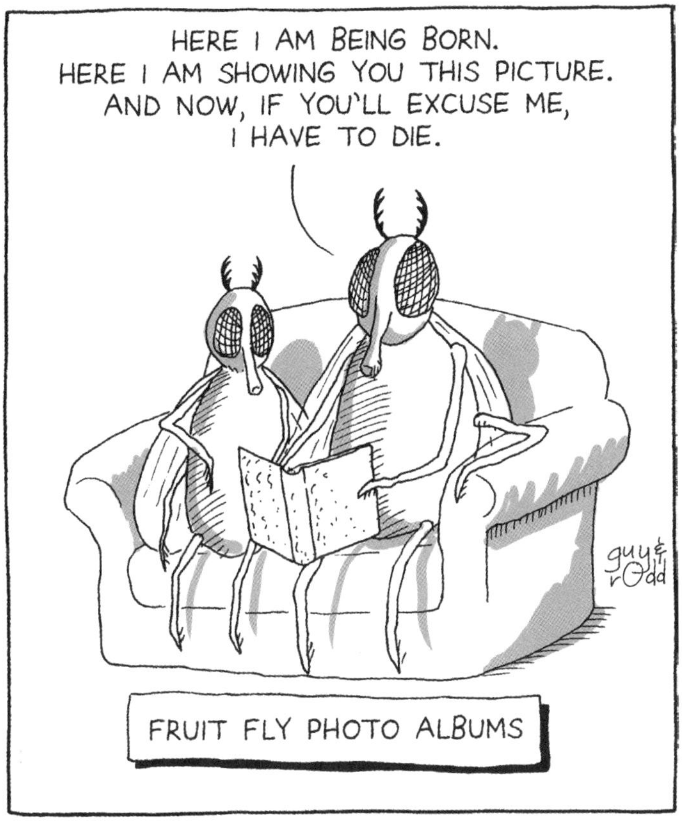
HERE I AM BEING BORN.
HERE I AM SHOWING YOU THIS PICTURE.
AND NOW, IF YOU'LL EXCUSE ME,
I HAVE TO DIE.

FRUIT FLY PHOTO ALBUMS

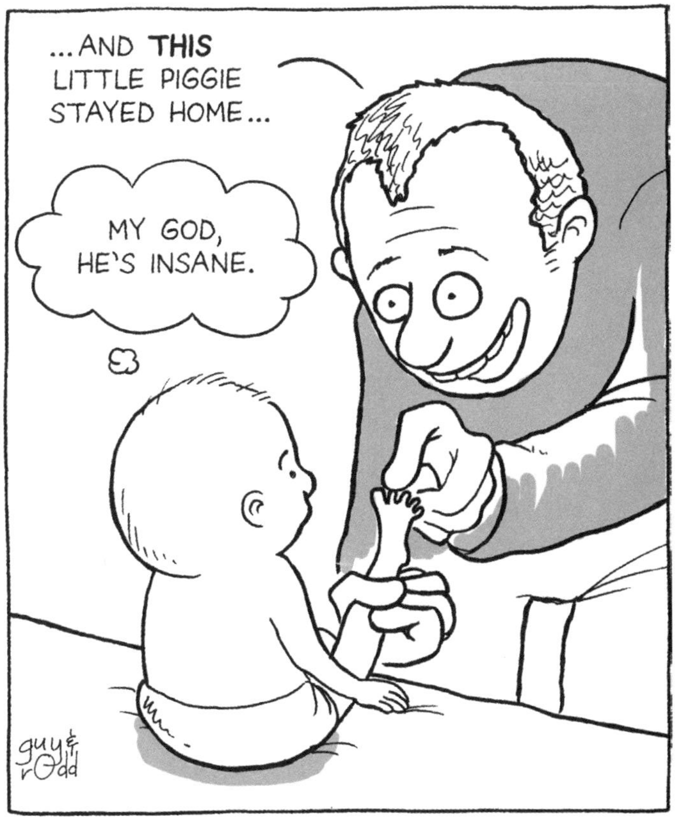
...AND **THIS** LITTLE PIGGIE STAYED HOME...
MY GOD, HE'S INSANE.

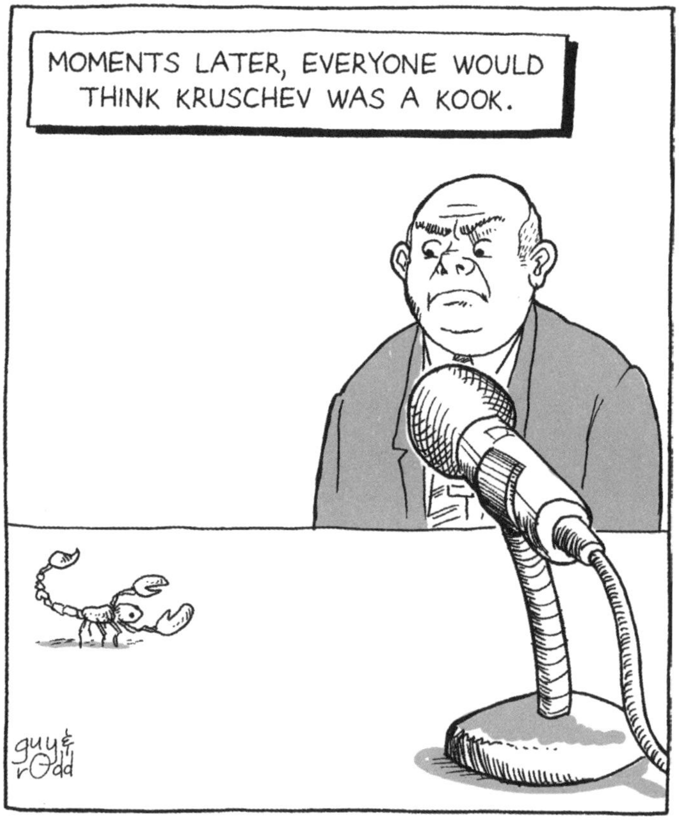
MOMENTS LATER, EVERYONE WOULD THINK KRUSCHEV WAS A KOOK.
guy & rOdd

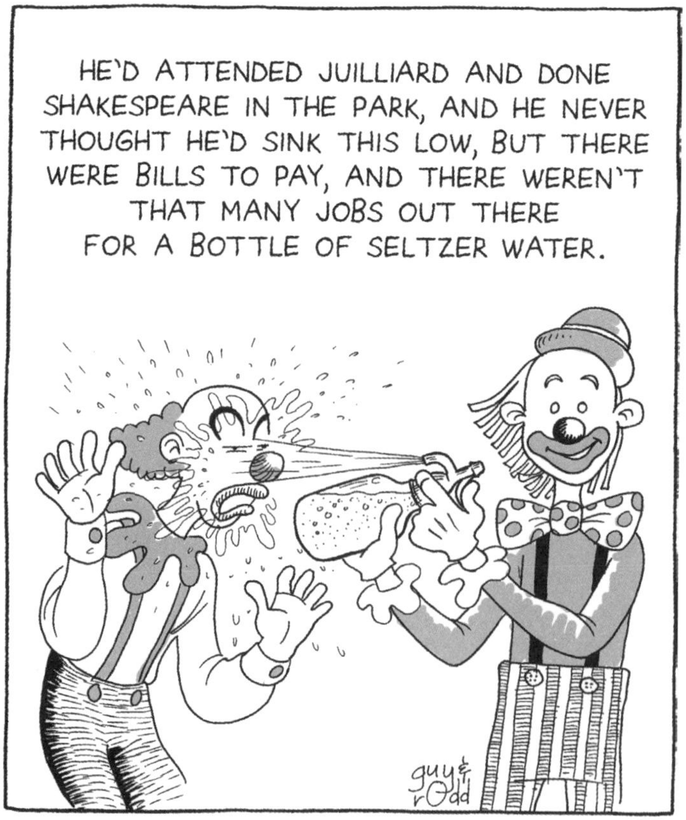
HE'D ATTENDED JUILLIARD AND DONE SHAKESPEARE IN THE PARK, AND HE NEVER THOUGHT HE'D SINK THIS LOW, BUT THERE WERE BILLS TO PAY, AND THERE WEREN'T THAT MANY JOBS OUT THERE FOR A BOTTLE OF SELTZER WATER.
guy & rOdd

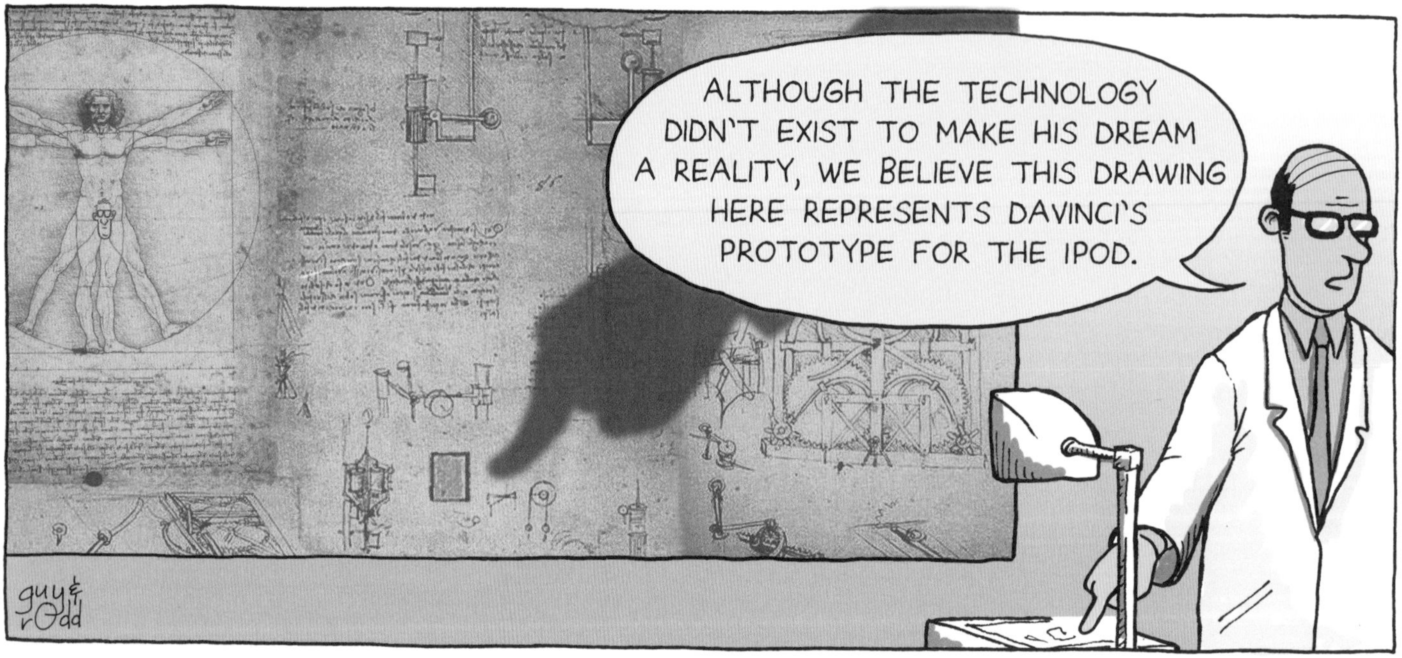
ALTHOUGH THE TECHNOLOGY DIDN'T EXIST TO MAKE HIS DREAM A REALITY, WE BELIEVE THIS DRAWING HERE REPRESENTS DAVINCI'S PROTOTYPE FOR THE IPOD.
guy & rOdd

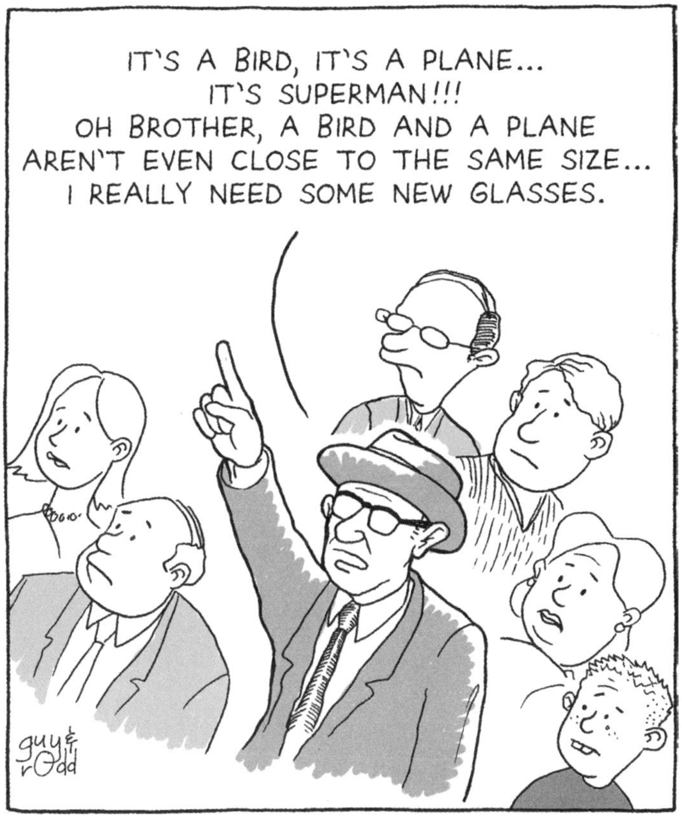
IT'S A BIRD, IT'S A PLANE...
IT'S SUPERMAN!!!
OH BROTHER, A BIRD AND A PLANE
AREN'T EVEN CLOSE TO THE SAME SIZE...
I REALLY NEED SOME NEW GLASSES.
guy & rodd

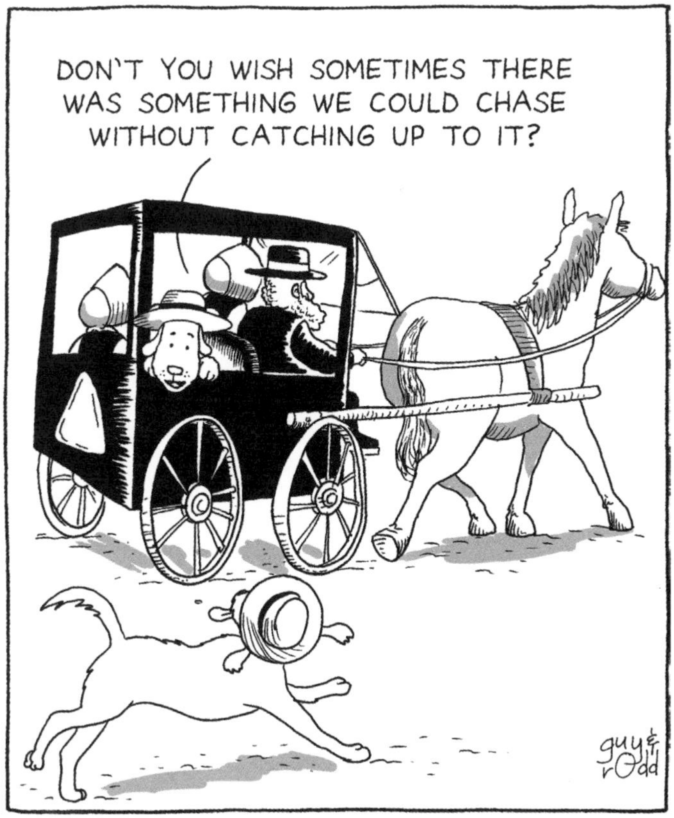
DON'T YOU WISH SOMETIMES THERE
WAS SOMETHING WE COULD CHASE
WITHOUT CATCHING UP TO IT?
guy & rodd

VIOLINS
FIDDLES
guy & rodd

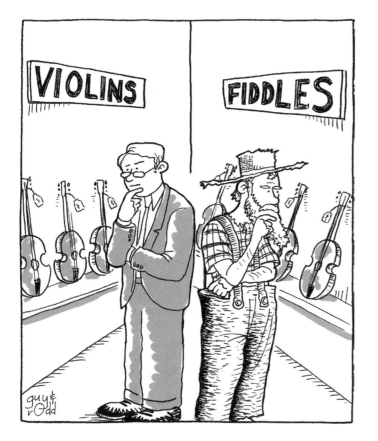

AFTER HE LOST THE RING OF POWER, GOLLUM WENT THROUGH A WEIRD PHASE WHERE HE BECAME TOTALLY OBSESSED WITH COSTUME JEWELRY.
guy & rodd

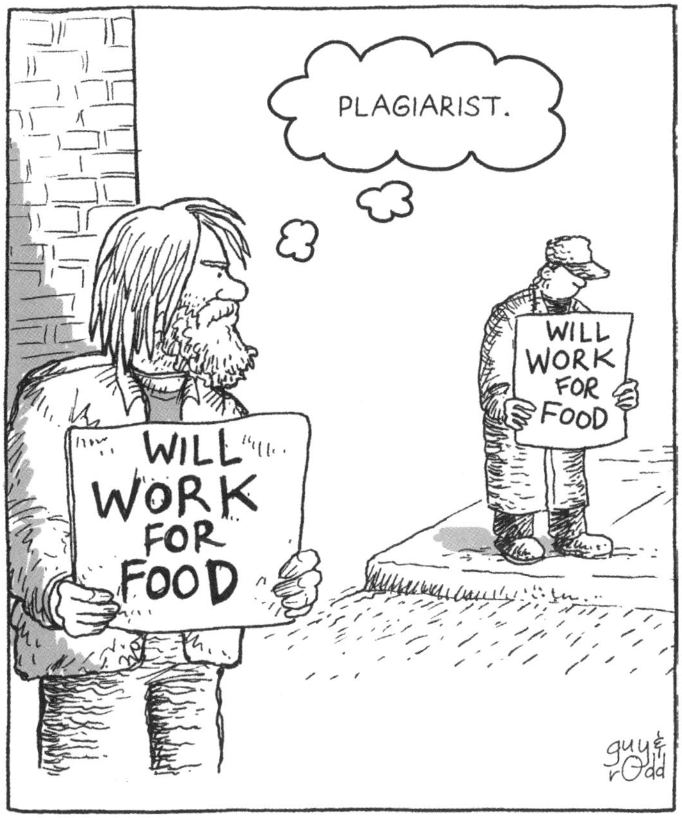
PLAGIARIST.
WILL WORK FOR FOOD
WILL WORK FOR FOOD

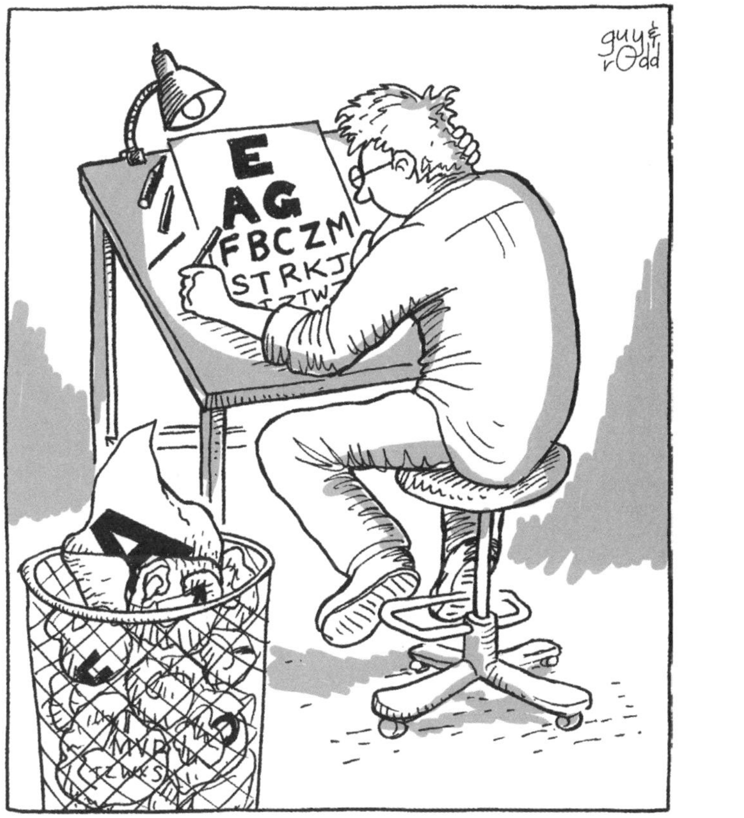
E
AG
FBCZM
STRKJ

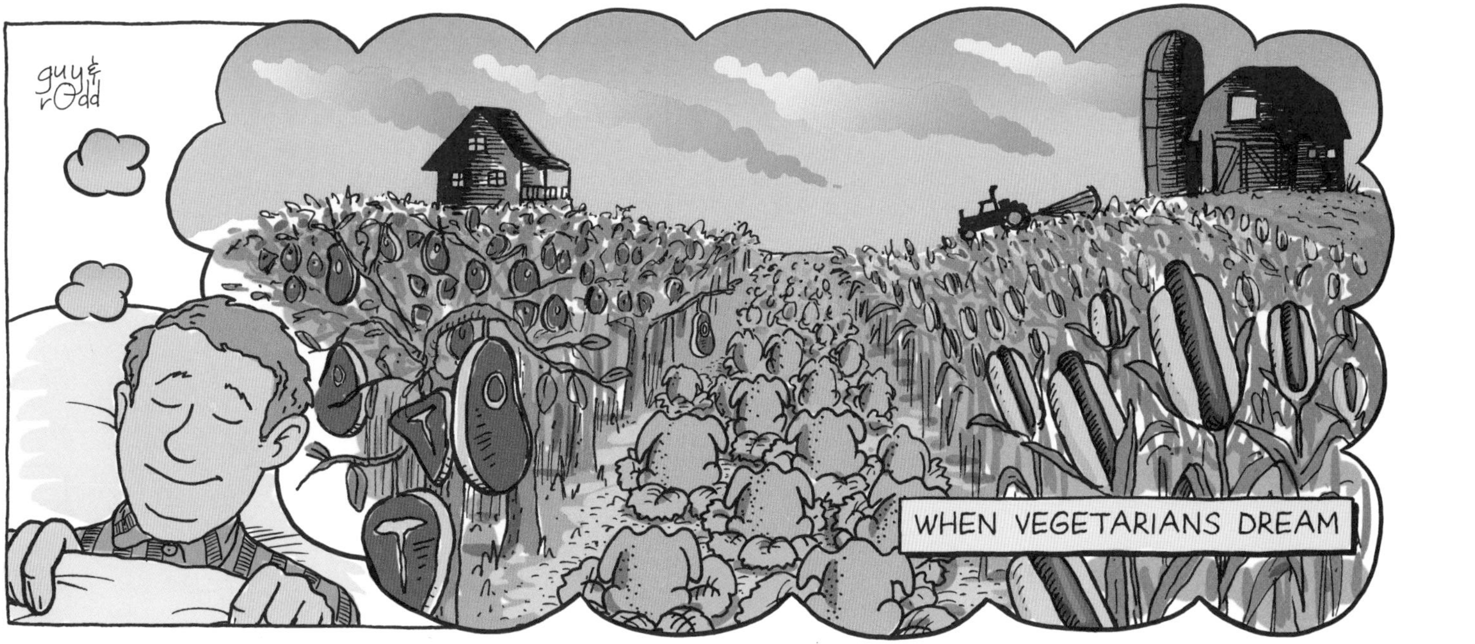
WHEN VEGETARIANS DREAM

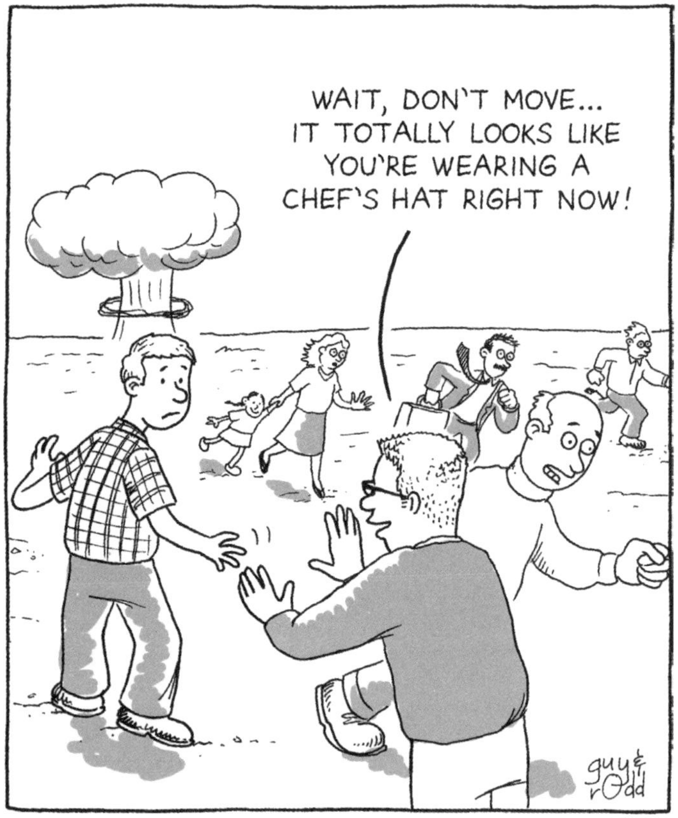
WAIT, DON'T MOVE... IT TOTALLY LOOKS LIKE YOU'RE WEARING A CHEF'S HAT RIGHT NOW!

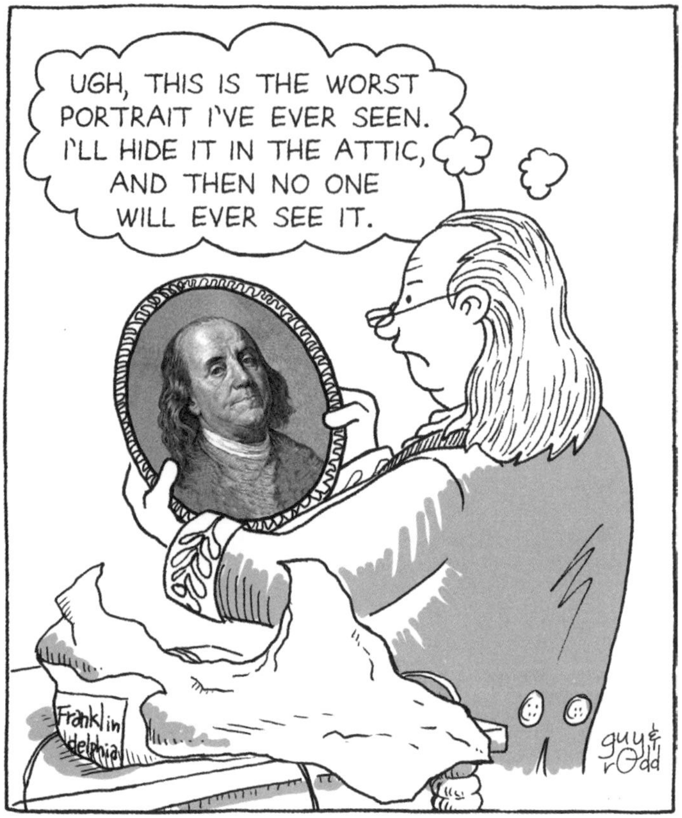
UGH, THIS IS THE WORST PORTRAIT I'VE EVER SEEN. I'LL HIDE IT IN THE ATTIC, AND THEN NO ONE WILL EVER SEE IT.

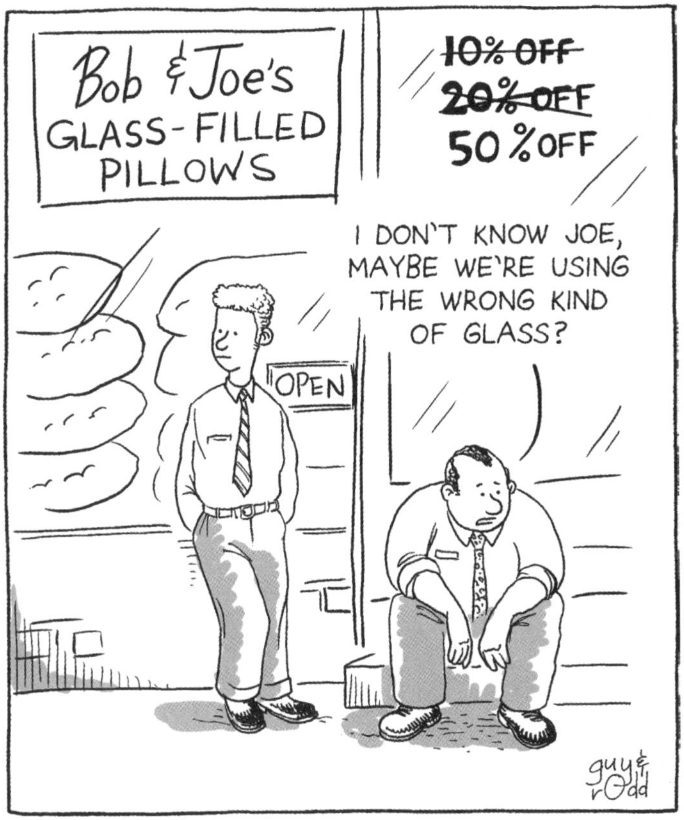
Bob & Joe's GLASS-FILLED PILLOWS
10% OFF
20% OFF
50% OFF
OPEN
I DON'T KNOW JOE, MAYBE WE'RE USING THE WRONG KIND OF GLASS?
guy & rOdd

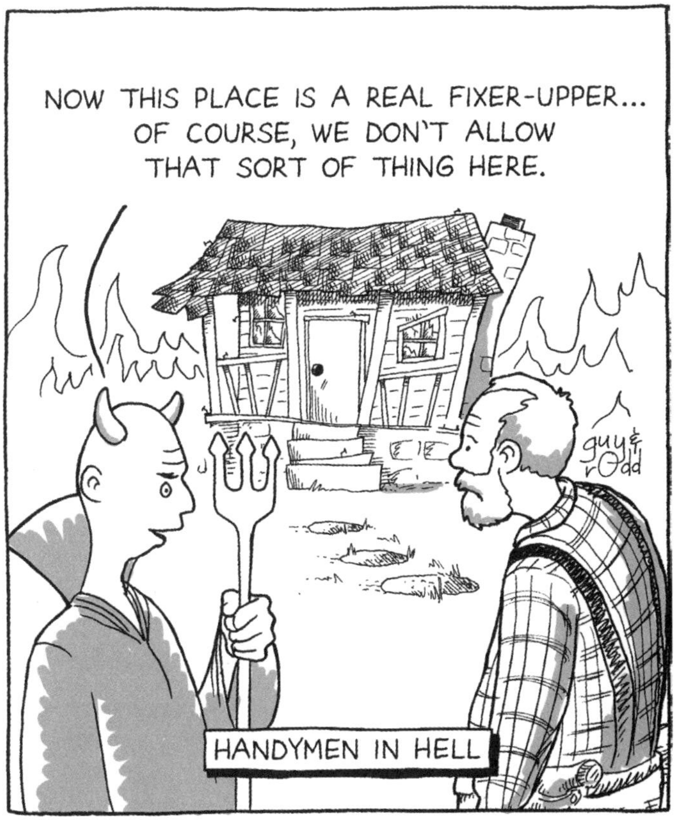
NOW THIS PLACE IS A REAL FIXER-UPPER... OF COURSE, WE DON'T ALLOW THAT SORT OF THING HERE.
HANDYMEN IN HELL
guy & rOdd

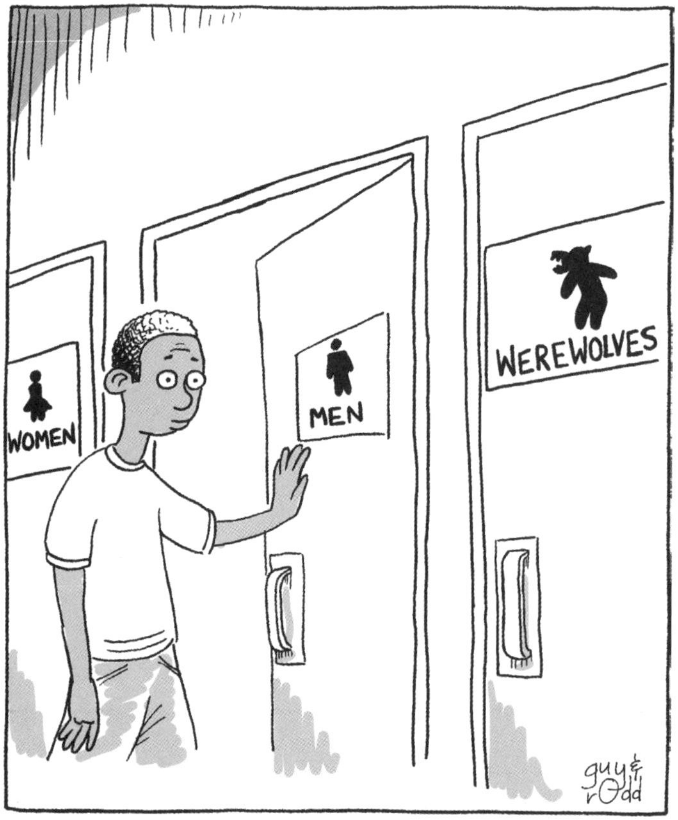
WOMEN
MEN
WEREWOLVES
guy & rOdd

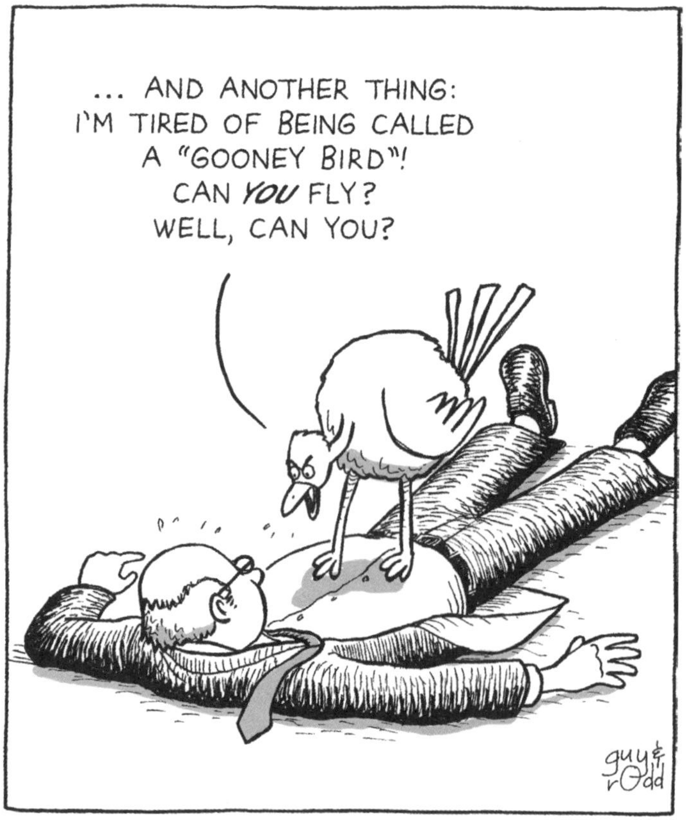
... AND ANOTHER THING: I'M TIRED OF BEING CALLED A "GOONEY BIRD"! CAN *YOU* FLY? WELL, CAN YOU?
guy & rOdd

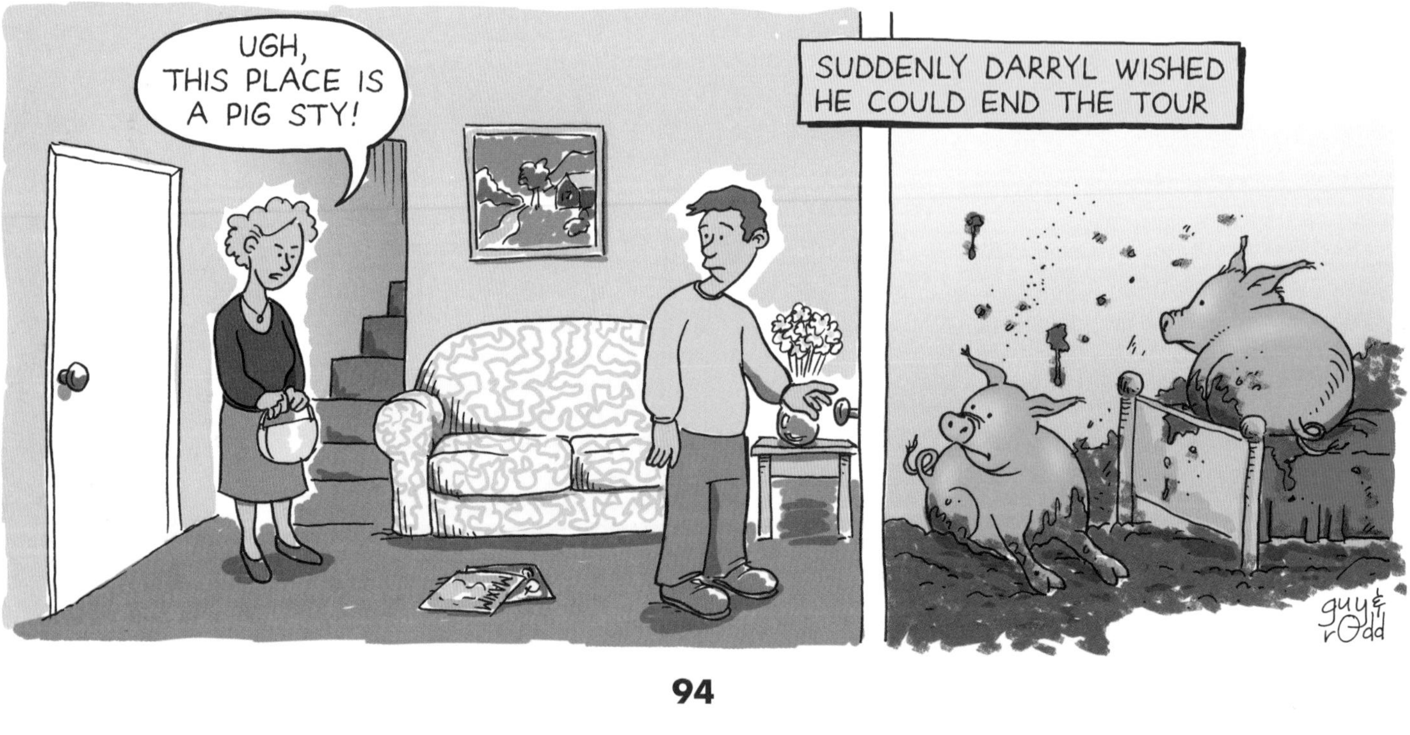
UGH, THIS PLACE IS A PIG STY!
MAXIM
SUDDENLY DARRYL WISHED HE COULD END THE TOUR
guy & rOdd

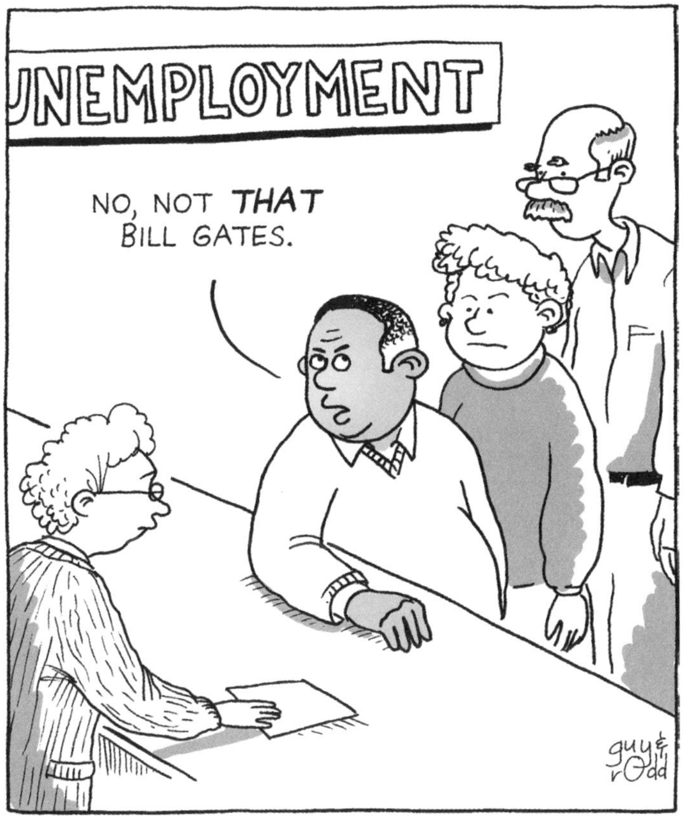
UNEMPLOYMENT
NO, NOT THAT BILL GATES.
guy & rOdd

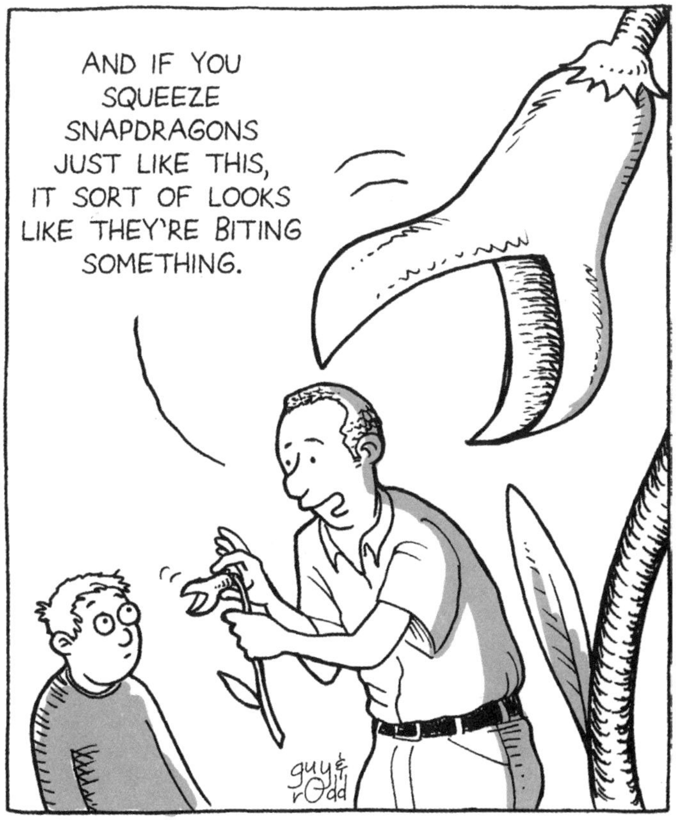
AND IF YOU SQUEEZE SNAPDRAGONS JUST LIKE THIS, IT SORT OF LOOKS LIKE THEY'RE BITING SOMETHING.
guy & rOdd

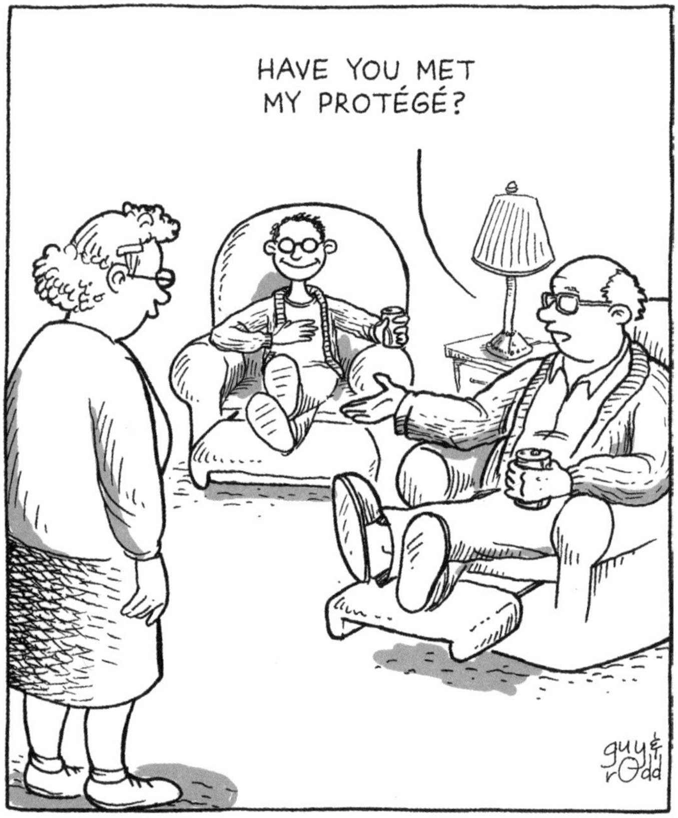
HAVE YOU MET
MY PROTÉGÉ?
guy & rOdd

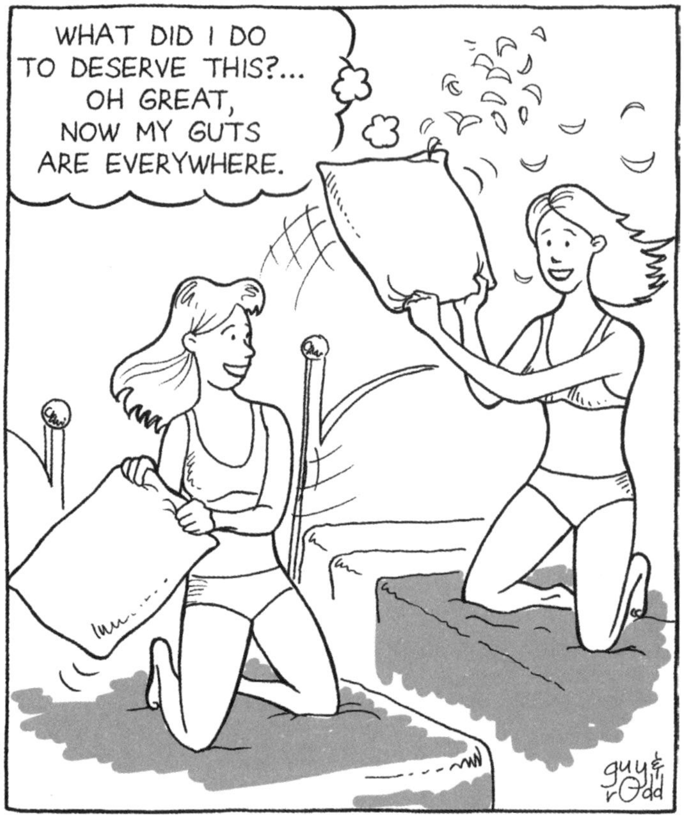
WHAT DID I DO
TO DESERVE THIS?...
OH GREAT,
NOW MY GUTS
ARE EVERYWHERE.
guy & rOdd

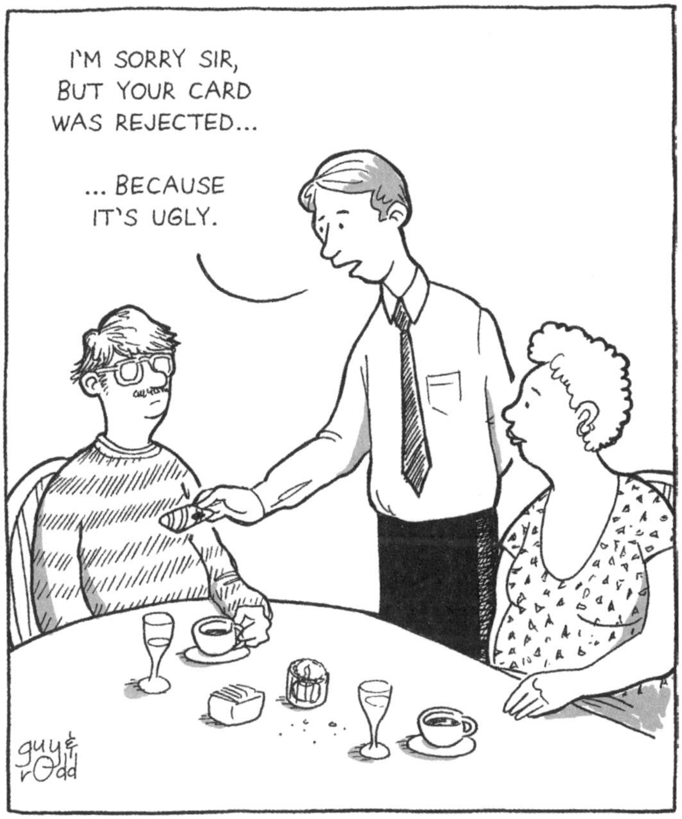
I'M SORRY SIR, BUT YOUR CARD WAS REJECTED...
... BECAUSE IT'S UGLY.
guy & rodd

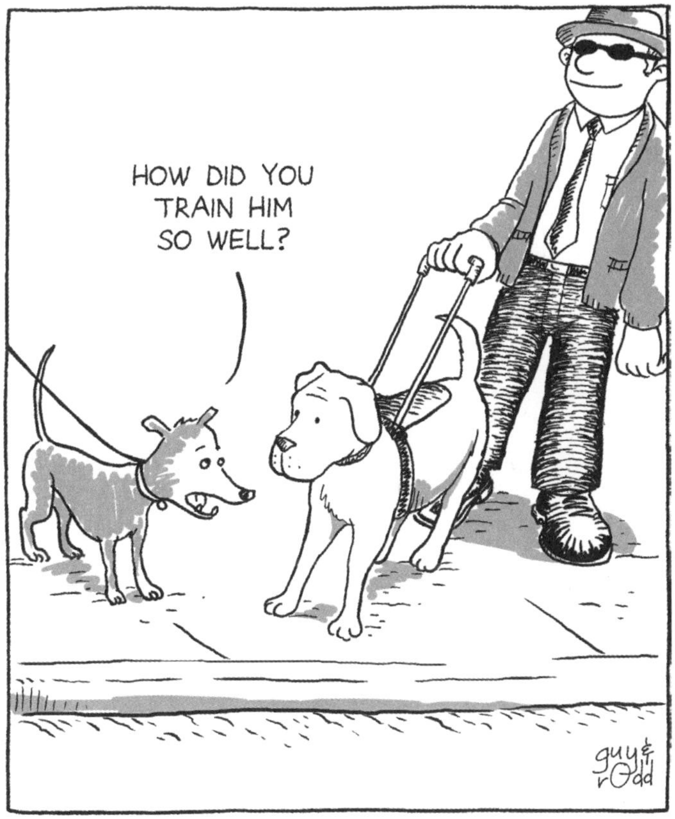
HOW DID YOU TRAIN HIM SO WELL?
guy & rodd

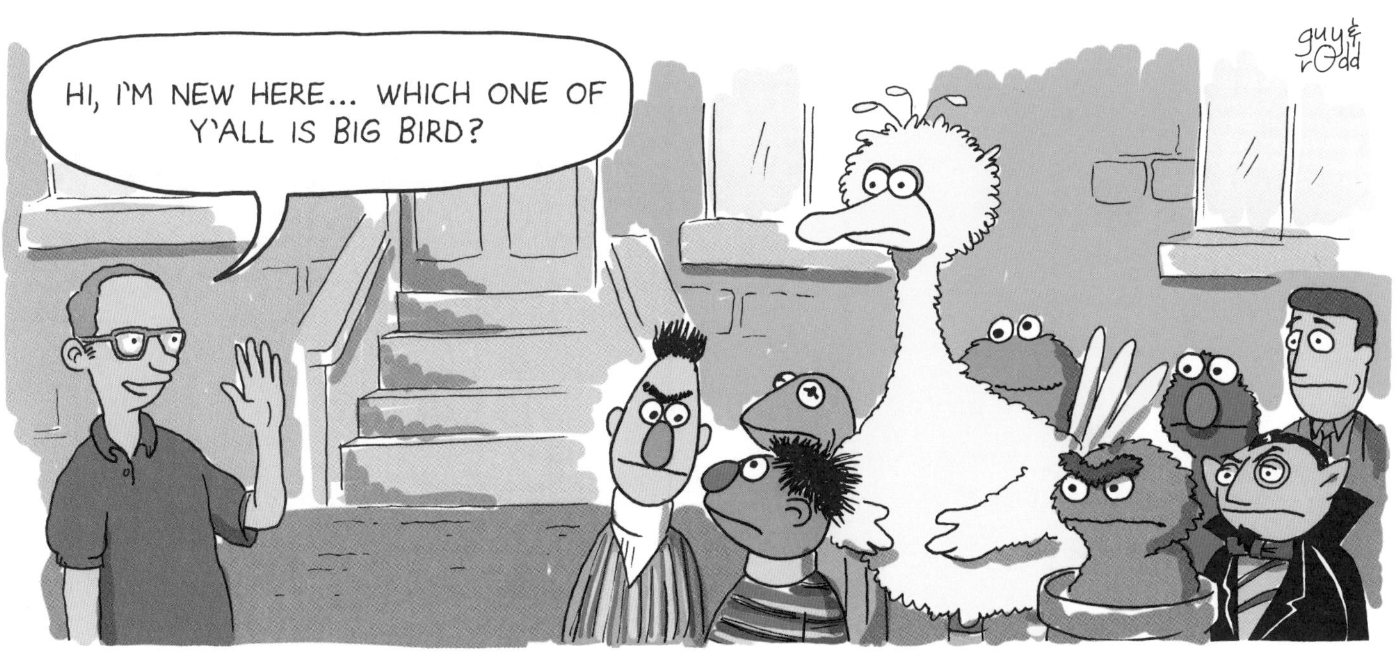
guy & rodd
HI, I'M NEW HERE... WHICH ONE OF Y'ALL IS BIG BIRD?

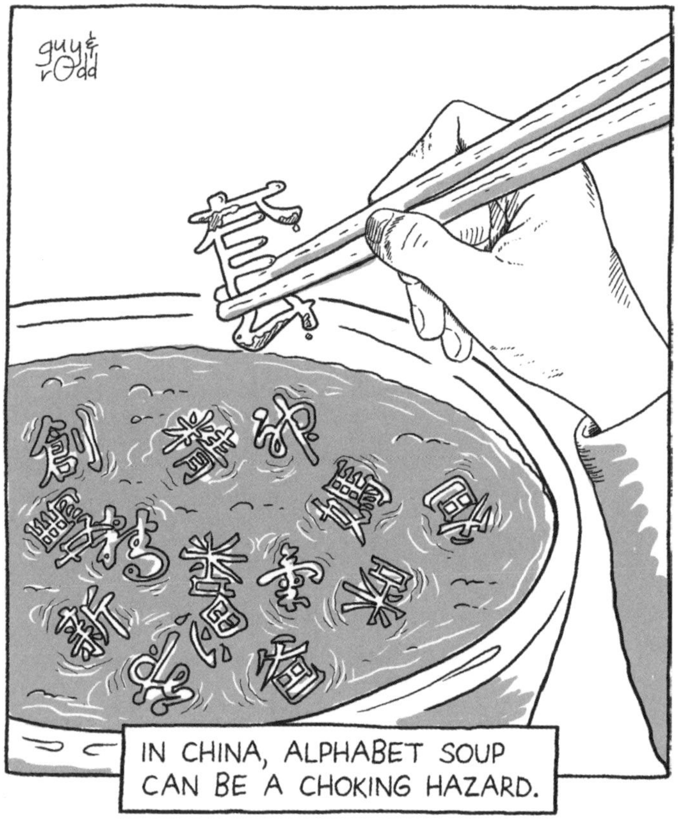
IN CHINA, ALPHABET SOUP CAN BE A CHOKING HAZARD.

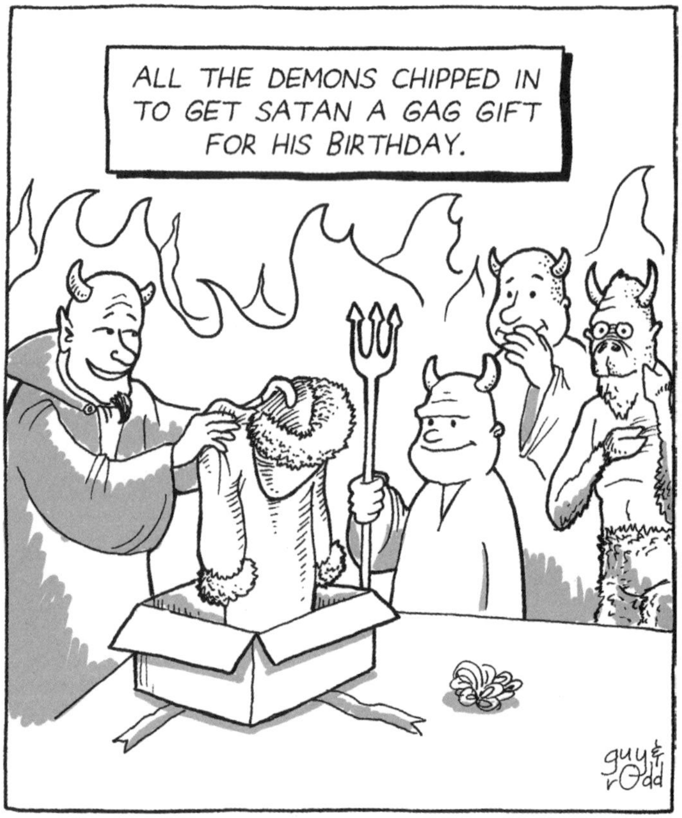
ALL THE DEMONS CHIPPED IN TO GET SATAN A GAG GIFT FOR HIS BIRTHDAY.

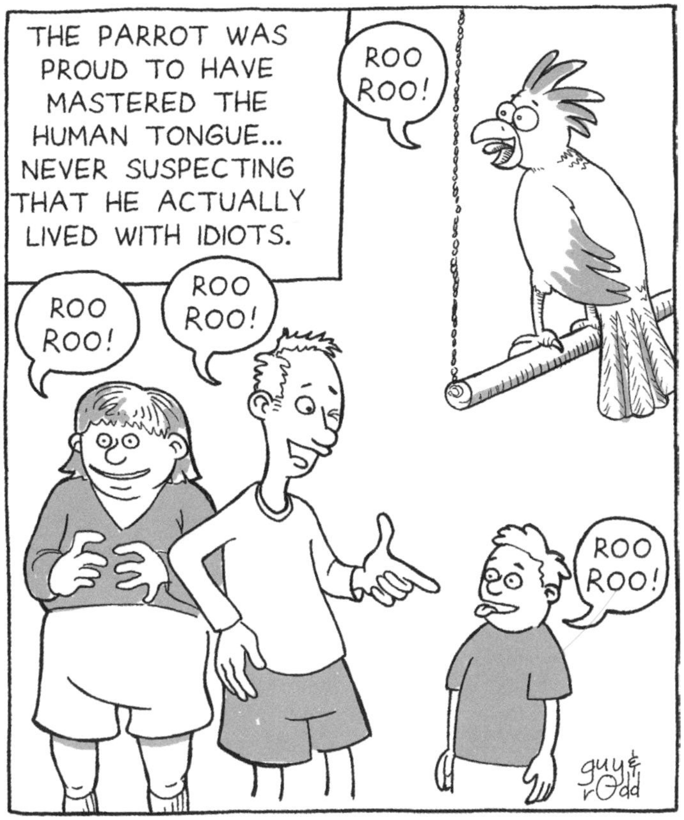
THE PARROT WAS PROUD TO HAVE MASTERED THE HUMAN TONGUE... NEVER SUSPECTING THAT HE ACTUALLY LIVED WITH IDIOTS.
ROO ROO!
ROO ROO!
ROO ROO!
ROO ROO!
guy & rOdd

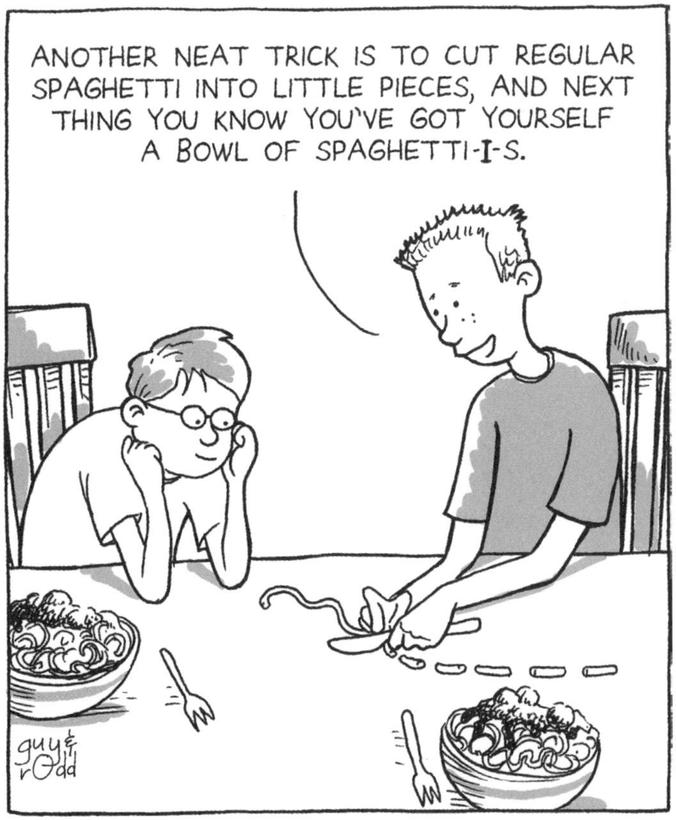
ANOTHER NEAT TRICK IS TO CUT REGULAR SPAGHETTI INTO LITTLE PIECES, AND NEXT THING YOU KNOW YOU'VE GOT YOURSELF A BOWL OF SPAGHETTI-I-S.
guy & rOdd

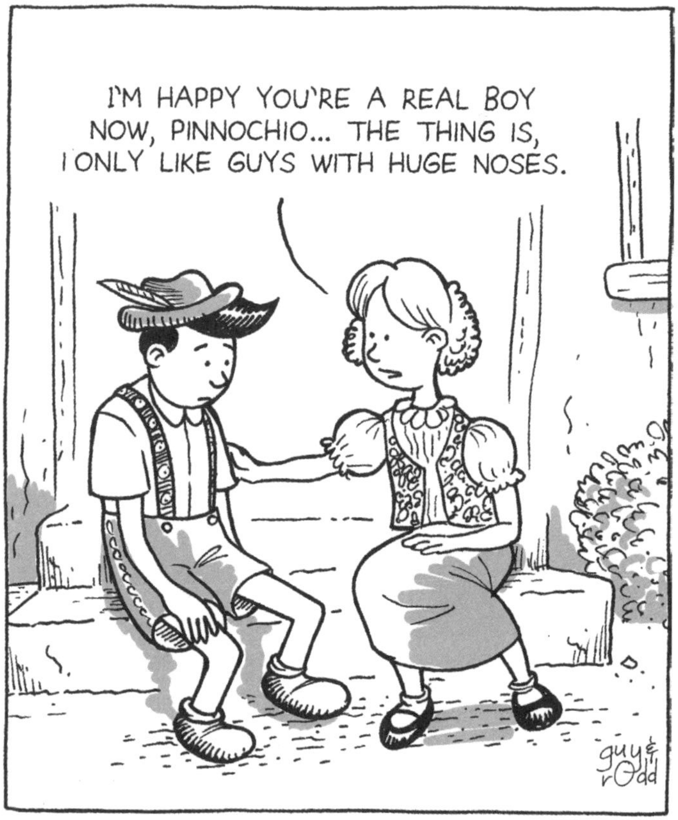
I'M HAPPY YOU'RE A REAL BOY NOW, PINNOCHIO... THE THING IS, I ONLY LIKE GUYS WITH HUGE NOSES.
guy & rOdd

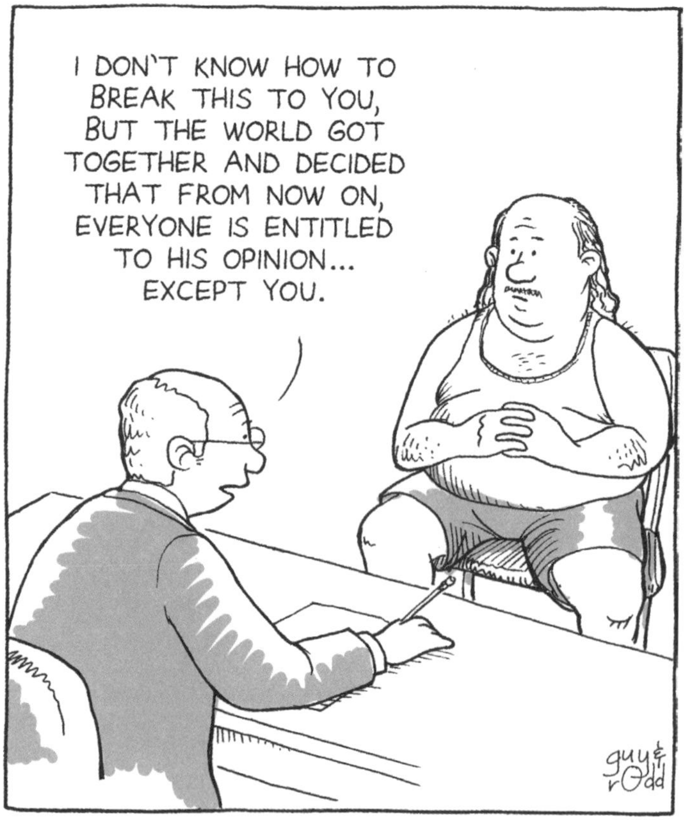
I DON'T KNOW HOW TO BREAK THIS TO YOU, BUT THE WORLD GOT TOGETHER AND DECIDED THAT FROM NOW ON, EVERYONE IS ENTITLED TO HIS OPINION... EXCEPT YOU.
guy & rOdd

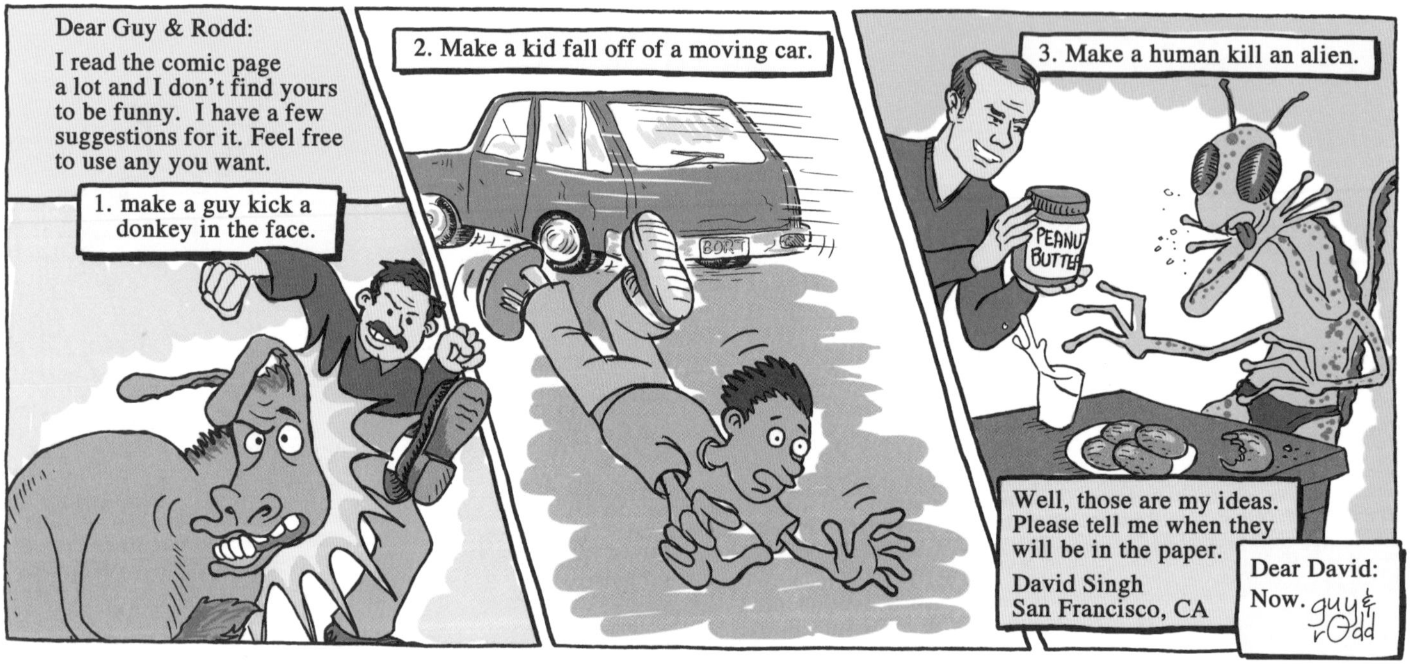
Dear Guy & Rodd:
I read the comic page a lot and I don't find yours to be funny. I have a few suggestions for it. Feel free to use any you want.
1. make a guy kick a donkey in the face.
2. Make a kid fall off of a moving car.
BORT
3. Make a human kill an alien.
PEANUT BUTTER
Well, those are my ideas. Please tell me when they will be in the paper.
David Singh
San Francisco, CA
Dear David:
Now.
guy & rOdd

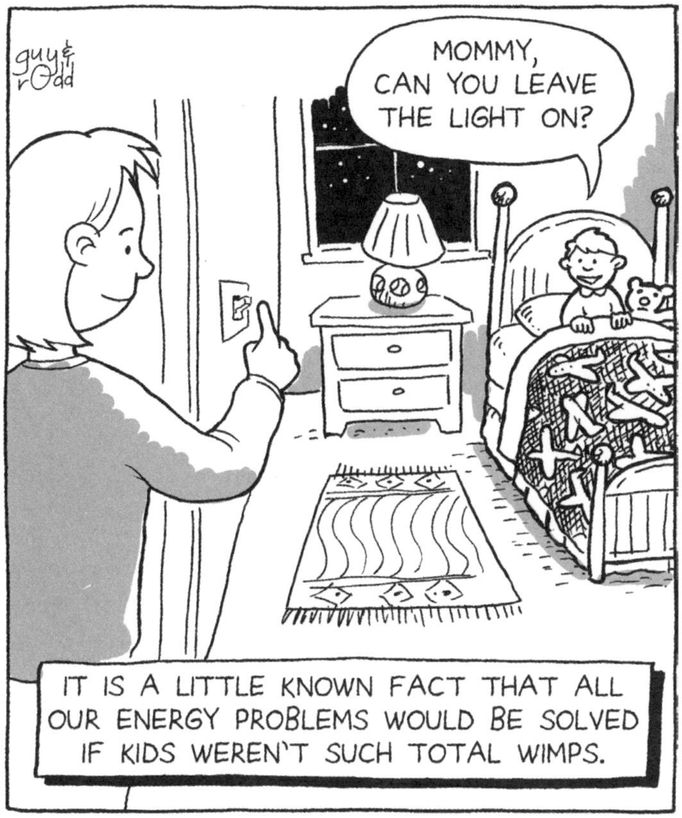
guy & rodd
MOMMY, CAN YOU LEAVE THE LIGHT ON?
IT IS A LITTLE KNOWN FACT THAT ALL OUR ENERGY PROBLEMS WOULD BE SOLVED IF KIDS WEREN'T SUCH TOTAL WIMPS.

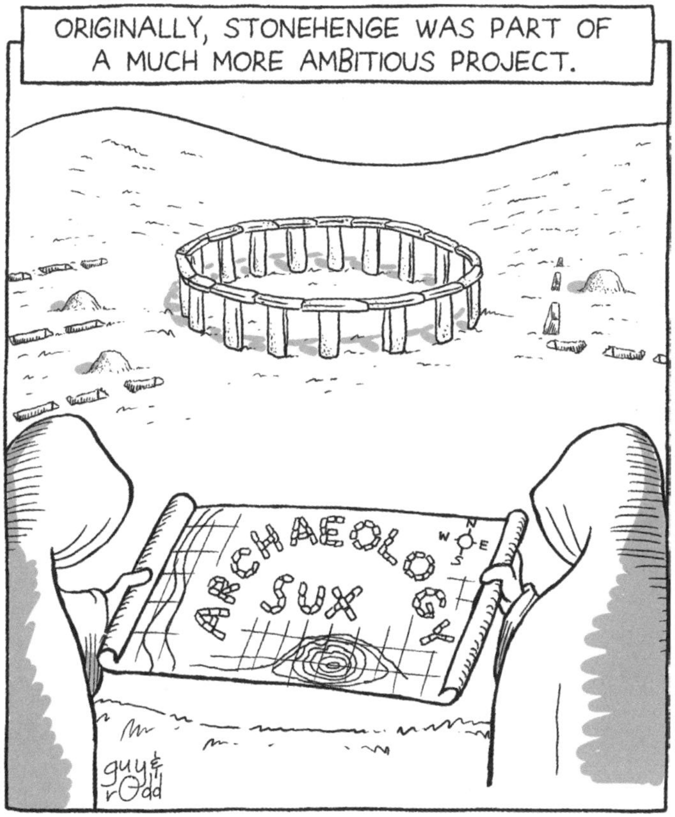
ORIGINALLY, STONEHENGE WAS PART OF A MUCH MORE AMBITIOUS PROJECT.
ARCHAEOLOGY SUX
N
W E
S
guy & rodd

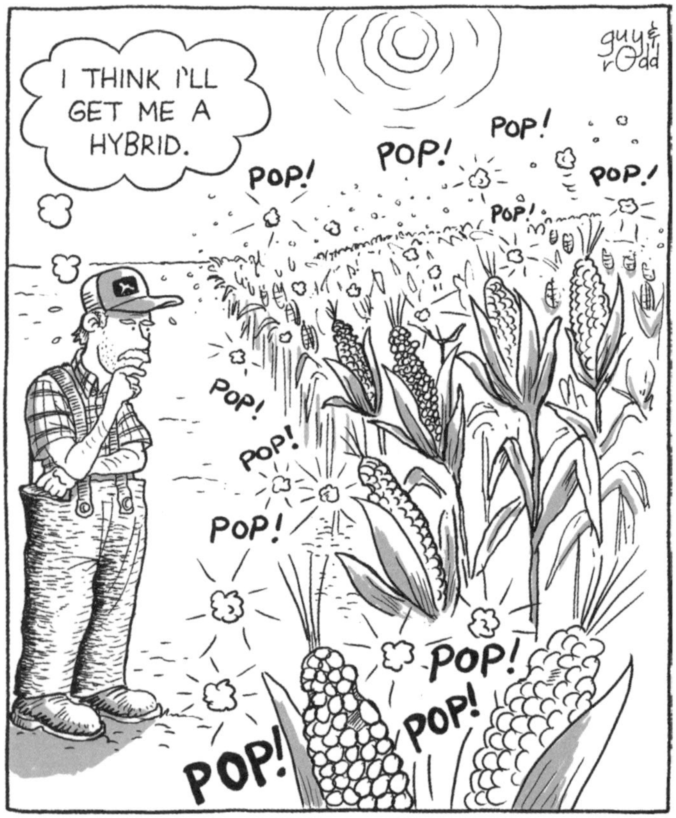
I THINK I'LL GET ME A HYBRID.
POP!
POP!
POP!
POP!
POP!
POP!
POP!
POP!
POP!
POP!
POP!
guy & rOdd

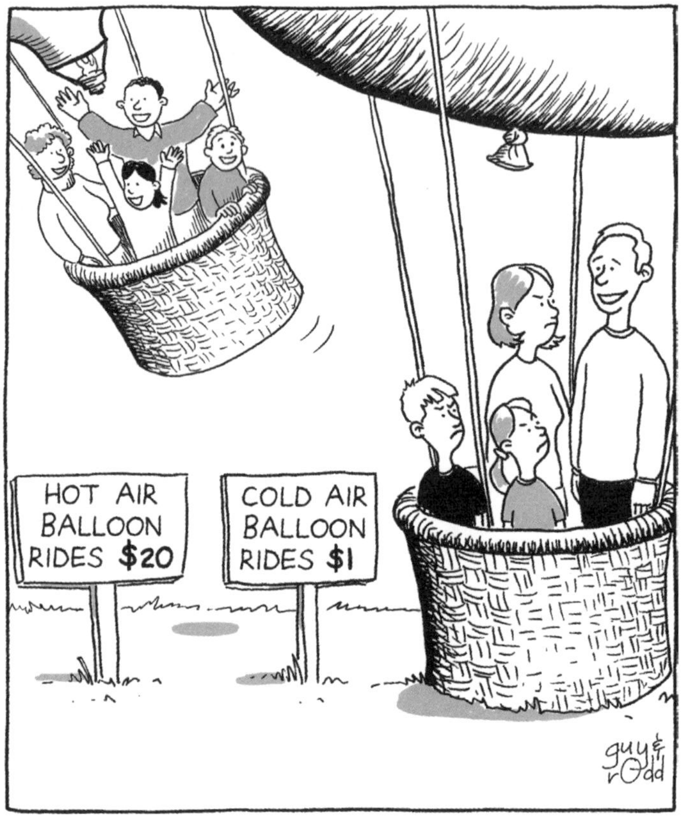
HOT AIR BALLOON RIDES $20
COLD AIR BALLOON RIDES $1
guy & rOdd

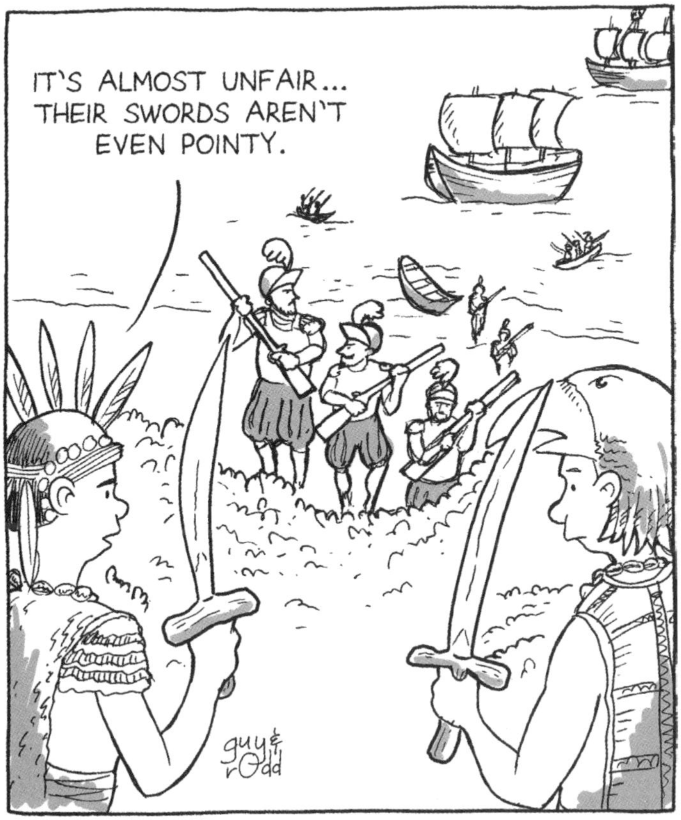
IT'S ALMOST UNFAIR... THEIR SWORDS AREN'T EVEN POINTY.
guy & rOdd

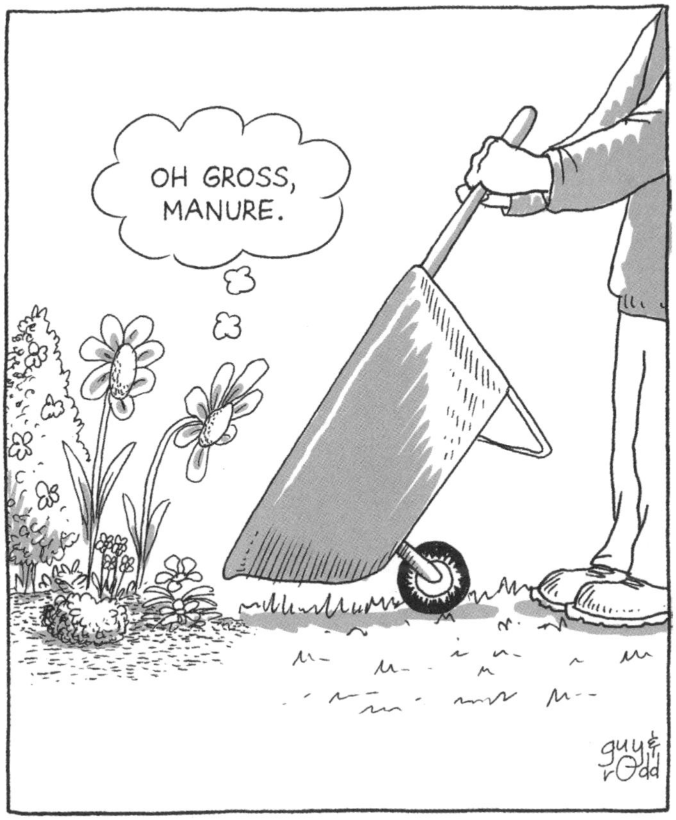
OH GROSS, MANURE.
guy & rOdd

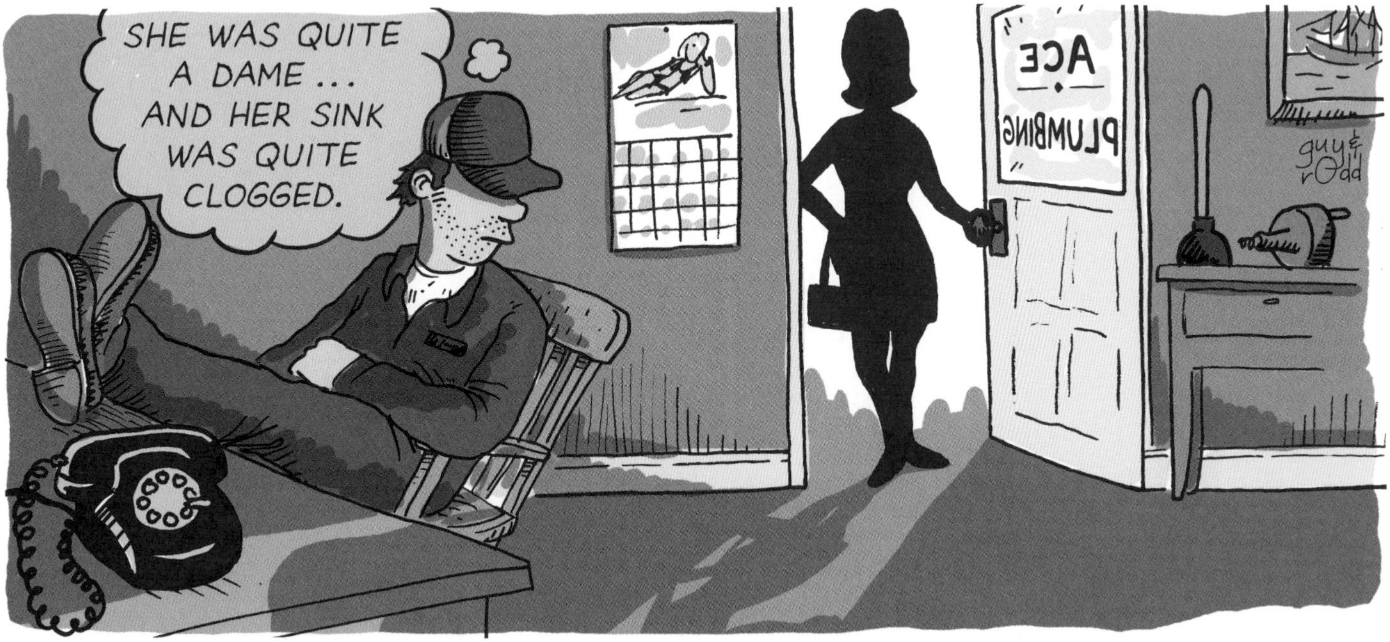
SHE WAS QUITE A DAME ... AND HER SINK WAS QUITE CLOGGED.
ACE • PLUMBING
guy & rOdd

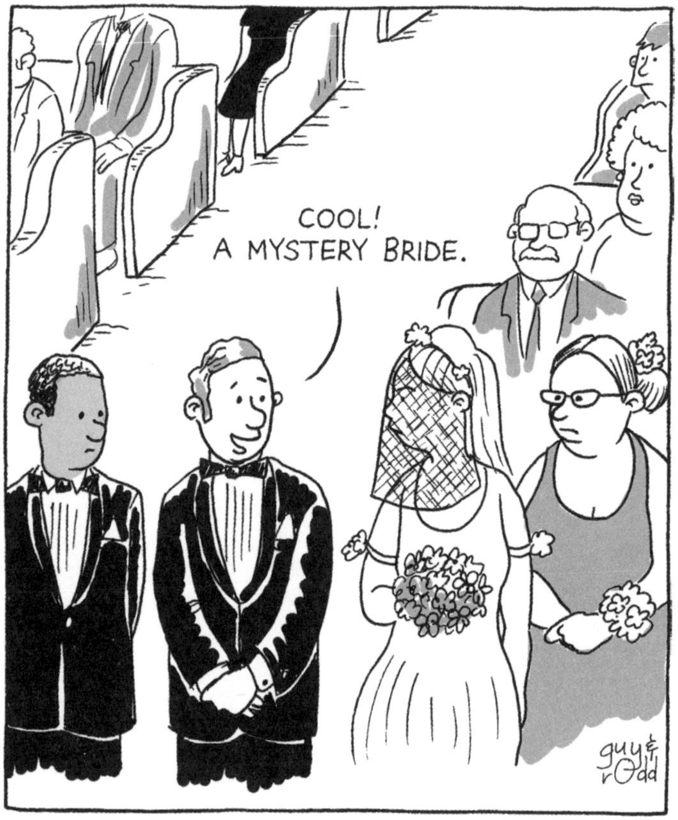
COOL!
A MYSTERY BRIDE.
guy & rOdd

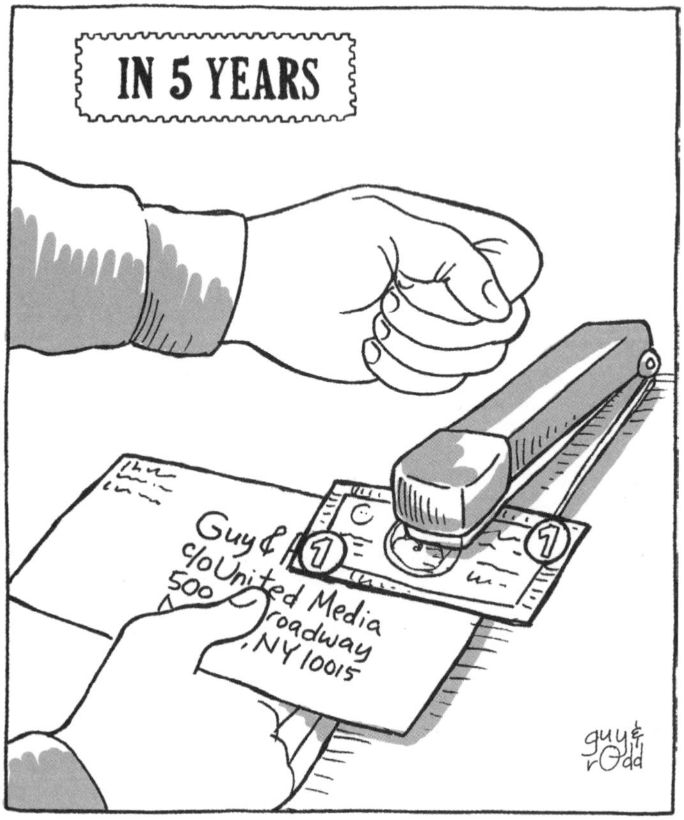
IN 5 YEARS
Guy &
c/o United Media
500
roadway
, NY 10015
guy & rOdd

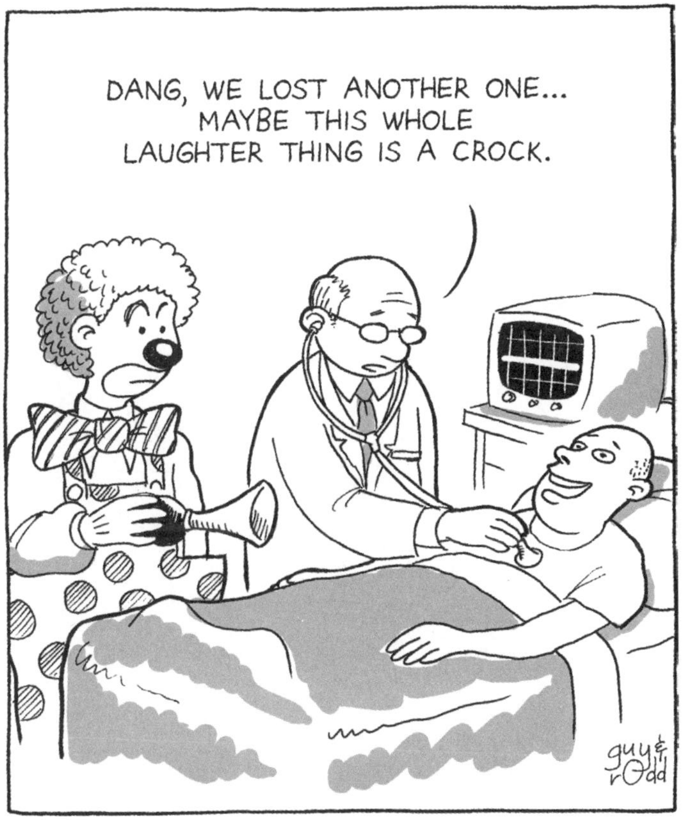
DANG, WE LOST ANOTHER ONE...
MAYBE THIS WHOLE
LAUGHTER THING IS A CROCK.
guy & rOdd

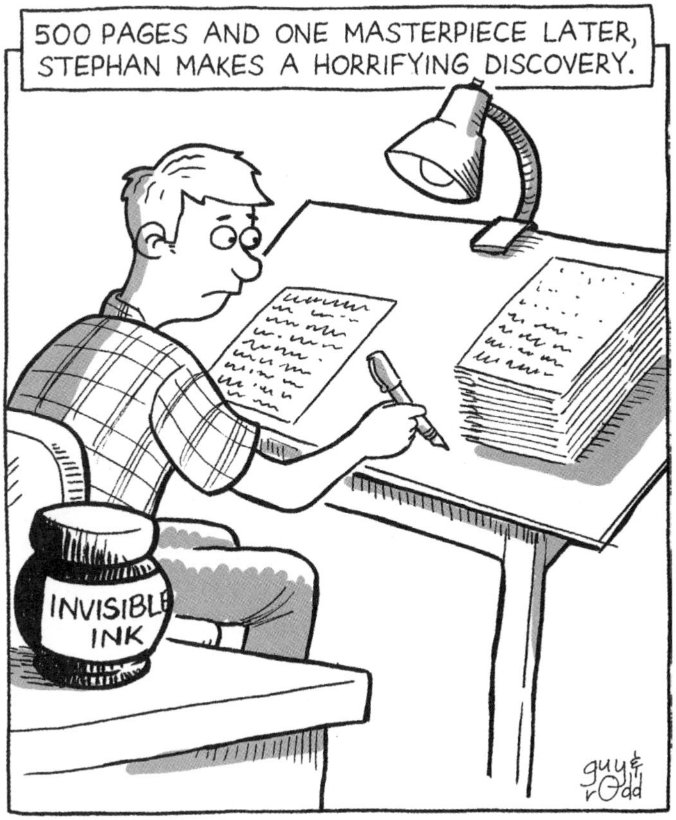
500 PAGES AND ONE MASTERPIECE LATER,
STEPHAN MAKES A HORRIFYING DISCOVERY.
INVISIBLE
INK
guy & rOdd

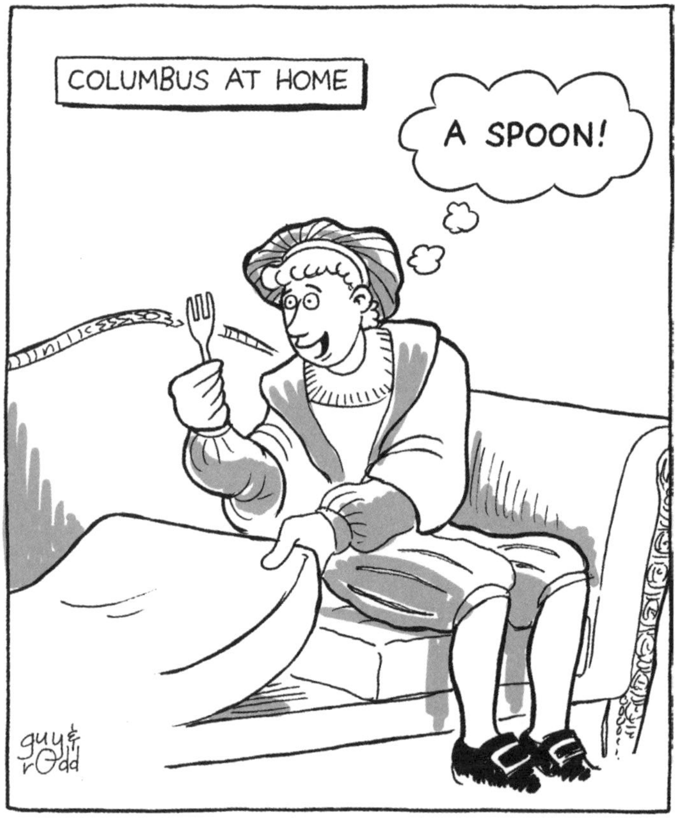
COLUMBUS AT HOME
A SPOON!
guy & rOdd

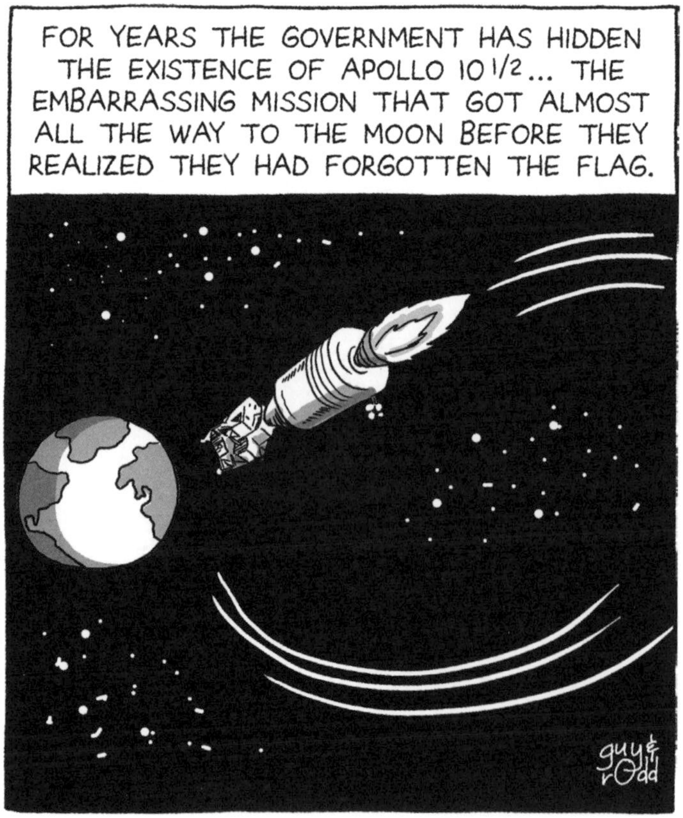
FOR YEARS THE GOVERNMENT HAS HIDDEN THE EXISTENCE OF APOLLO 10 1/2... THE EMBARRASSING MISSION THAT GOT ALMOST ALL THE WAY TO THE MOON BEFORE THEY REALIZED THEY HAD FORGOTTEN THE FLAG.
guy & rOdd

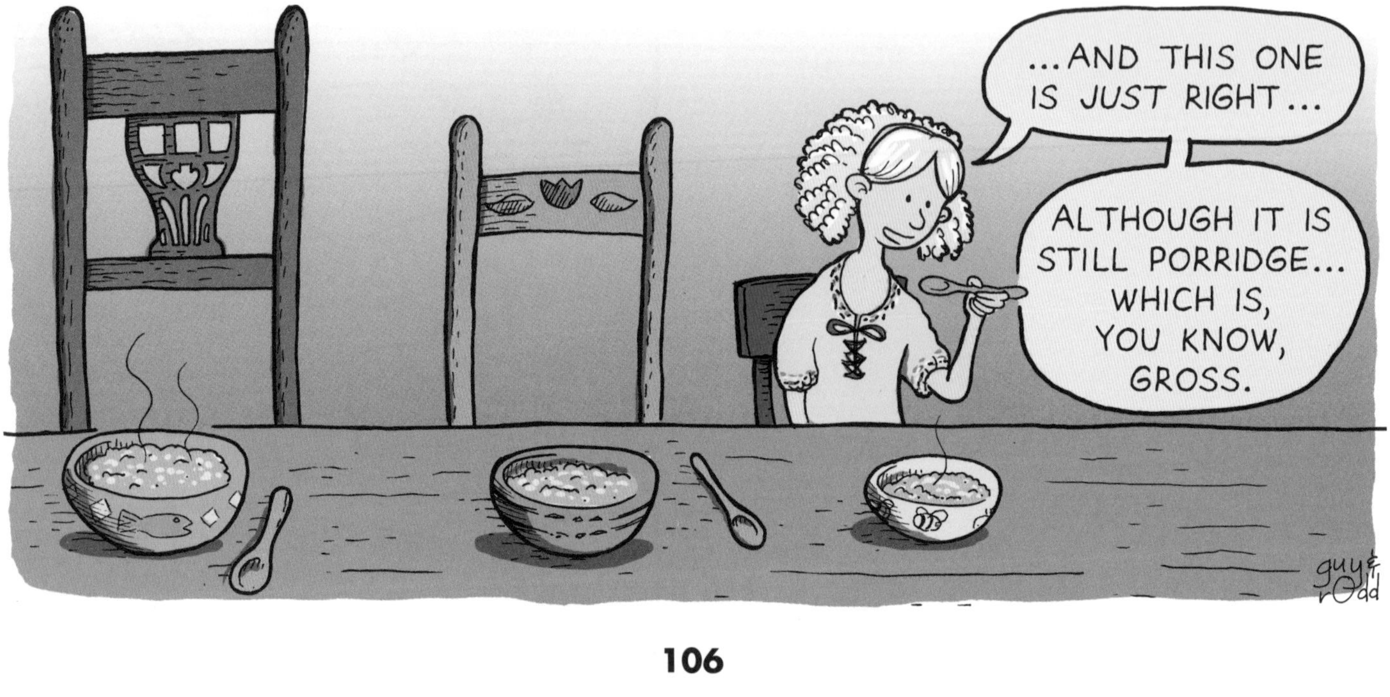
...AND THIS ONE IS JUST RIGHT...
ALTHOUGH IT IS STILL PORRIDGE... WHICH IS, YOU KNOW, GROSS.
guy & rOdd

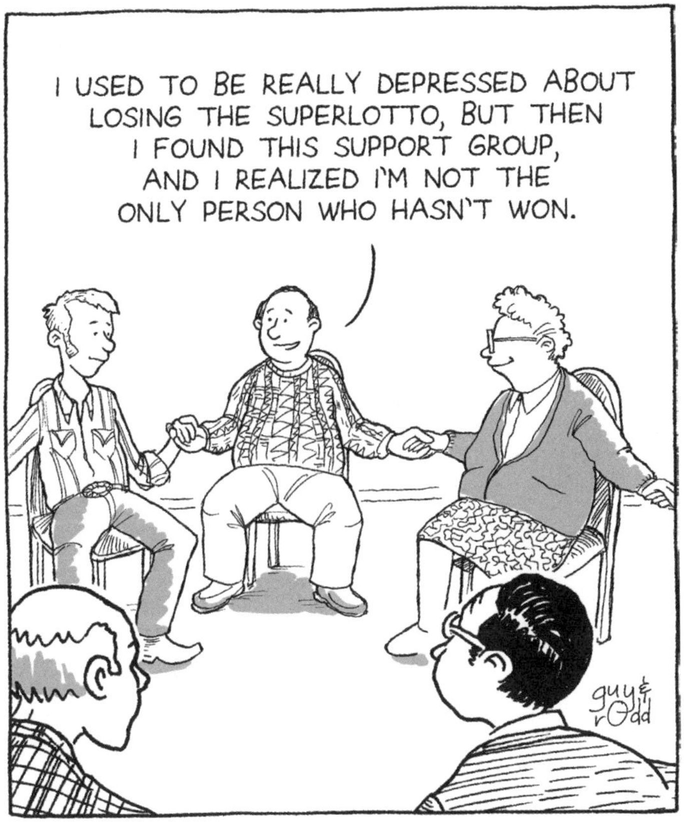
I USED TO BE REALLY DEPRESSED ABOUT LOSING THE SUPERLOTTO, BUT THEN I FOUND THIS SUPPORT GROUP, AND I REALIZED I'M NOT THE ONLY PERSON WHO HASN'T WON.
guy & rOdd

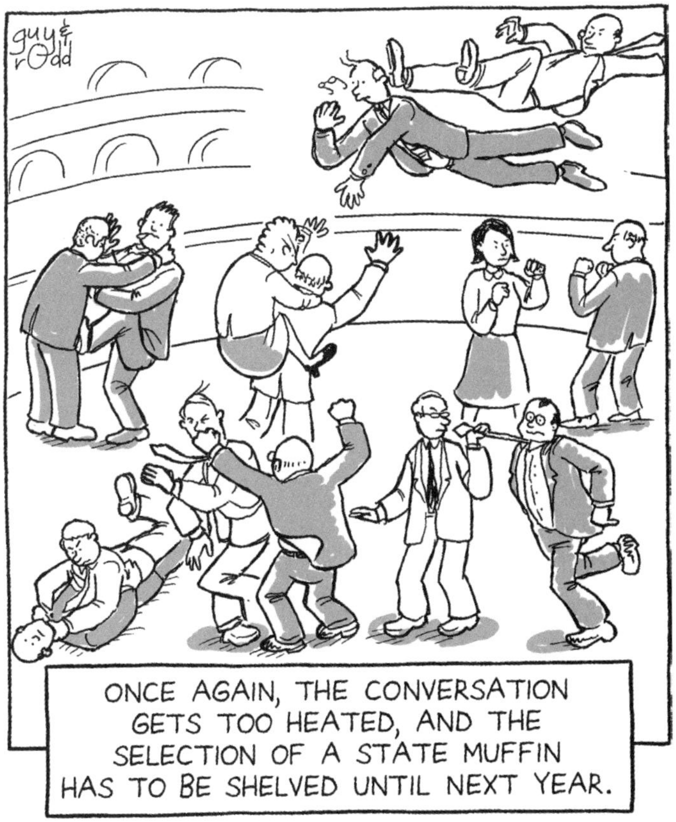
guy & rOdd
ONCE AGAIN, THE CONVERSATION GETS TOO HEATED, AND THE SELECTION OF A STATE MUFFIN HAS TO BE SHELVED UNTIL NEXT YEAR.

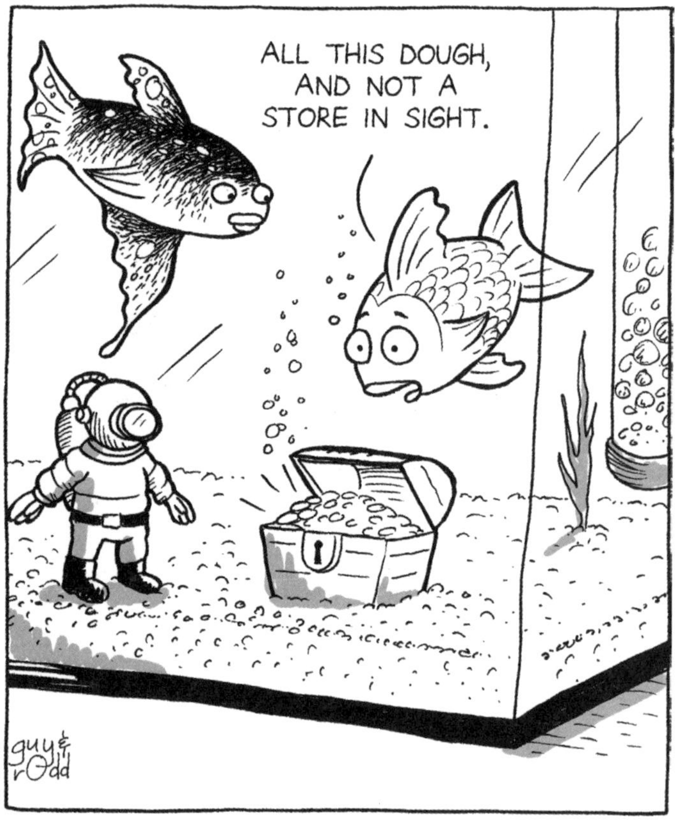
ALL THIS DOUGH, AND NOT A STORE IN SIGHT.
guy & rOdd

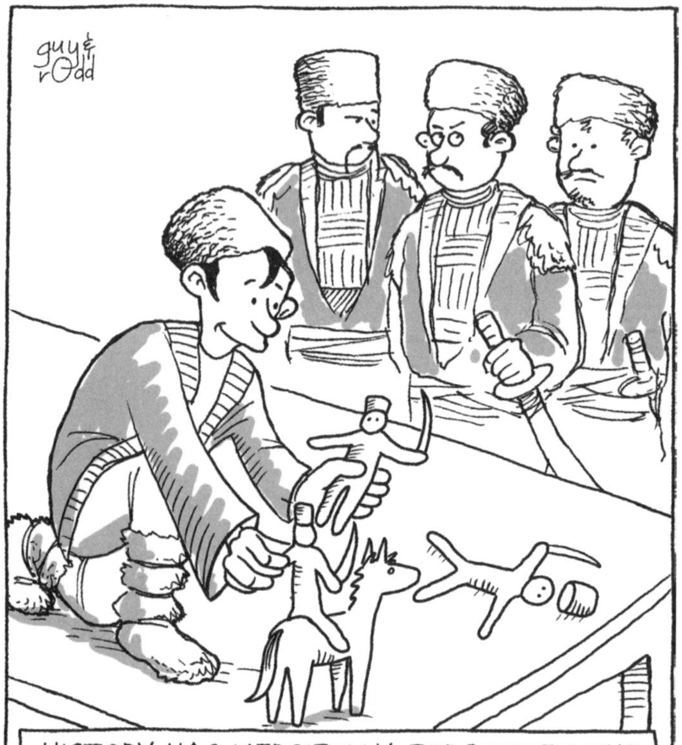
guy & rOdd

HISTORY HAS MERCIFULLY FORGOTTEN THE INCREDIBLY BRIEF REIGN OF DINGUS KHAN.

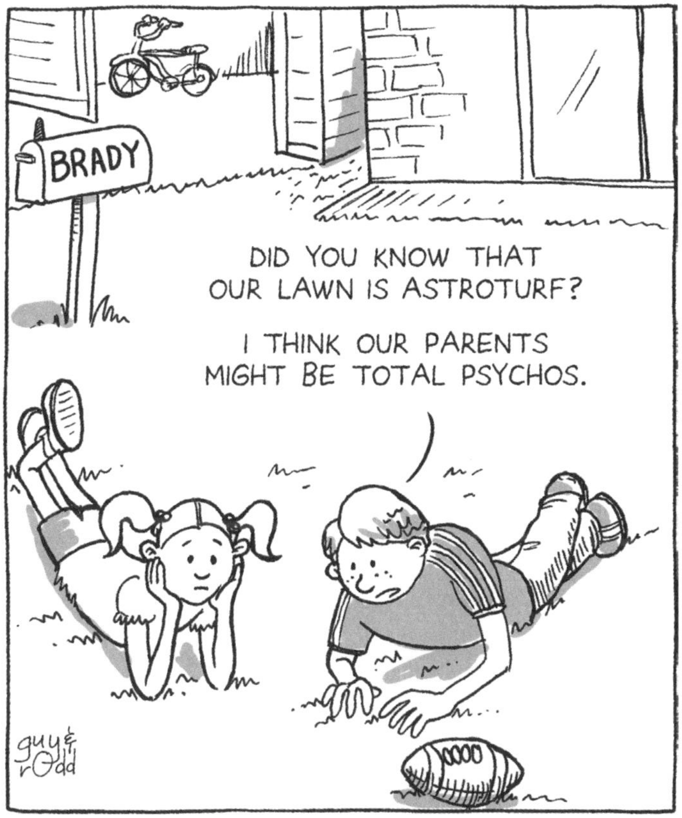
BRADY
DID YOU KNOW THAT OUR LAWN IS ASTROTURF?
I THINK OUR PARENTS MIGHT BE TOTAL PSYCHOS.
guy & rOdd

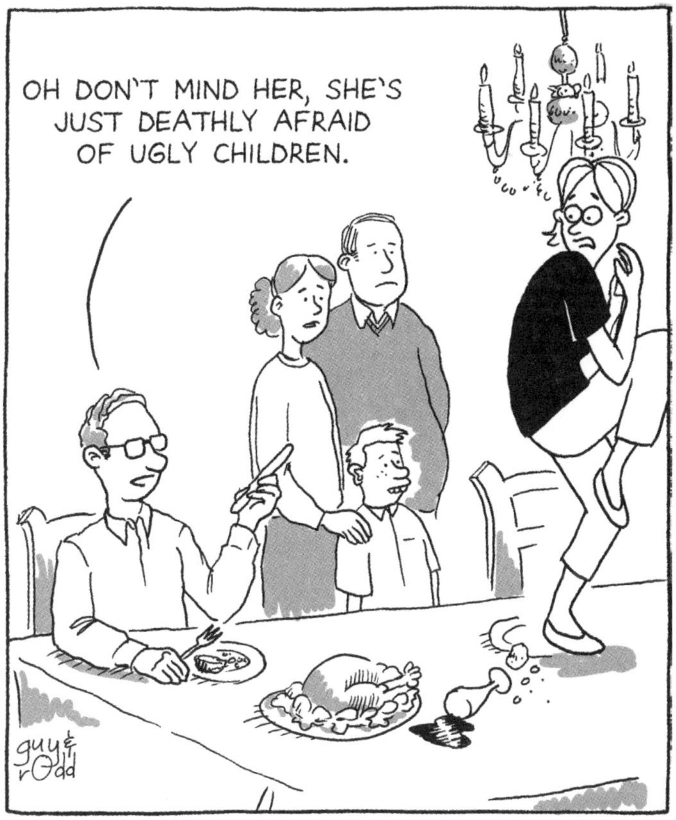
OH DON'T MIND HER, SHE'S JUST DEATHLY AFRAID OF UGLY CHILDREN.
guy & rOdd

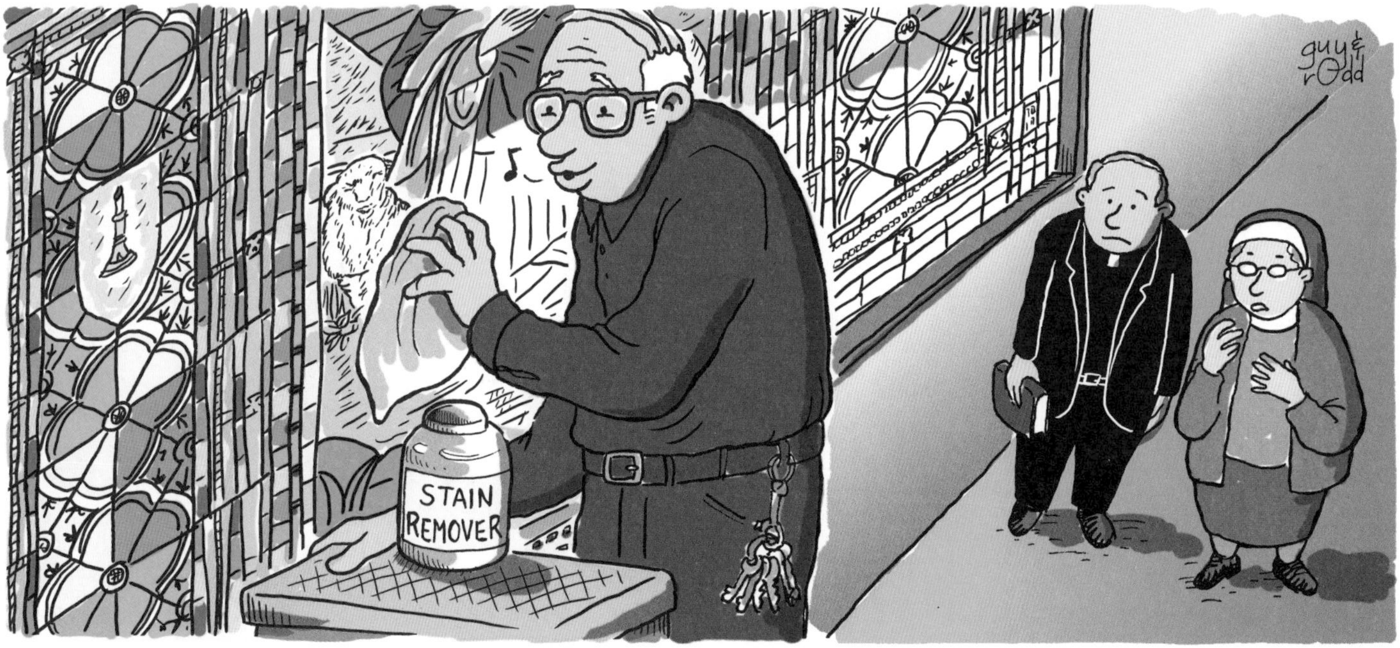
guy & rOdd
STAIN REMOVER

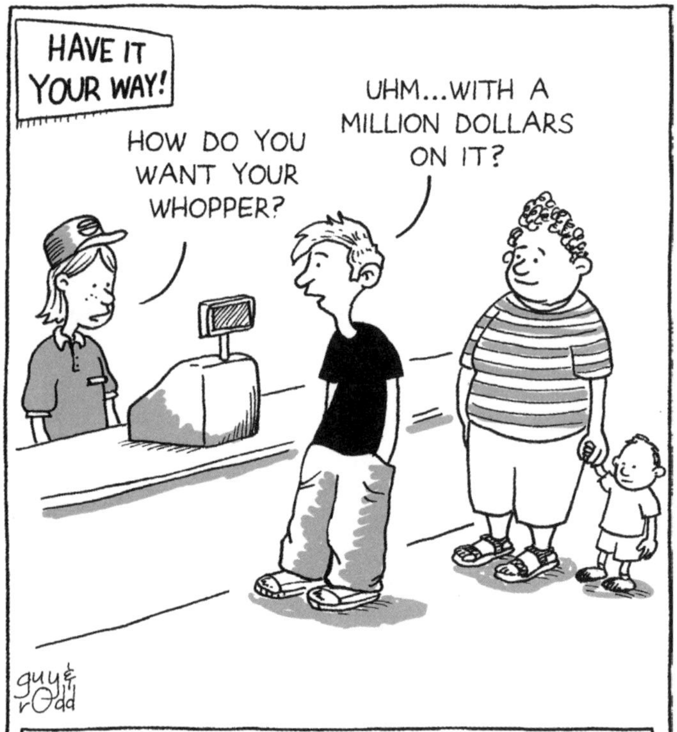
HAVE IT YOUR WAY!
HOW DO YOU WANT YOUR WHOPPER?
UHM...WITH A MILLION DOLLARS ON IT?

SHORTLY THEREAFTER, THEY WOULD MAKE SWEEPING CHANGES TO THEIR POLICIES.

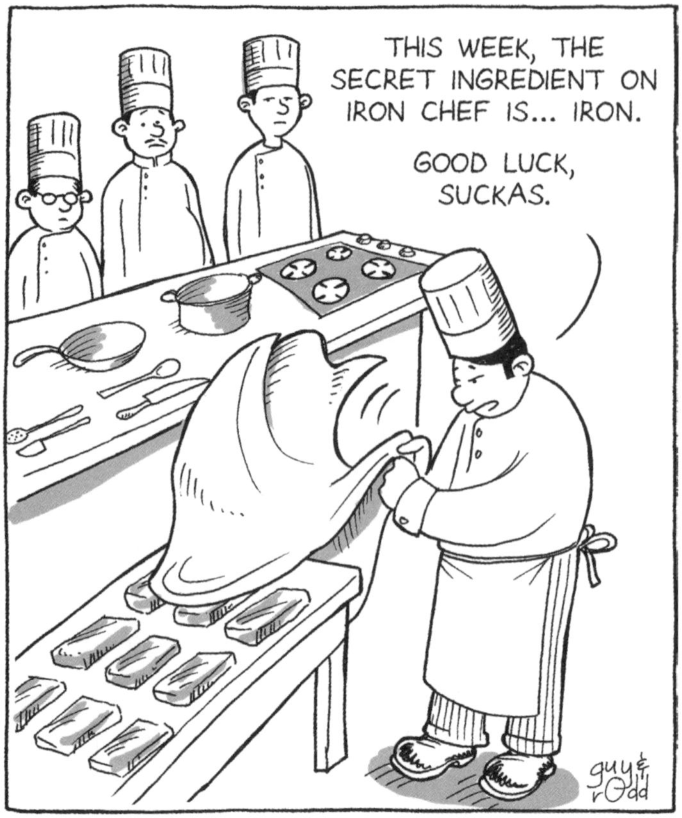
THIS WEEK, THE SECRET INGREDIENT ON IRON CHEF IS... IRON.
GOOD LUCK, SUCKAS.

YEAH, I KNOW I'M GENERALLY RECOGNIZED AS THE TOUGHEST BUTTERFLY ON THE BLOCK... BUT WHAT DOES THAT REALLY MEAN AT THE END OF THE DAY?

UIDANCE
UNSELOR
OH YEAH, EVERYONE LOVES AUDITORS. YOU'LL BE SUPER POPULAR!

SECRETLY SHE'D ALWAYS HATED YOUNG ADAM KASSAN.

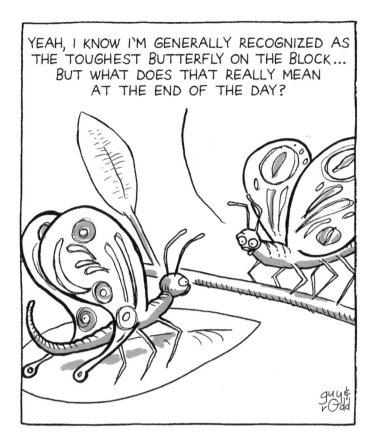

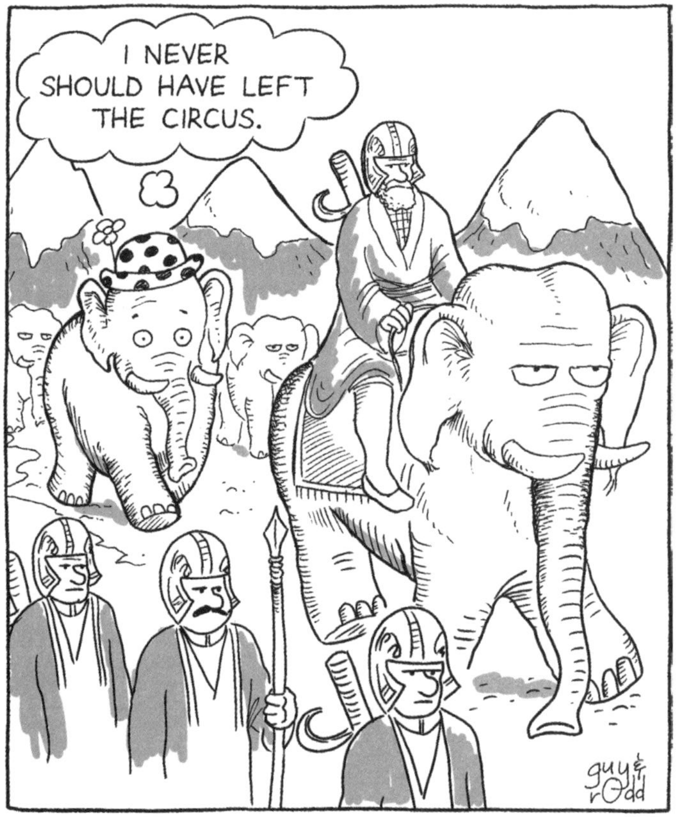
I NEVER SHOULD HAVE LEFT THE CIRCUS.
guy & rodd

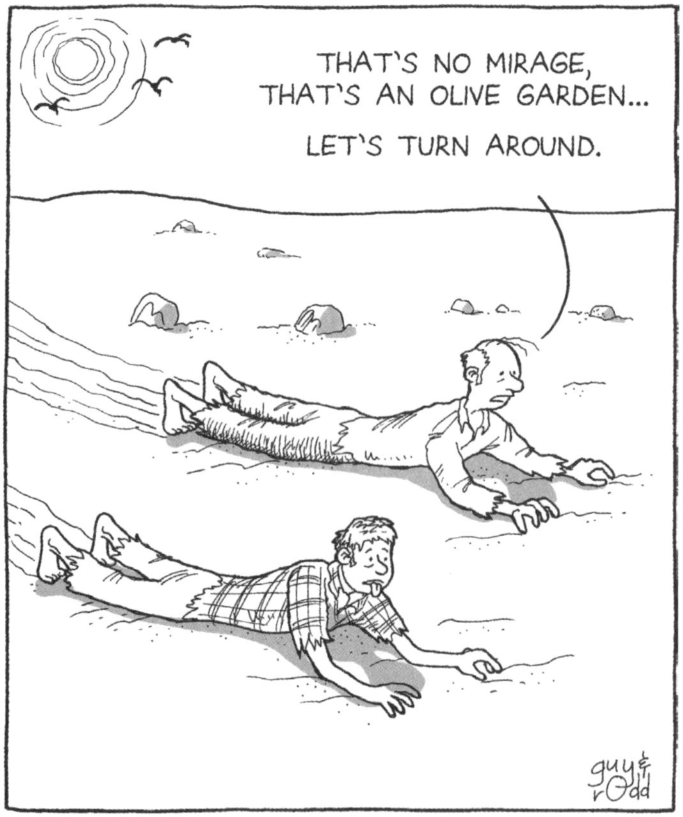
THAT'S NO MIRAGE, THAT'S AN OLIVE GARDEN...
LET'S TURN AROUND.
guy & rodd

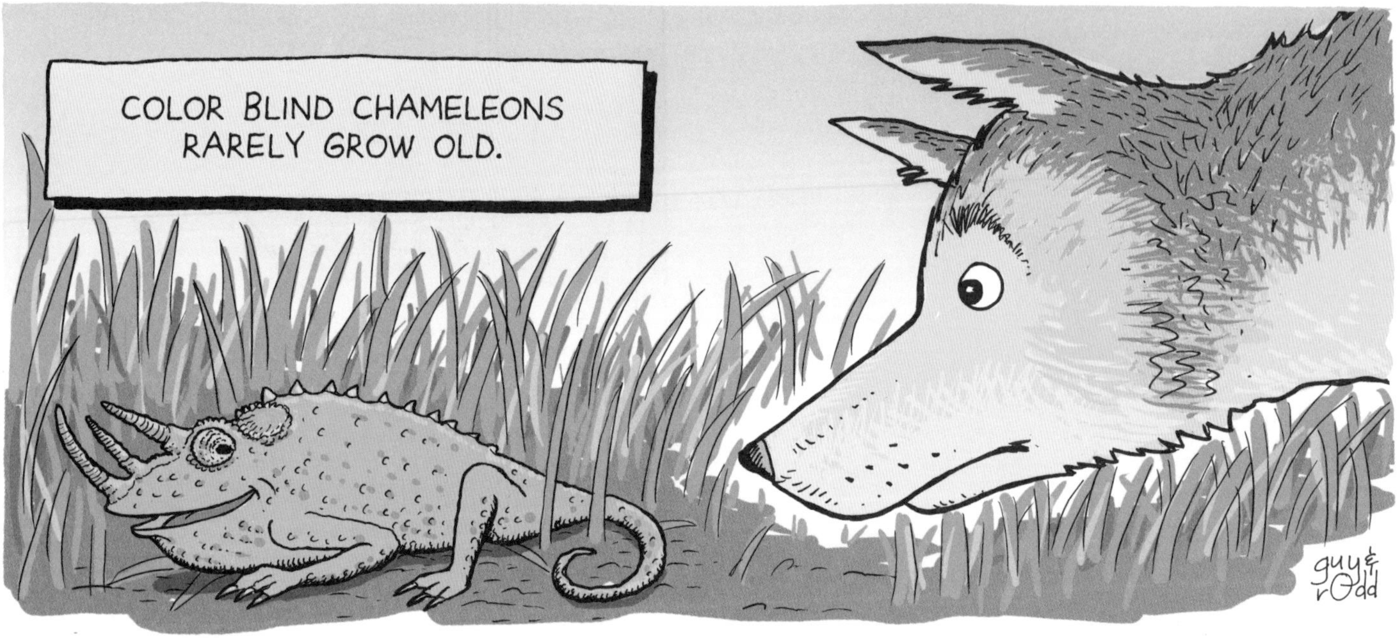
COLOR BLIND CHAMELEONS RARELY GROW OLD.
guy & rodd

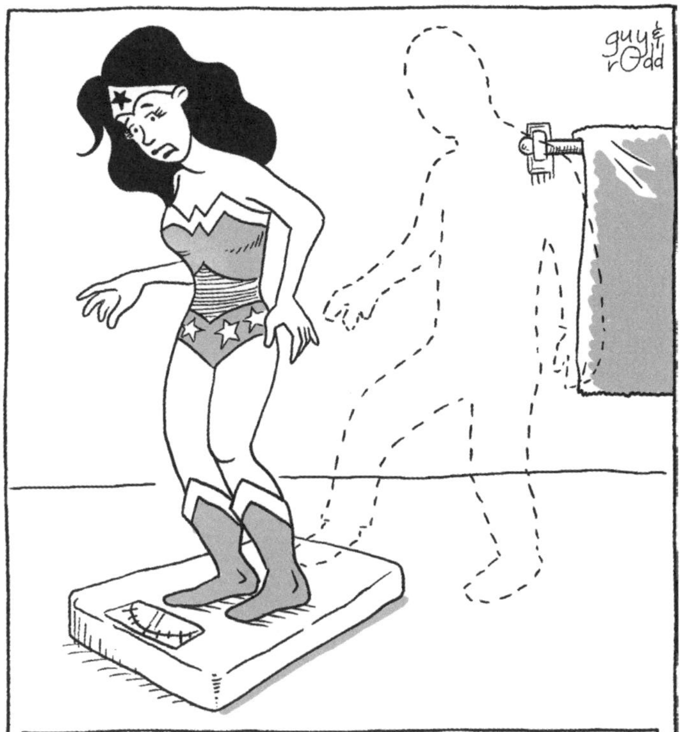

THE INVISIBLE MAN LOVED TO MESS WITH WONDER WOMAN.

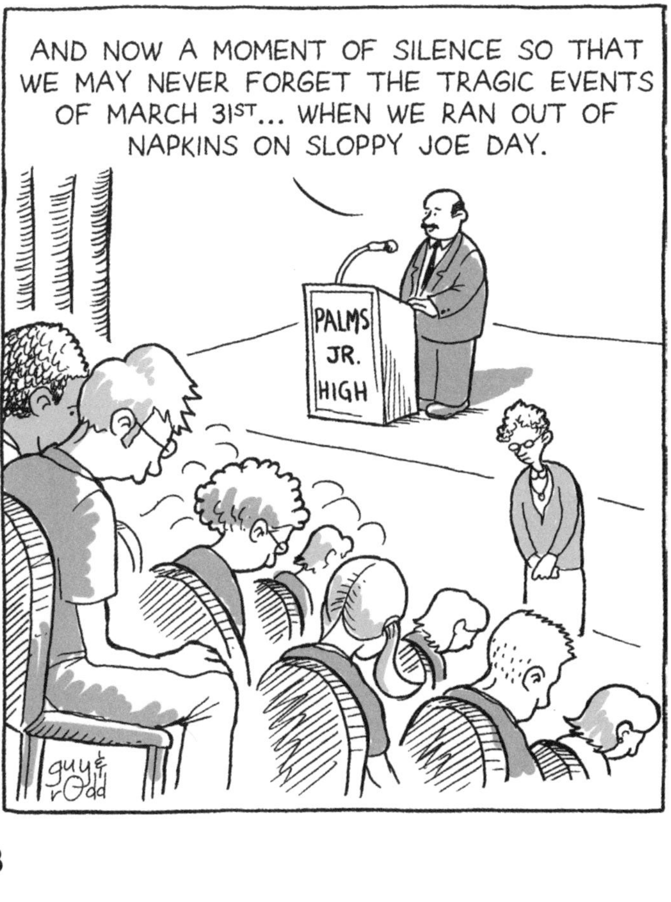
AND NOW A MOMENT OF SILENCE SO THAT WE MAY NEVER FORGET THE TRAGIC EVENTS OF MARCH 31ST... WHEN WE RAN OUT OF NAPKINS ON SLOPPY JOE DAY.
PALMS
JR.
HIGH

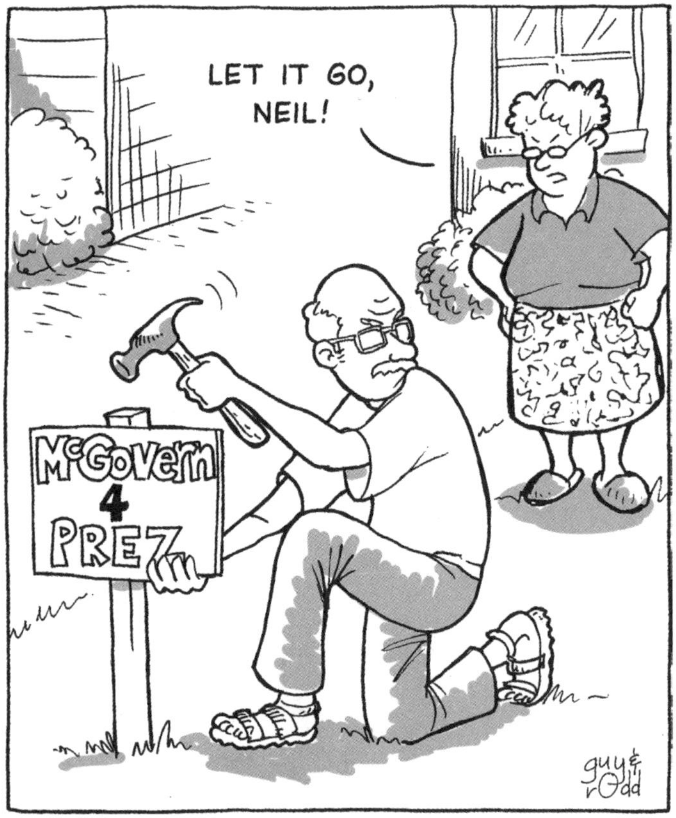
LET IT GO, NEIL!
McGovern 4 PREZ
guy & rodd

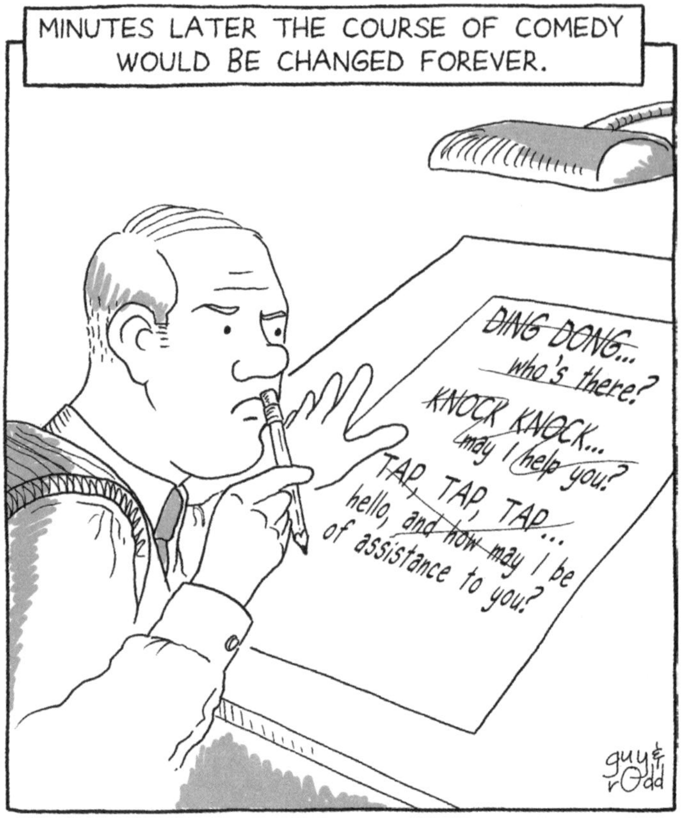
MINUTES LATER THE COURSE OF COMEDY WOULD BE CHANGED FOREVER.
DING DONG... who's there?
KNOCK KNOCK... may I help you?
TAP, TAP, TAP... hello, and how may I be of assistance to you?
guy & rodd

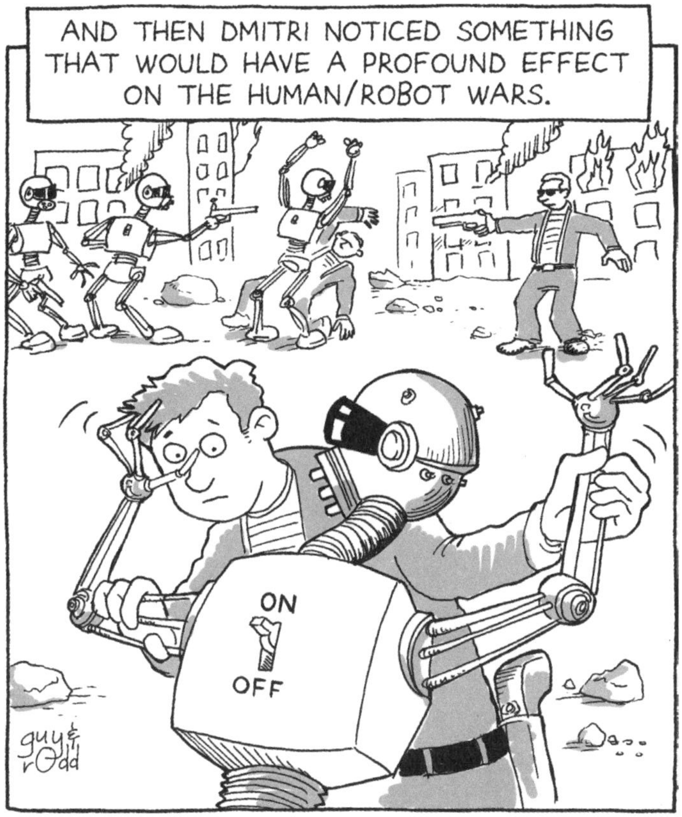
AND THEN DMITRI NOTICED SOMETHING THAT WOULD HAVE A PROFOUND EFFECT ON THE HUMAN/ROBOT WARS.
ON
OFF
guy & rOdd

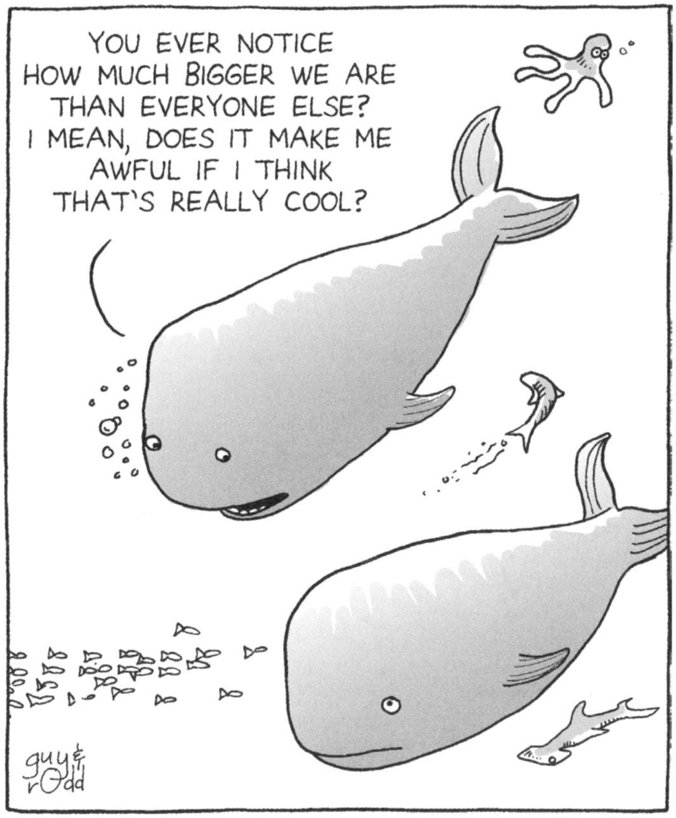
YOU EVER NOTICE HOW MUCH BIGGER WE ARE THAN EVERYONE ELSE? I MEAN, DOES IT MAKE ME AWFUL IF I THINK THAT'S REALLY COOL?
guy & rOdd

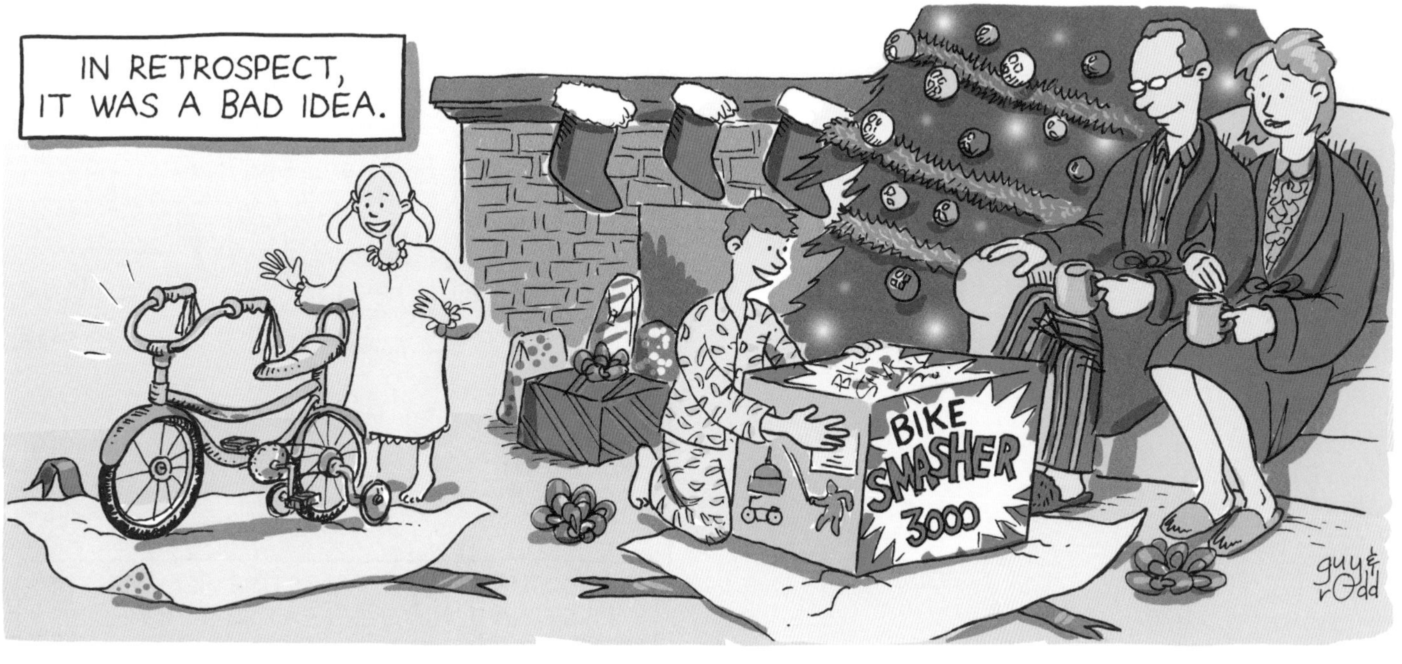
IN RETROSPECT, IT WAS A BAD IDEA.
BIKE SMASHER 3000
guy & rOdd

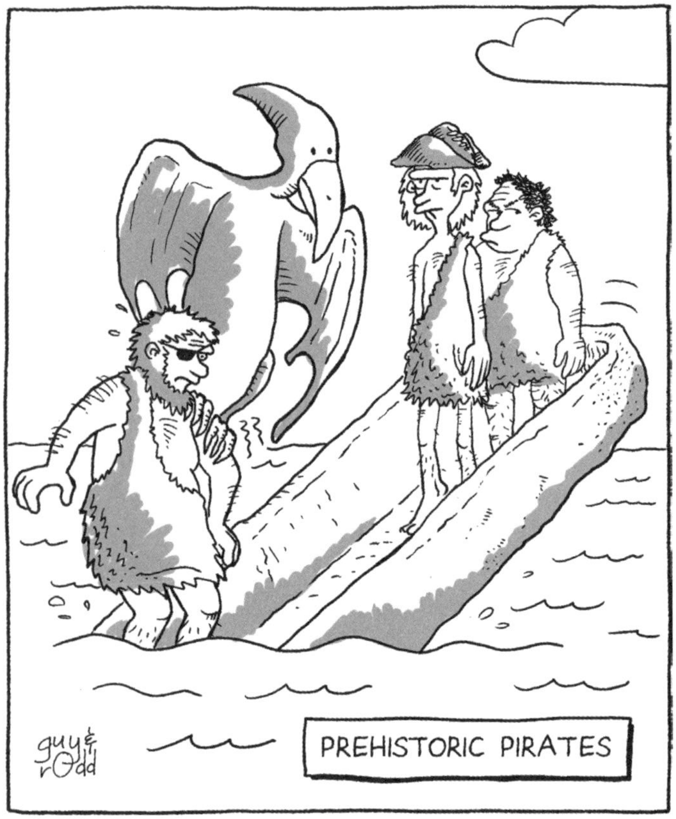
guy & rodd
PREHISTORIC PIRATES

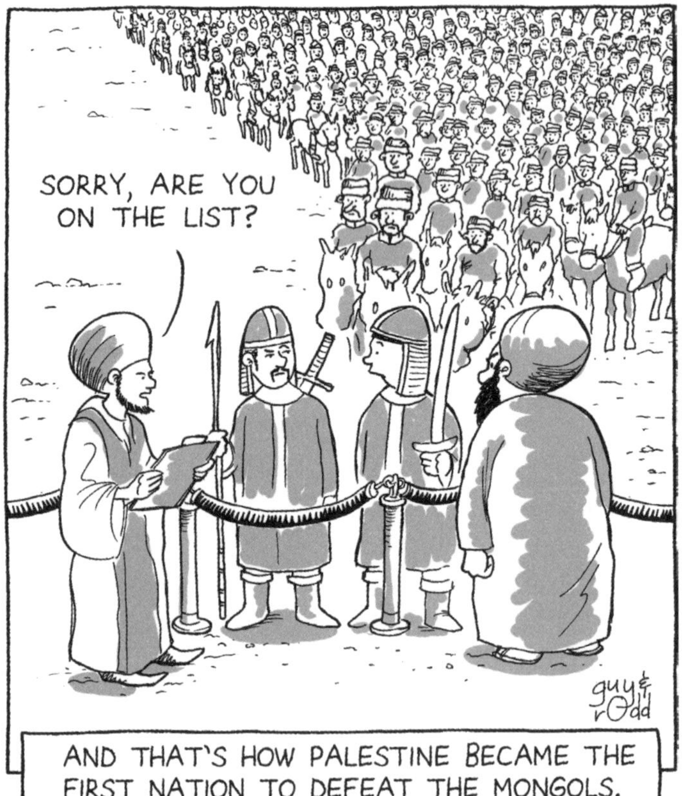
SORRY, ARE YOU ON THE LIST?
guy & rodd
AND THAT'S HOW PALESTINE BECAME THE FIRST NATION TO DEFEAT THE MONGOLS.

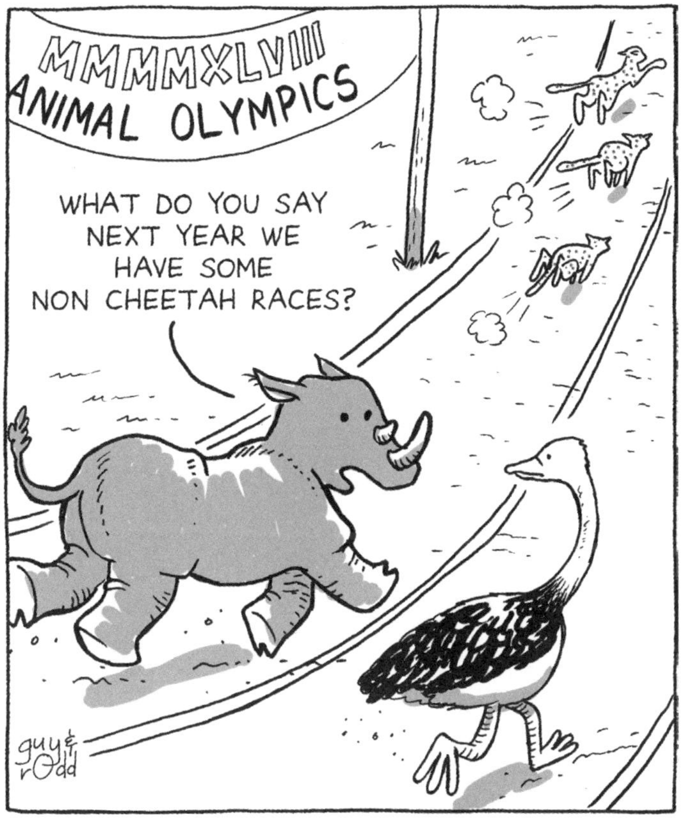
MMMMXLVIII
ANIMAL OLYMPICS
WHAT DO YOU SAY NEXT YEAR WE HAVE SOME NON CHEETAH RACES?
guy & rodd

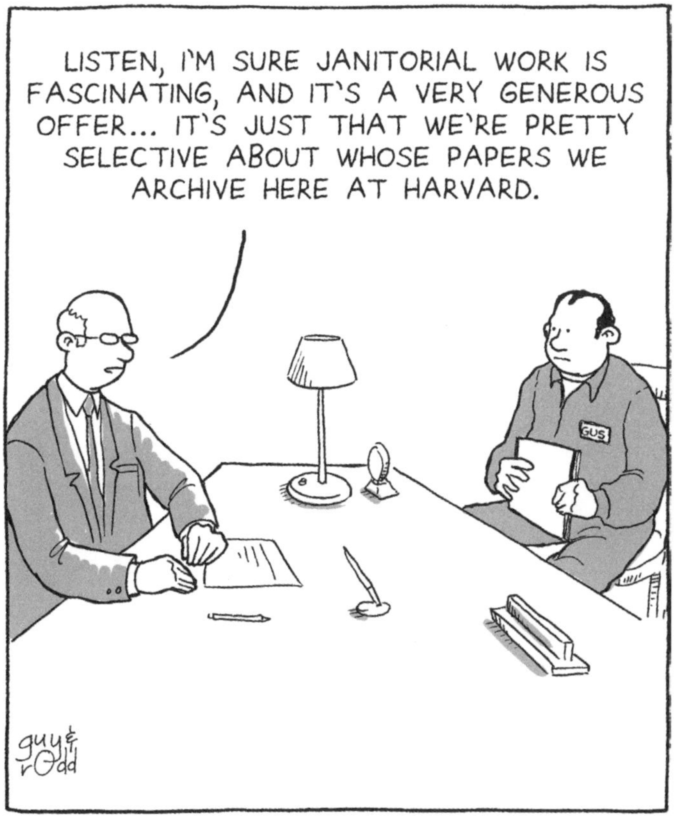
LISTEN, I'M SURE JANITORIAL WORK IS FASCINATING, AND IT'S A VERY GENEROUS OFFER... IT'S JUST THAT WE'RE PRETTY SELECTIVE ABOUT WHOSE PAPERS WE ARCHIVE HERE AT HARVARD.
GUS
guy & rodd

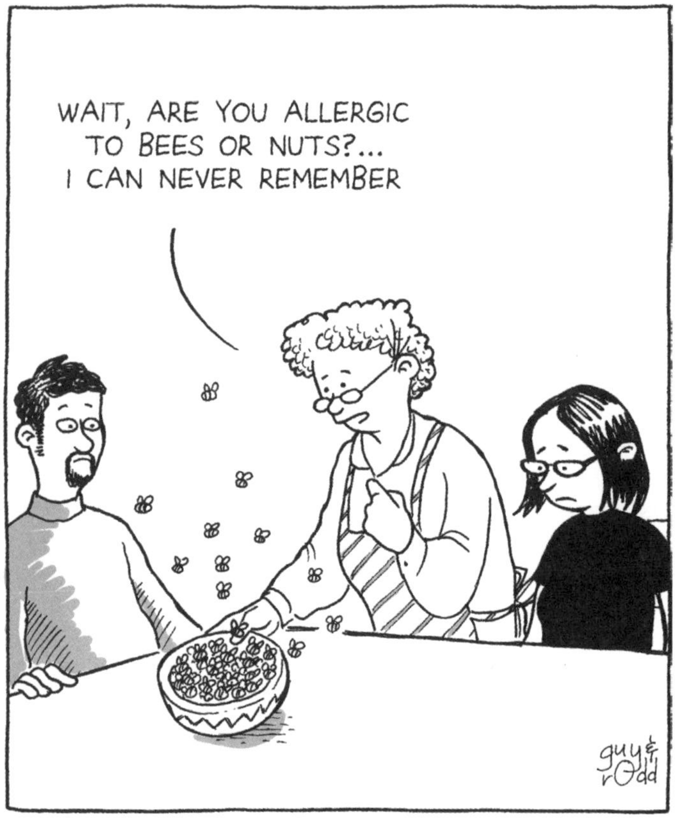
WAIT, ARE YOU ALLERGIC TO BEES OR NUTS?... I CAN NEVER REMEMBER
guy & rOdd

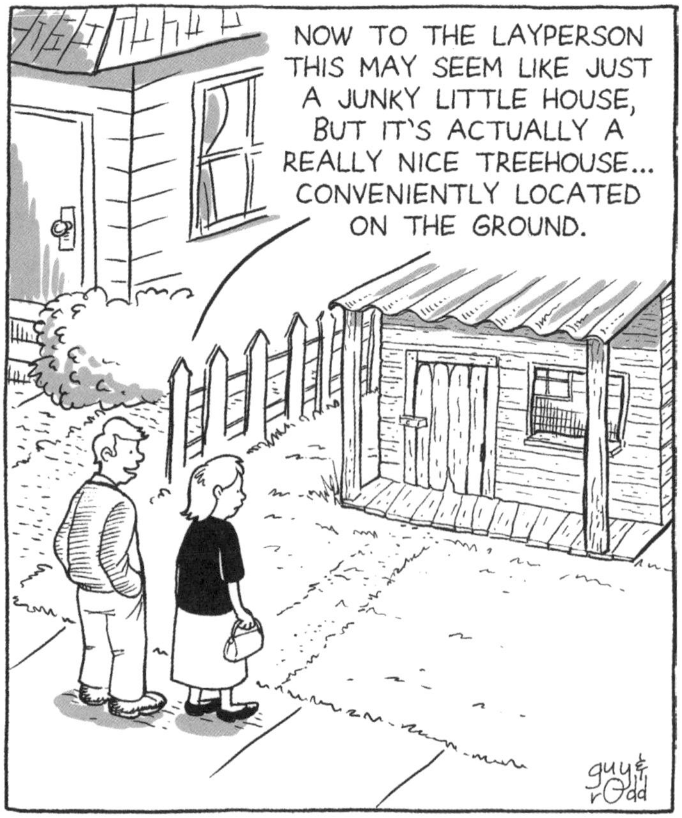
NOW TO THE LAYPERSON THIS MAY SEEM LIKE JUST A JUNKY LITTLE HOUSE, BUT IT'S ACTUALLY A REALLY NICE TREEHOUSE... CONVENIENTLY LOCATED ON THE GROUND.
guy & rOdd

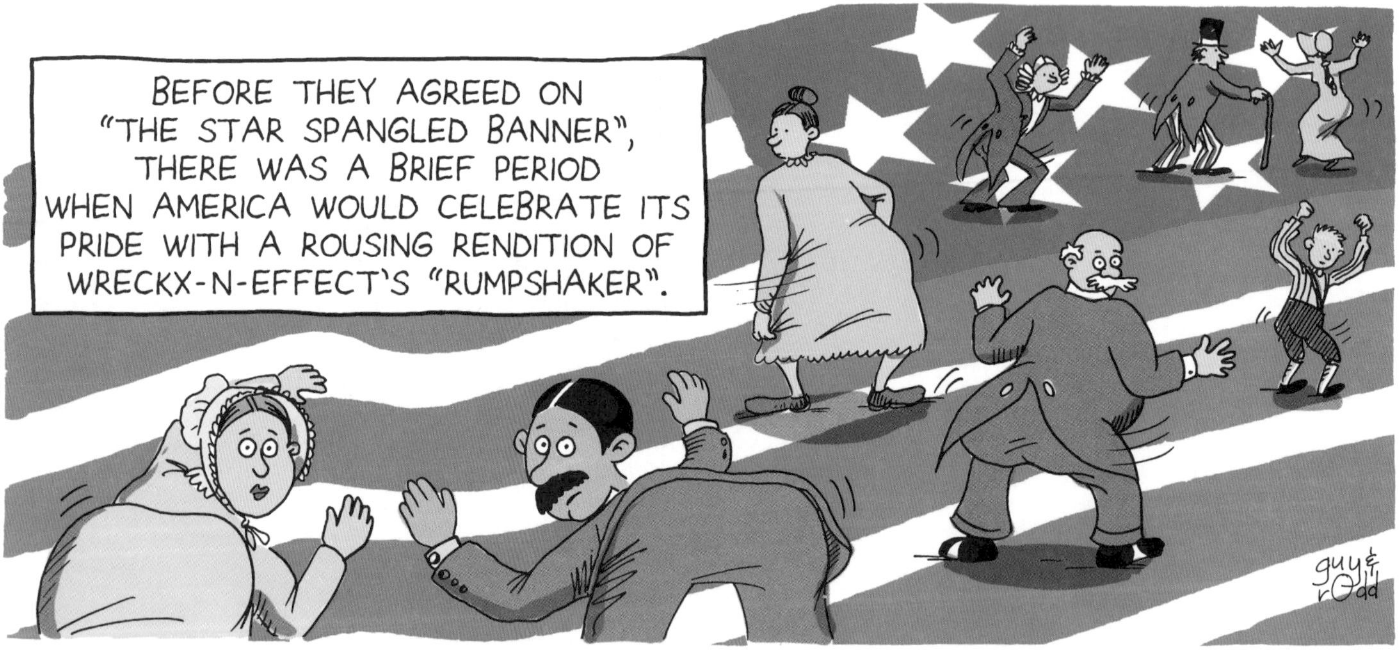
BEFORE THEY AGREED ON "THE STAR SPANGLED BANNER", THERE WAS A BRIEF PERIOD WHEN AMERICA WOULD CELEBRATE ITS PRIDE WITH A ROUSING RENDITION OF WRECKX-N-EFFECT'S "RUMPSHAKER".
guy & rOdd

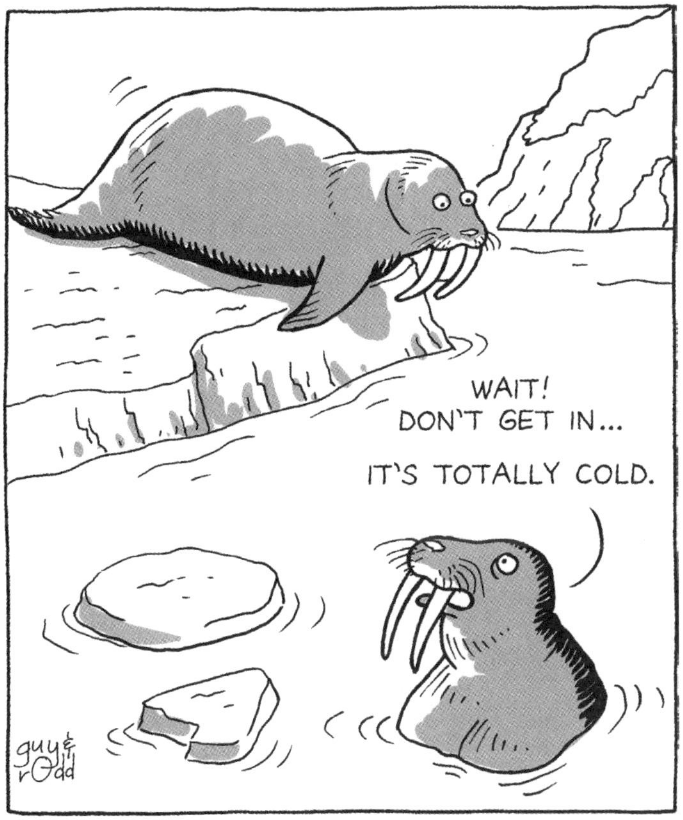
WAIT!
DON'T GET IN...
IT'S TOTALLY COLD.
guy & rOdd

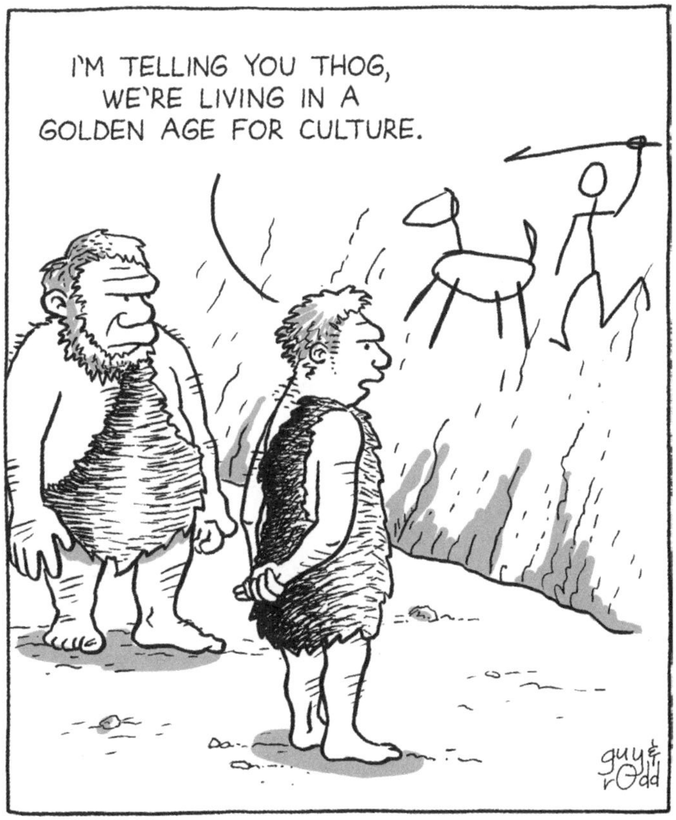
I'M TELLING YOU THOG, WE'RE LIVING IN A GOLDEN AGE FOR CULTURE.
guy & rOdd

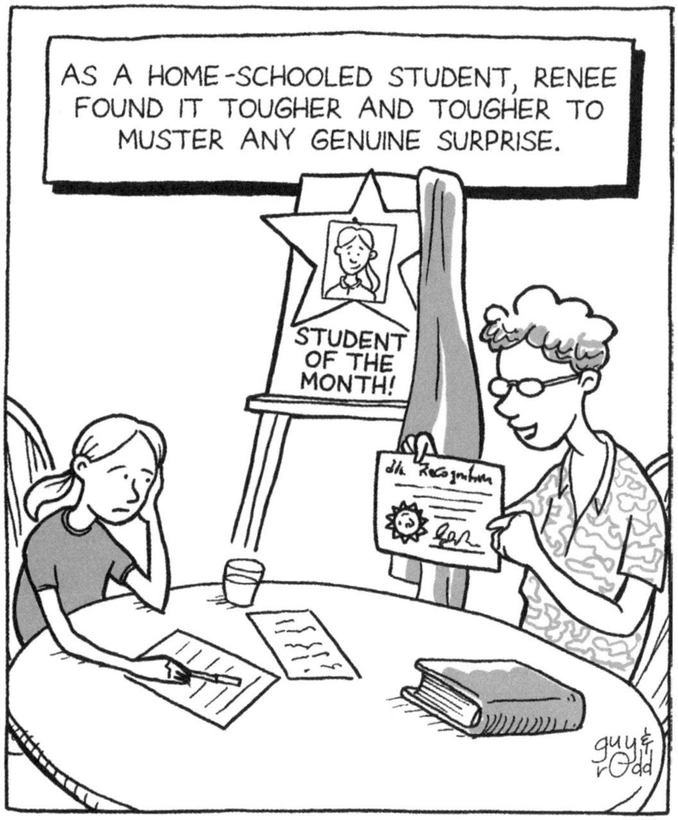
AS A HOME-SCHOOLED STUDENT, RENEE FOUND IT TOUGHER AND TOUGHER TO MUSTER ANY GENUINE SURPRISE.
STUDENT OF THE MONTH!
guy & rOdd

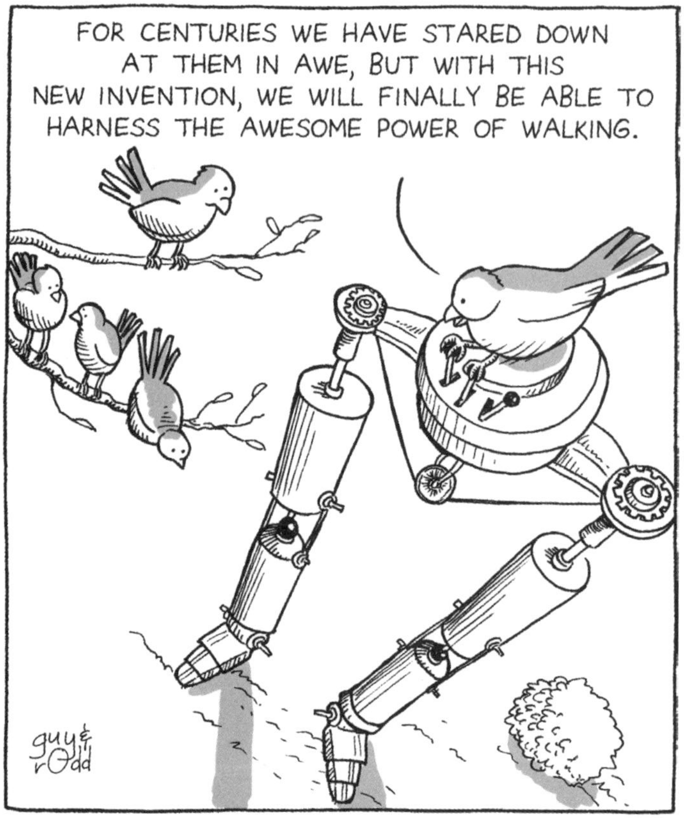
FOR CENTURIES WE HAVE STARED DOWN AT THEM IN AWE, BUT WITH THIS NEW INVENTION, WE WILL FINALLY BE ABLE TO HARNESS THE AWESOME POWER OF WALKING.
guy & rOdd

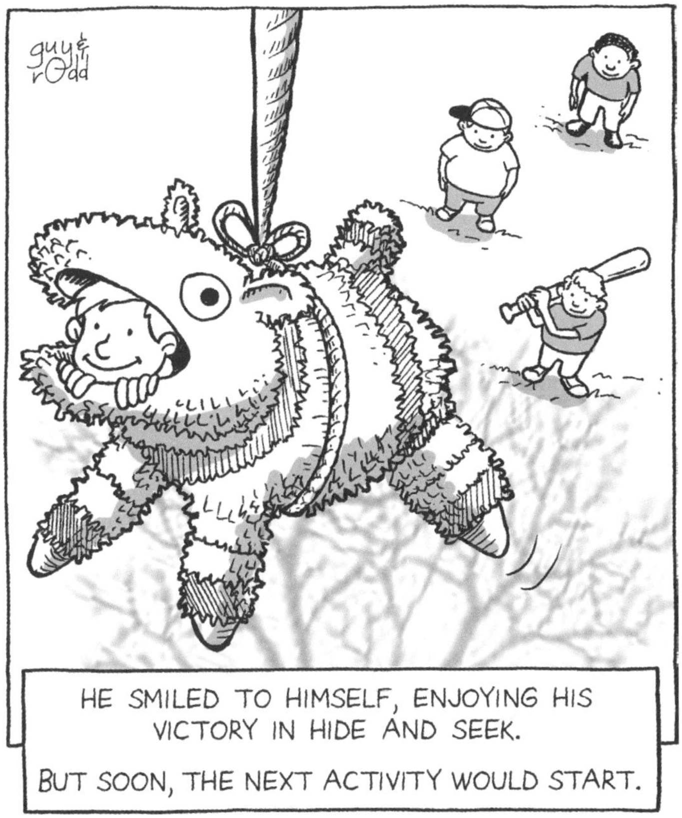
HE SMILED TO HIMSELF, ENJOYING HIS VICTORY IN HIDE AND SEEK.
BUT SOON, THE NEXT ACTIVITY WOULD START.

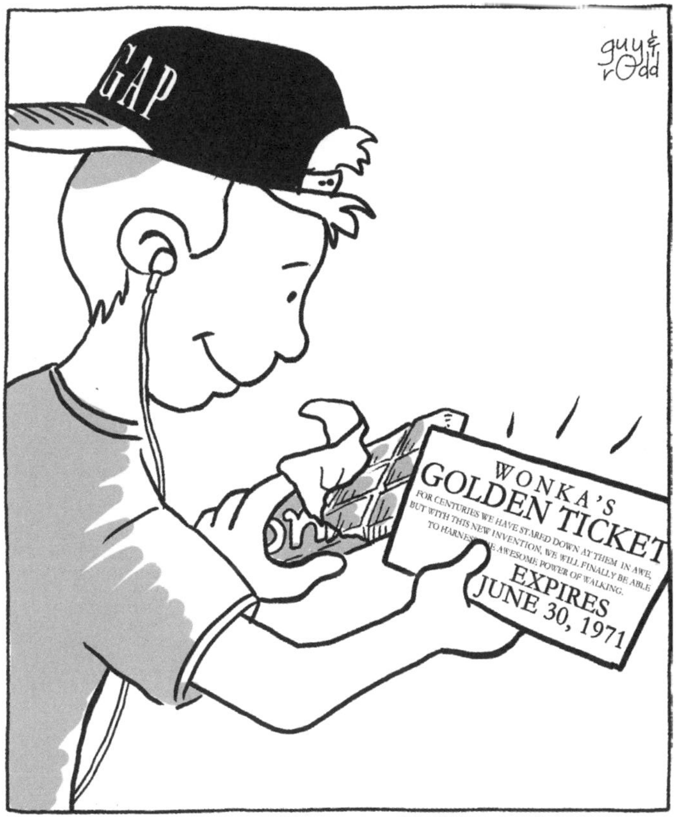
GAP
WONKA'S
GOLDEN TICKET
FOR CENTURIES WE HAVE STARED DOWN AT THEM IN AWE,
BUT WITH THIS NEW INVENTION, WE WILL FINALLY BE ABLE
EXPIRES
JUNE 30, 1971

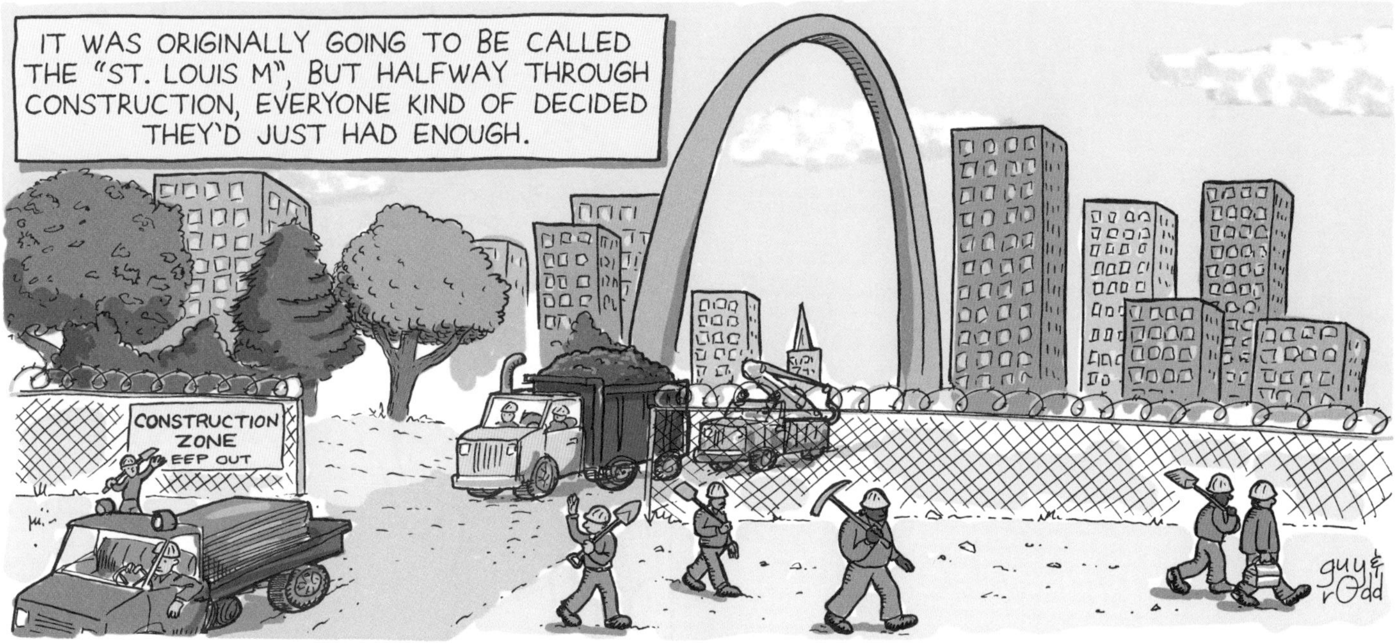
IT WAS ORIGINALLY GOING TO BE CALLED THE "ST. LOUIS M", BUT HALFWAY THROUGH CONSTRUCTION, EVERYONE KIND OF DECIDED THEY'D JUST HAD ENOUGH.
CONSTRUCTION ZONE
EEP OUT

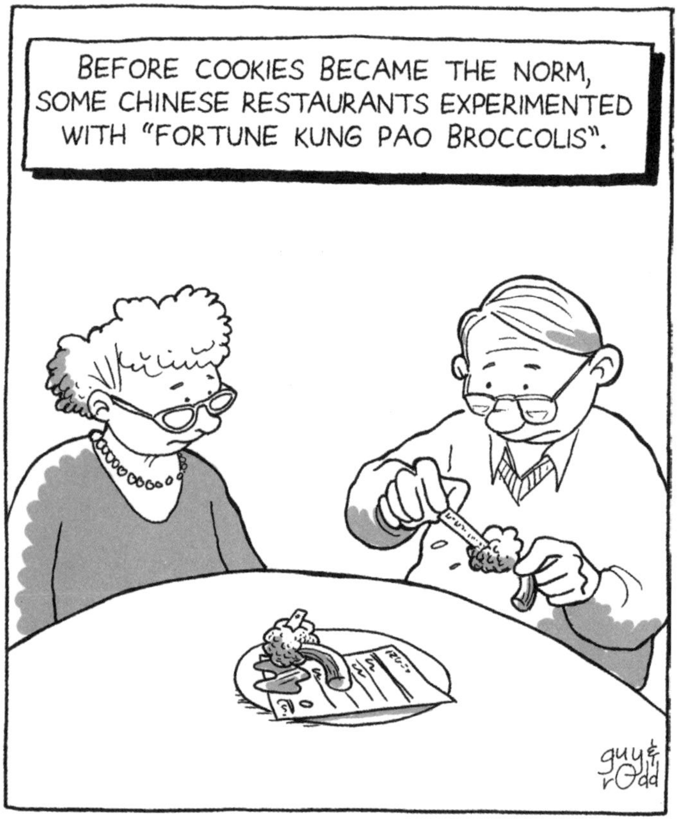
BEFORE COOKIES BECAME THE NORM, SOME CHINESE RESTAURANTS EXPERIMENTED WITH "FORTUNE KUNG PAO BROCCOLIS".
guy & rOdd

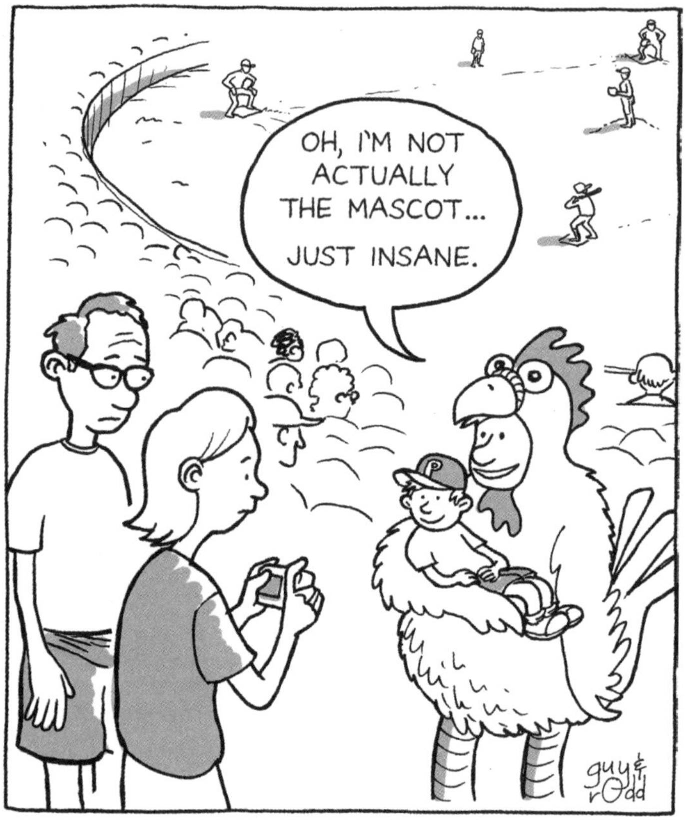
OH, I'M NOT ACTUALLY THE MASCOT... JUST INSANE.
guy & rOdd

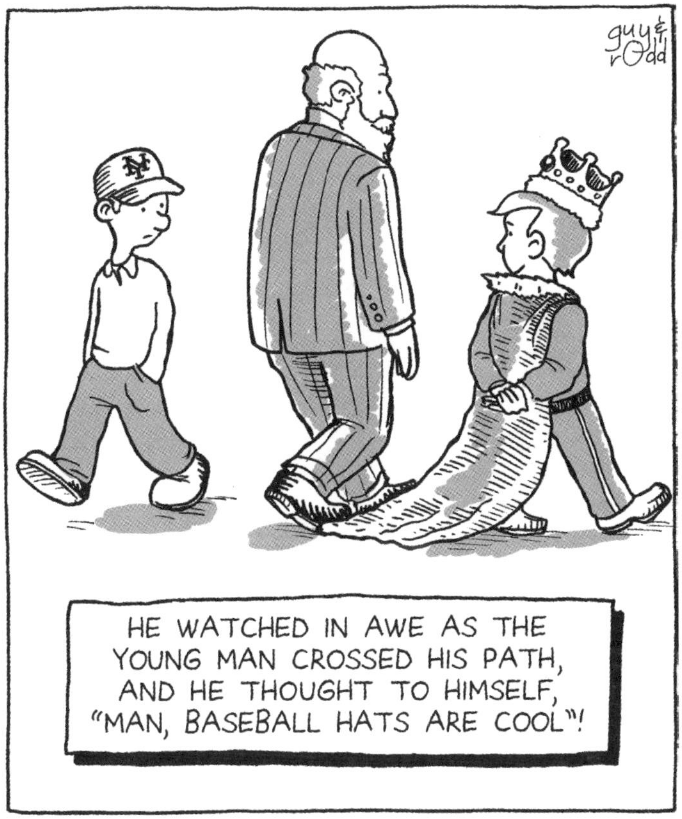
guy & rodd
HE WATCHED IN AWE AS THE YOUNG MAN CROSSED HIS PATH, AND HE THOUGHT TO HIMSELF, "MAN, BASEBALL HATS ARE COOL"!

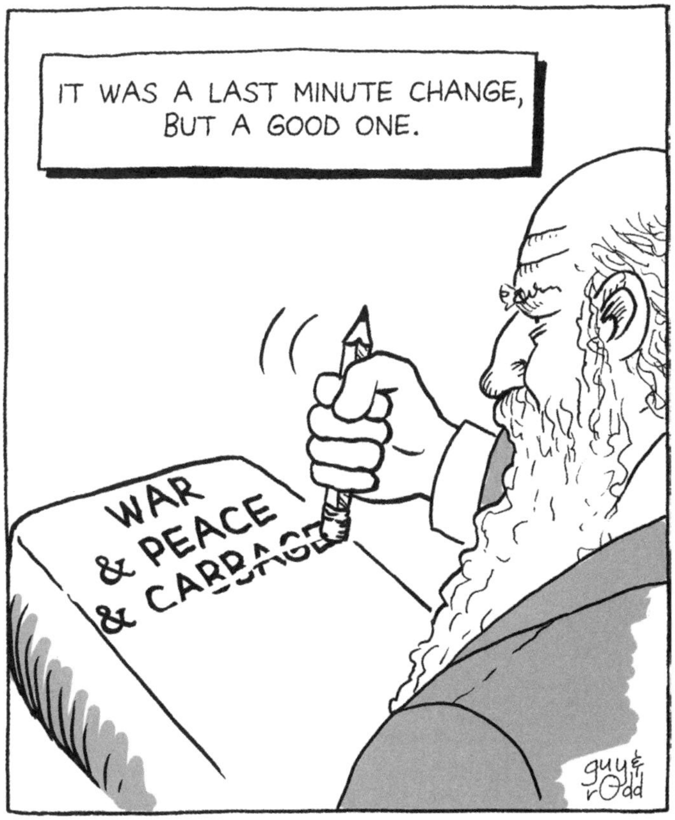
IT WAS A LAST MINUTE CHANGE, BUT A GOOD ONE.
WAR & PEACE & CABBAGE
guy & rodd

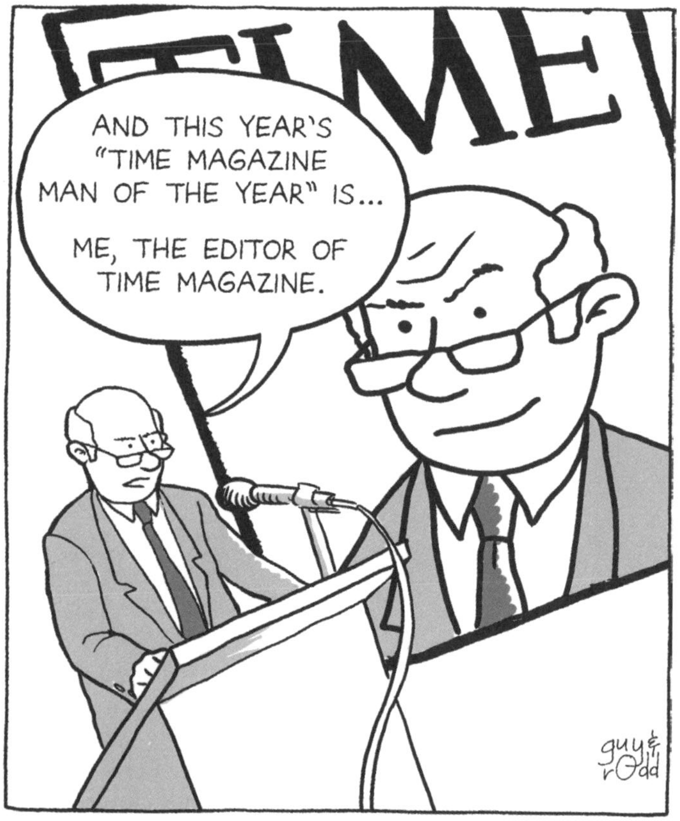
TIME
AND THIS YEAR'S "TIME MAGAZINE MAN OF THE YEAR" IS...
ME, THE EDITOR OF TIME MAGAZINE.

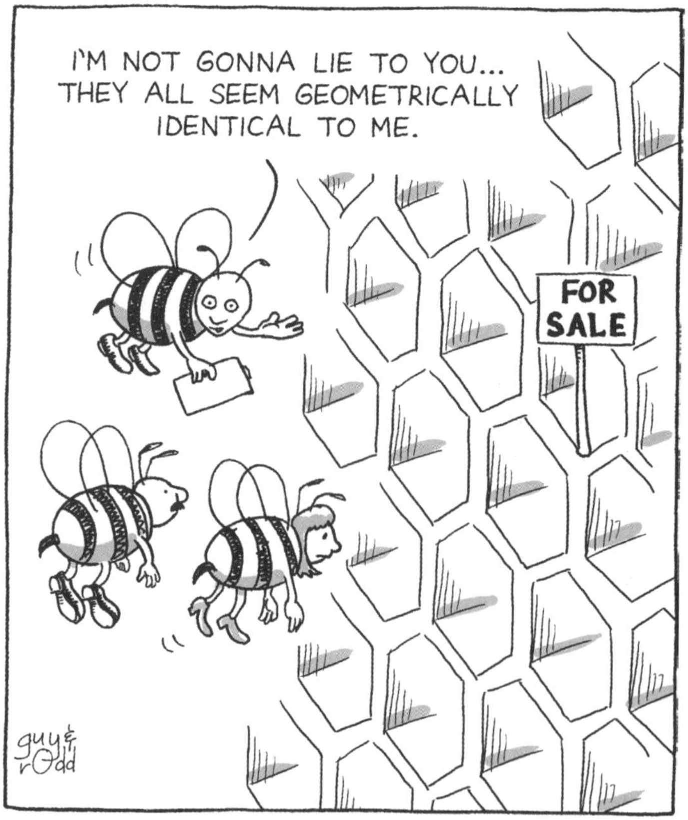
I'M NOT GONNA LIE TO YOU... THEY ALL SEEM GEOMETRICALLY IDENTICAL TO ME.
FOR SALE

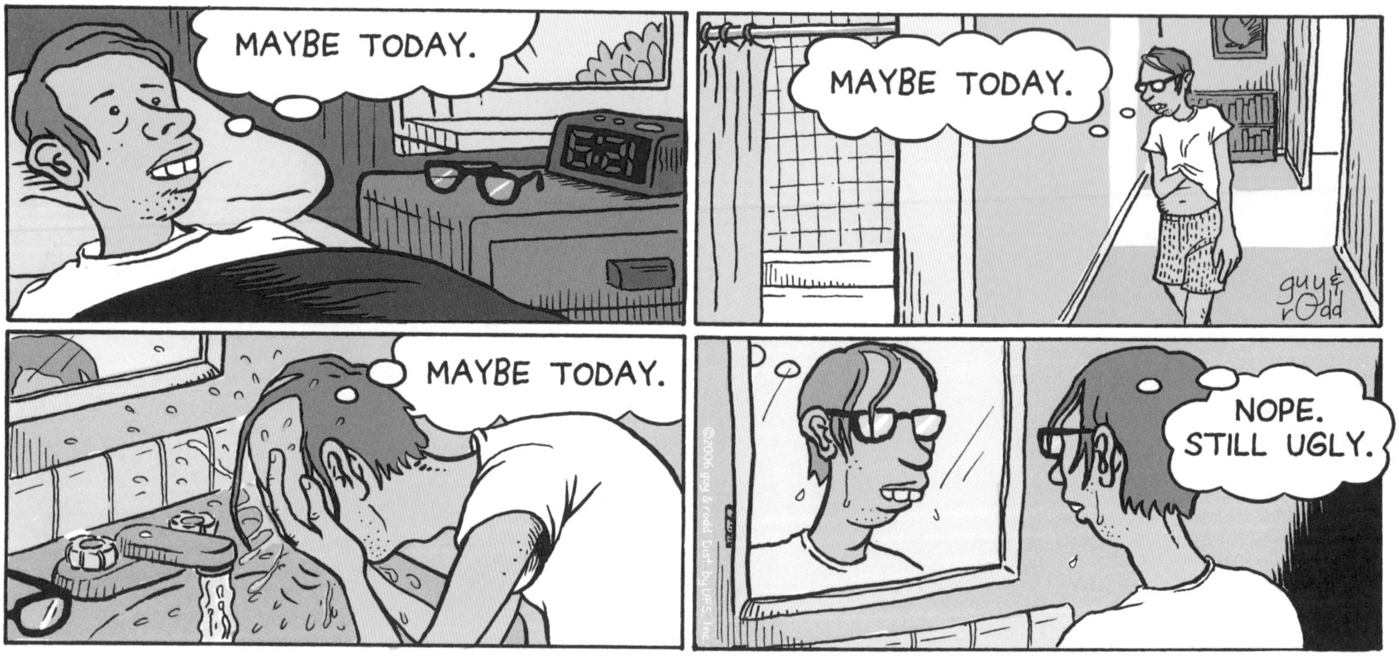
MAYBE TODAY.
MAYBE TODAY.
MAYBE TODAY.
NOPE. STILL UGLY.

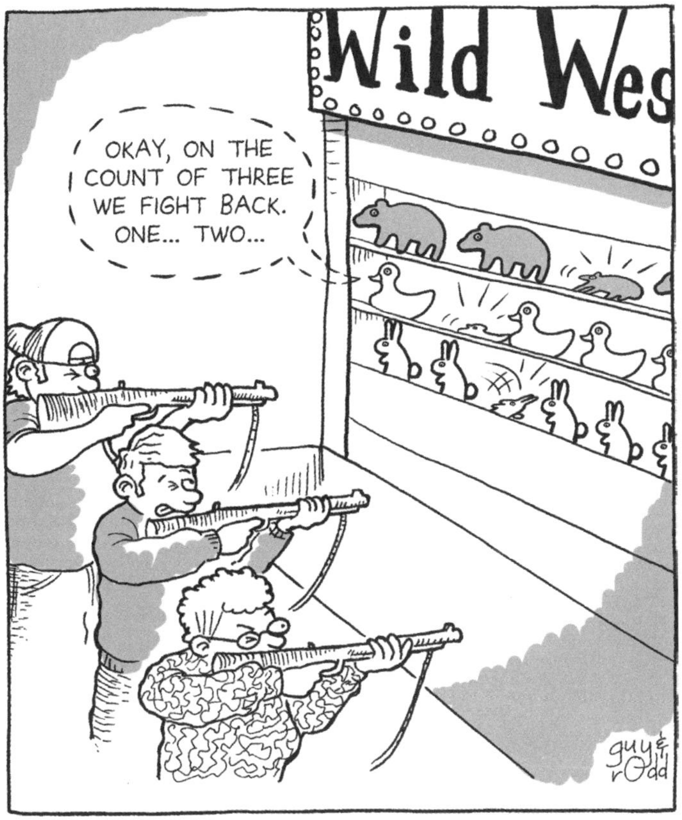
Wild Wes
OKAY, ON THE COUNT OF THREE WE FIGHT BACK. ONE... TWO...
guy & rOdd

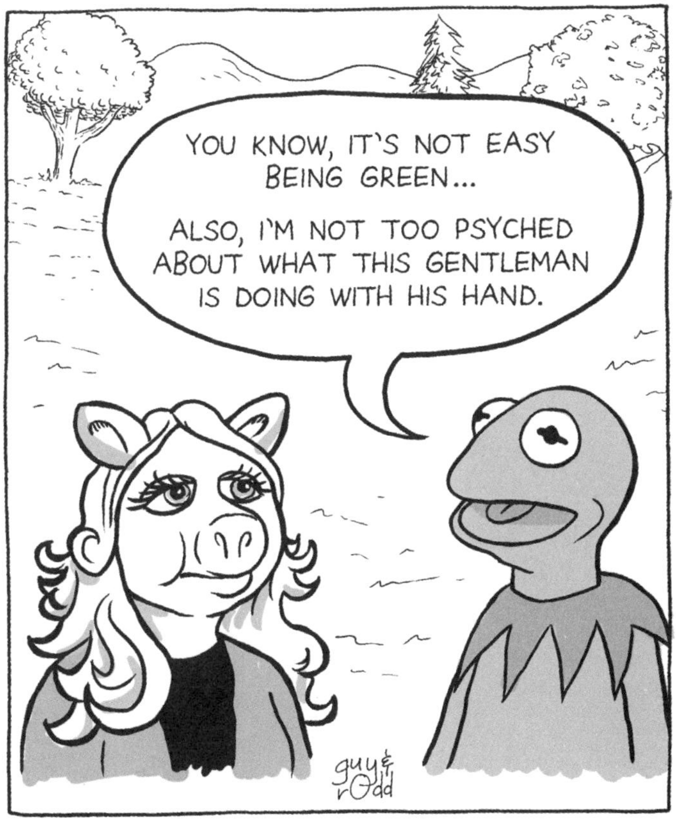
YOU KNOW, IT'S NOT EASY BEING GREEN...
ALSO, I'M NOT TOO PSYCHED ABOUT WHAT THIS GENTLEMAN IS DOING WITH HIS HAND.
guy & rOdd

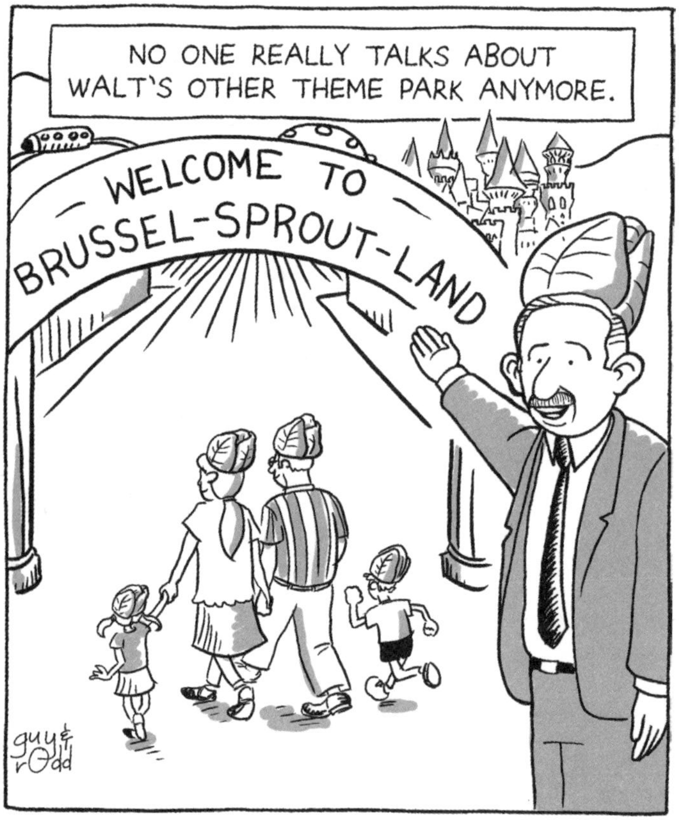

NO ONE REALLY TALKS ABOUT WALT'S OTHER THEME PARK ANYMORE.
WELCOME TO BRUSSEL-SPROUT-LAND
guy & rOdd

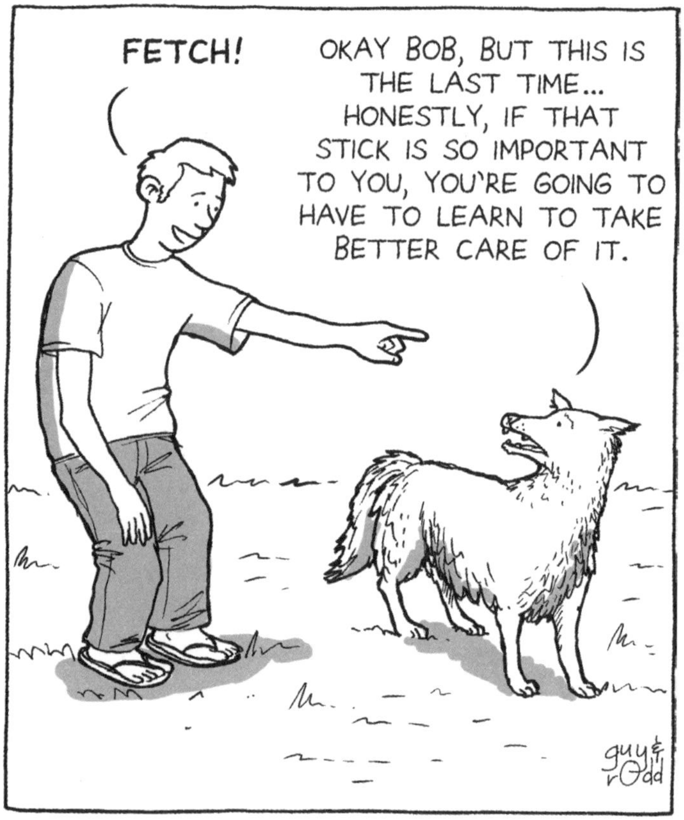

FETCH!
OKAY BOB, BUT THIS IS THE LAST TIME... HONESTLY, IF THAT STICK IS SO IMPORTANT TO YOU, YOU'RE GOING TO HAVE TO LEARN TO TAKE BETTER CARE OF IT.
guy & rOdd

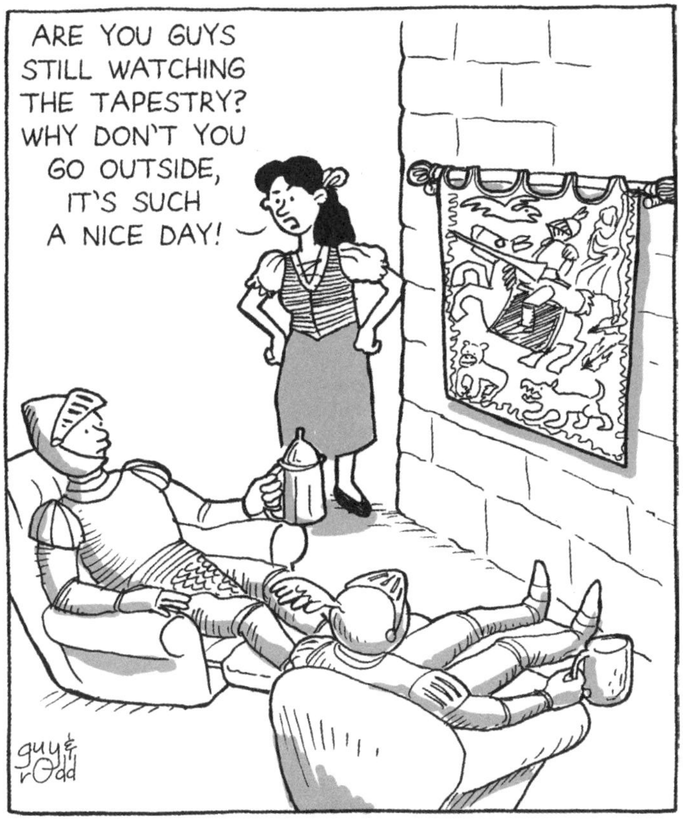
ARE YOU GUYS STILL WATCHING THE TAPESTRY? WHY DON'T YOU GO OUTSIDE, IT'S SUCH A NICE DAY!
guy & rOdd

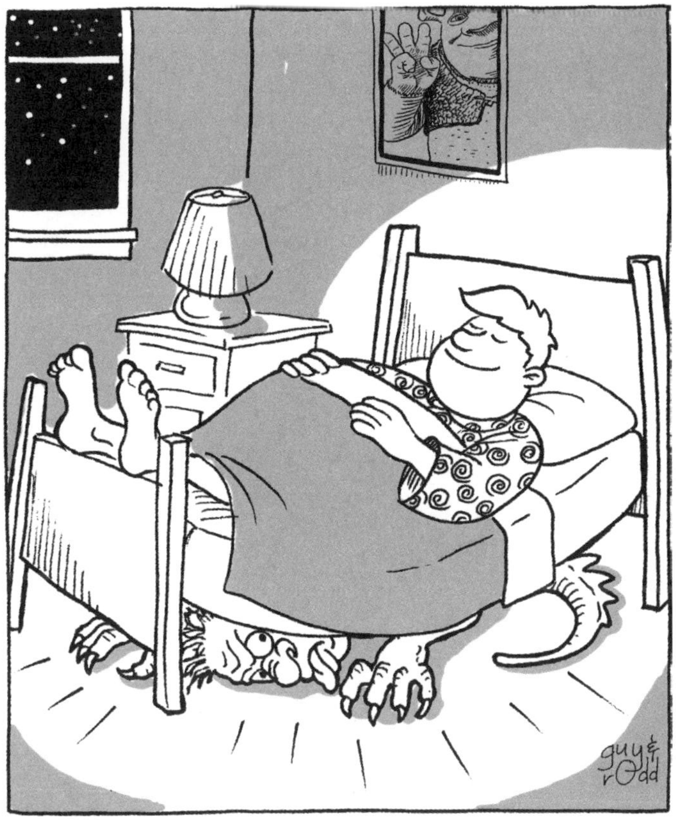
guy & rOdd

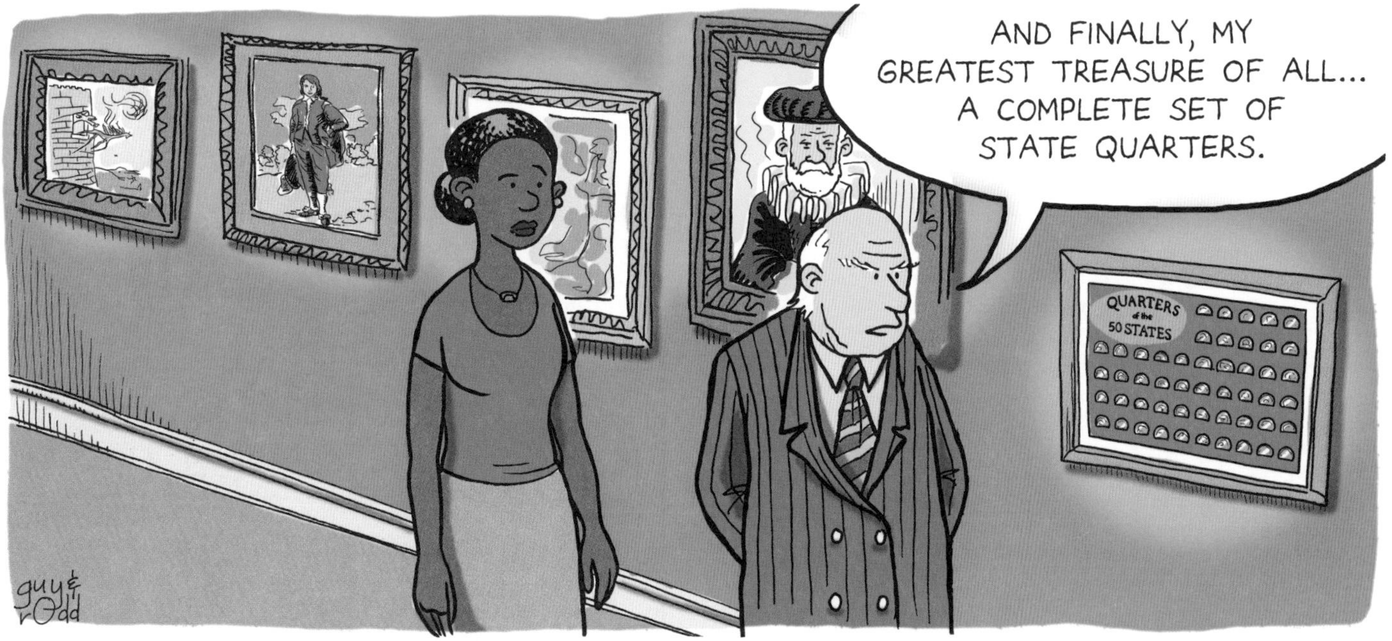
AND FINALLY, MY GREATEST TREASURE OF ALL... A COMPLETE SET OF STATE QUARTERS.
QUARTERS of the 50 STATES
guy & rOdd

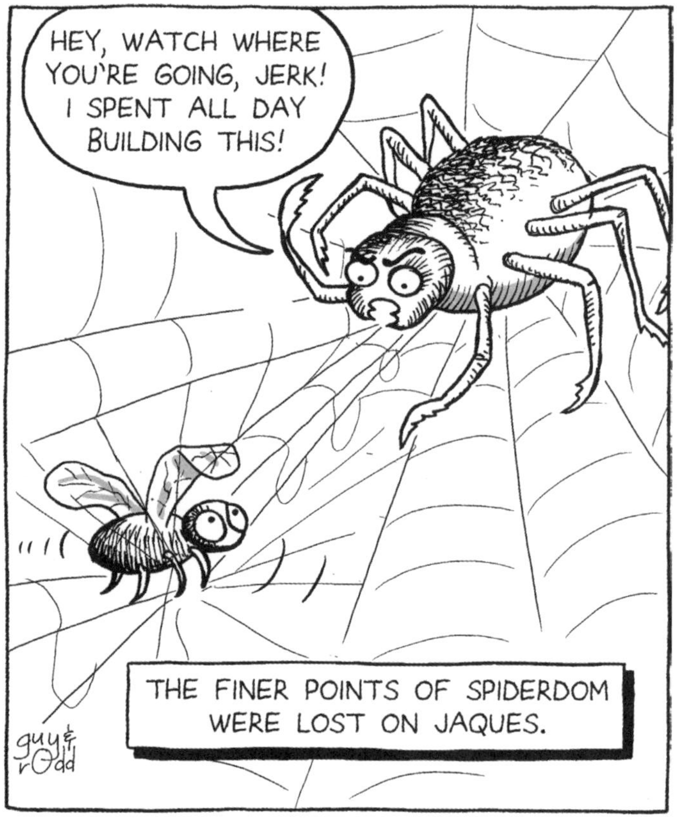
HEY, WATCH WHERE YOU'RE GOING, JERK! I SPENT ALL DAY BUILDING THIS!
THE FINER POINTS OF SPIDERDOM WERE LOST ON JAQUES.
guy & rOdd

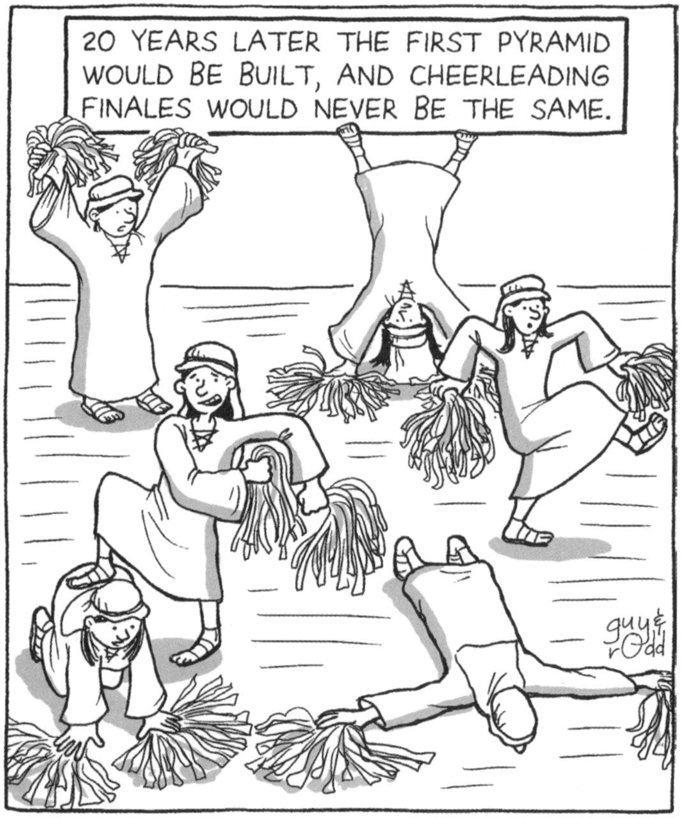
20 YEARS LATER THE FIRST PYRAMID WOULD BE BUILT, AND CHEERLEADING FINALES WOULD NEVER BE THE SAME.
guy & rOdd